Van Johnson

Hollywood Legends Series
Ronald L. Davis, General Editor

Van Johnson

MGM's Golden Boy

Ronald L. Davis

UNIVERSITY PRESS OF MISSISSIPPI   JACKSON

www.upress.state.ms.us

Copyright © 2001 by University Press of Mississippi
All rights reserved
Manufactured in the United States of America

09 08 07 06 05 04 03 02 01   4 3 2 1
∞

Library of Congress Cataloging-in-Publication Data

Davis, Ronald L.
Van Johnson: MGM's golden boy / by Ronald L. Davis.
p.   cm. — (Hollywood legends series)
Includes bibliographical references and index.
ISBN 1-57806-377-9 (cloth : alk. paper)
1. Johnson, Van, 1916–   2. Motion picture actors and actresses—United
States—Biography. I. Title. II. Series.

PN2287.J58 V38   2001
791.43'028'092—dc21
[B]
00-054541

British Library Cataloging-in-Publication Data available

In memory of...
Robert Randall Wade,
who traveled best

CONTENTS

PREFACE

A product of his time, Van Johnson illustrates the fantasy world that Hollywood projected during the 1940s and 1950s. Johnson came into movies unencumbered by the methods of acting and the claptrap taught in professional drama schools; he succeeded by letting the pure personality show through in the parts he played. Any dishonesty in his life was part of a desire, dominant during the heyday of Hollywood's big studios, to produce pristine likenesses of an idealized society in which all but the most indolent sought the glories and riches of the American dream fulfilled. That Van Johnson tried to internalize deceit in his own life and make the mask his reality became a principal factor in his personal difficulties. Few people truly knew Van Johnson; it is unlikely that the man ever came to know himself deeply. The visage of the freckled boy next door that so enchanted movie audiences in the 1940s was advantageous and comfortable to hide behind; it won the young actor fame, approval, and wealth in record time. The hurt in Johnson's private life was offset by the adulation of his adoring public. He did his crying in seclusion, and the walls around his solitary person were seldom broken.

Johnson was lucky in his career, soaring to popularity during World War II on the crest of a boy-next-door image that Metro-Goldwyn-Mayer created for him. He remains fortunate in having loyal friends who wish to do nothing to displease him. Although their devotion speaks well of Johnson and his relationships with colleagues, their reticence does not help a biographer whose aim is to write a truthful book about the man who once was the bobby-soxers' heartthrob. Time and again I found potential sources unwilling to talk to me or reluctant to reveal information that

Johnson himself had not approved. Those willing to discuss Johnson's life and career were generally cooperative until the question of his sexuality was raised. At that point, most told me politely that that area was taboo.

Writing an honest book about a living subject invariably poses problems for an author. If the subject collaborates, the biographer can easily lose objectivity or feel like a betrayer when unauthorized material is included. Manuscript sources frequently are incomplete if the subject is still alive, since personal correspondence and business records may not yet have found their way into public archives. Those documents that have reached archival collections may be closed to users until some time in the future. If there is an undisclosed side to the subject's personality, the problems a biographer faces are all the greater.

I never intended to write anything other than a sympathetic book about Van Johnson. Yet as a professional historian I felt an obligation to construct a three-dimensional portrait of one of the most popular screen legends from Hollywood's golden age. Writing about Johnson in depth meant delving behind the boyish image depicted in fan magazines and asking probing questions about the man whose celluloid reflection still enchants audiences who watch classic movie channels. Although I had no desire to dwell on Johnson's secret life, neither could I ignore that side of his personality or be naive about it.

As with my biographies of Linda Darnell, John Ford, and John Wayne, I began research on this book by first consulting the Southern Methodist University Oral History Collection on the Performing Arts, which I have directed for more than twenty-five years. Interviewees who shed particular light on Johnson's life and career include George Abbott, Leon Ames, Lucille Ball, Pandro S. Berman, Ralph Blane, Frederick Brisson, Robert Buckner, Lillian Burns, Edward Buzzell, Joseph J. Cohn, Donald Curtis, Arlene Dahl, Dan Dailey, Rosemary DeCamp, Don DeFore, Armand Deutsch, Edward Dmytryk, Stanley Donen, Joanne Dru, Irene Dunne, Julius J. Epstein, Mike Frankovich, John Green, Henry Hathaway, June Havoc, Marsha Hunt, Martha Hyer, Gene Kelly, Ruth Kobart, Stanley

Kramer, Fernando Lamas, Piper Laurie, Mervyn LeRoy, Norman Lloyd, Mary Anita Loos, John Lund, Betty Lynn, Mary Martin, Dorothy McGuire, Vincente Minnelli, Tharon Musser, Robert Nathan, Barry Nelson, Richard Ney, Robert Pirosh, Jean Porter, Ella Raines, Joseph Ruttenberg, Lizabeth Scott, Vivienne Segal, Melville Shavelson, George Sidney, Leonard Sillman, Robert Stack, Ann Straus, Marshall Thompson, Emily Torchia, Al Trescony, Nancy Walker, Hal B. Wallis, Charles Walters, Marie Windsor, and Keenan Wynn. I remain grateful to these luminaries for granting me and my staff the privilege of taping their professional memoirs for the university's archives.

When I first contacted Van Johnson about writing this book, I received no reply. A second letter produced a telephone call from Alan Foshko, Johnson's business manager. When told of the biography I was preparing, Foshko asked if Johnson would share in the book's profits should he cooperate. I explained that profits were rarely involved in works published by university presses. Foshko then asked if Johnson would have the right to approve my final manuscript. I said I doubted that any university press would grant such permission, since scholarly editors and their boards demand objectivity and a historical perspective in the books they publish. Foshko's reply was that Johnson would not want me prying into his private life, at which point I realized that I faced problems in writing the kind of biography that the University Press of Mississippi intended for its Hollywood Legends series.

Eve Wynn Johnson, Van's ex-wife, wrote me a lengthy note in response to my letter of inquiry to her, agreed to be interviewed for this book, then canceled after I had made reservations to visit with her in Florida, claiming that an in-depth session would be too painful for her. She did agree to answer questions over the telephone and graciously did so.

Those whom I interviewed expressly for this book include Eddie Bracken, Mildred (Toddy) Burns, Rosemary Clooney, Sandy Descher, Anne Dimery, Giuliano Gemma, Martin and Erin-Jo Jurow, Richard Lederer, Janet Leigh, Leonard J. Panaggio, Elliott Reid, Mary Sharmat, Barbara

(Mrs. Marshall) Thompson, Frank Vohs, and Jane Wyman. Their help was invaluable although sometimes guarded.

More revealing was *We Will Always Live in Beverly Hills: Growing Up Crazy in Hollywood,* a sensitive and commendable book by Ned Wynn, Van Johnson's older stepson. Without this personal insight into Johnson's family life, my biography would have been severely diminished. Also helpful was an interview with Tracy Keenan Wynn, Johnson's younger stepson, which was printed in Raymond Strait's book *Hollywood's Children.* Both Wynn sons remembered Johnson with respect but with exceptional candor.

My gratitude extends to the excellent and courteous staff of the Margaret Herrick Library of the Academy of Motion Picture Arts and Sciences (especially Barbara Hall in Special Collections), Ned Comstock in the Doheny Library at the University of Southern California, the gracious personnel of the Mayer Library at the American Film Institute in Los Angeles, Ronald Grele and his associates in the Columbia University Oral History Collection, the several workers in the New York Public Library for the Performing Arts, and the capable staff of the Fine Arts division of the Dallas Public Library. In Newport my work was made pleasurable and productive by curators in the Redwood Library, the Newport Historical Society, and the Rogers High School Alumni Association. At SMU I had the benefit of efficient librarians in Fondren Library (most notably Billie Stovall in Interlibrary Loan), the Hamon Arts Library (especially Sam Ratcliffe), and the DeGolyer Library (in particular Kay Bost and Betty Friedrich).

In England an energetic Carolyn Wilson took time out from her own research to check the British Film Institute's holdings on Van Johnson and gather data for me that appeared in the press during Johnson's appearances on the London stage in *The Music Man.* She has my undying appreciation and friendship.

Personal thanks go to Judy Bland (my secretary), Gail Alpert, Sally Caldwell, Dana and John Pickett, Brenda Cooper, Mildred Pinkston, Jane Elder, Marilynn Hill, Diana Serra Cary, Robert Nott, Charles Cooper, Steven Simonson, James O. Breeden (my chairman in the William P. Clements

Department of History at SMU), and Jay Fultz (who gave the manuscript a thorough and judicious reading). There could be no more cooperative editor than Seetha Srinivasan at the University Press of Mississippi. Seetha has been the instigation and force behind launching the Hollywood Legends series, and her dignity matches her knowledge.

Ronald L. Davis

Van Johnson

Introduction

In the fall of 1946, at the height of his popularity, Van Johnson went to Santa Cruz, California, to film *The Romance of Rosy Ridge*. The production company was housed in a hotel overlooking a pier and an amusement park with a spectacular roller coaster. Van loved riding roller coasters even more than he loved going to circuses and staring at the electric signs in New York's Times Square. He wanted desperately to walk down to the roller coaster in Santa Cruz and give it a try, but knew that he would be mobbed by his fans if he did. Night after night he watched the joyriders from his hotel room, longing to participate in the fun. One evening during dinner in his room with Marshall Thompson, Janet Leigh, and other Metro-Goldwyn-Mayer contract players who were working on the picture, Van kept eyeing the roller coaster through the window with mounting enthusiasm. "Maybe I could go down for a quick ride if I disguised myself," he finally ventured.

So Thompson and some others put a stocking cap on Johnson, painted a dark mustache on him with a pencil, and gave him a pair of glasses to wear. "I thought it was kind of silly," Thompson recalled, "but I went along with the gag. We covered his red hair, put a heavy coat on him, and went down to the amusement park with him." At first nobody seemed to notice the actors, although a couple did look at them in a peculiar way. But no one did anything that suggested recognition.

3

The Metro group got aboard the roller coaster, and the car started up the first incline. "The next thing we knew," Thompson remembered, "they had to stop us about halfway through the ride because by then the word was out that Van Johnson was on board." It took a cordon of firemen and policemen to get people off the tracks and scaffold of the roller coaster and a ladder to get Van and his fellow actors down from the ride with the help of firemen. Johnson and the Metro gang were quickly taken to the fire station on the pier, but fans followed in such growing numbers that the crowd broke the glass door of the station when people tried to force their way inside. A police car finally arrived, and with the help of a police escort, Van Johnson, the bobby-soxers' heartthrob, was taken safely back to his hotel.

"That's how popular this man was," said Thompson, who a few hours before the commotion had thought all the caution was silly and had urged his celebrated friend to go to the park and enjoy himself. "I was just dumbfounded," Thompson said. "I'd never seen anything like that. Van was quite right; he couldn't go out in public without creating a riot. He was the nation's sweetheart."

Fourteen years later Van Johnson, the former Metro superstar, was alone in another hotel room in Geneva, Switzerland. Depressed and feeling desolate, Johnson left the room and walked moodily along the dark shore of Lake Geneva. Nobody seemed to recognize him, but Johnson was too preoccupied with his own gloom to care. He and his wife of twelve years had separated, and he did not know where to turn for comfort. He appeared to have lost everything—his movie career, his family, his self-esteem, his sense of direction. Van stood alone on the water's edge in Switzerland and felt like walking into Lake Geneva. "Is this the way it's going to end," he thought, "just nothing?" All he could think about were his misery and the mistakes he had made. His mind turned back to the near-fatal automobile accident that had propelled him to fame in 1943. He reviewed his unhappy childhood in Newport, Rhode Island, abandoned by his mother and raised cheerlessly by his father. The toughest memories were those of a sexual ambivalence that still tortured him, an arranged marriage after a near-ruinous brush with scandal, and the gulf between his public and private life. He lamented the demise of the Hollywood system that had brought him fame and the realization that the image he had brought to the screen no longer appeared to be in demand. The losses he had experienced were overwhelming. Johnson's future looked so hopeless as he stood looking at the murky waters of Lake Geneva that disappearing into the lake became a temptation. Yet something held him back. As he examined his life, a vague response started to crystallize. Maybe it was time for a change, Johnson thought, time to find another way, another lifestyle. He had lived so long in fantasy; perhaps it was time to grow up and get honest with himself. Van returned to his hotel, picked up an envelope that had arrived for him from the United States, and found an offer inside that could lead to his return to the stage and a second career. Accepting the offer would require courage, but he had never shrunk from challenges in his work. He read the missive again. If it did not hold the key to sustained happiness, it might at least suggest a route to his survival.

CHAPTER 1

Newport

Most tourists think of Newport, Rhode Island, as a resort community famous for its mansions, its yacht races, and its tennis tournaments. But there is a blue-collar side to the island city, and that is the Newport in which Van Johnson grew up. His father was a plumber, and Van spent his youth living in a boarding house on Ayrault Street, just a few blocks from the ornate castles that line Bellevue Avenue. Van and his father were year-round residents of the port city who stayed behind to brave the icy New England winters after the summer colony had left.

Settled in 1639, Newport benefited from an accessible harbor that permitted the town to become a thriving colonial seaport and shipbuilding center. Its wharves were tentacles of trade and commerce, and fishermen unloaded their catch on its docks. Mariners lined the waterfront streets of the town, waiting to depart as crew members of Newport-based ships. By the eighteenth century a merchant aristocracy dominated the city, yet the community was already noted for its artists and craftsmen.

Irish, Italians, Portuguese, and Greeks later came to work in the local textile mills, to fish, and to farm the adjacent countryside. By the time Van Johnson was born on the eve of America's entry into World War I, Newport contained enough of a Swedish population to support two Swedish churches. The community had also become a significant U.S. Navy town, and sailors and their dependents made up a visible component of the city's thriving population.

Van's father, Charles E. Johnson, had come to the United States from Sweden while still a babe in his mother's arms. As a youth in Newport, Charlie Johnson developed into a powerfully built, bull-necked athlete who gave tumbling exhibitions and parallel bar performances for enjoyment. He served as catcher for a YMCA baseball team and at one time was gymnastic instructor of the Algonquin Club at Emmanuel Church. Raised in an austere, Calvinistic environment, Charles grew into a tough-minded, pragmatic New Englander who valued thrift over material comfort. True to his Swedish heritage, he lived simply and honestly, more given to self-effacement than to self-assertion. Achievement and success were far less important to Charlie than were privacy, discipline, self-control, and spiritual conviction.

Imbued with such rigid beliefs, Charles was unfortunate in his choice of mates. Loretta Johnson, who came from a Pennsylvania Dutch background, was miserable in her marriage to the humorless Swede and in the spartan living quarters he provided. With little more than a housekeeper's chores to keep her busy, Loretta soon became an alcoholic. Tension between the young couple existed from the outset but grew worse when their only child, christened Charles Van Dell Johnson, was born at Newport Hospital on August 25, 1916.

His birth took place shortly before dawn on a howling, rainy night. The arrival of a son merely added more pressure to his mismatched parents' dismal relationship, and Loretta's discontent and drinking sprees intensified. When Van was three years old, his still-attractive mother abandoned her family and fled to Brooklyn, New York, in pursuit of a livelier existence. Her son would not see her again until he was a late teenager. Commenting on his parents' divorce years later, Van said, "I was too young to comprehend it then and today I deliberately don't try." His father did not believe in airing such private matters and refused to talk about the marital rift.

Van stayed in Newport with his dad, who continued to live in the boardinghouse at 16 Ayrault Street, up the hill from the beach, where he had lived with Loretta. The two-and-a-half-story structure, with its pitched roof and clapboard siding, later would be converted into an apartment building, and Charlie Johnson, who never veered from his belief in plain living, resided there the rest of his life.

Soon after his mother's departure, Van's paternal grandmother came to live with her son and his shy three-year-old boy. Van remembered his grandmother as a tiny, tidy woman who wore bustling black taffeta dresses and used orange water as a scent on special occasions. She was also an orderly housekeeper and a fabulous cook whose Swedish meatballs, yellow cheese, and frosted cookies were beyond comparison. Born in Sweden, Grandma Johnson spoke English with an accent and sometimes reverted to her native tongue when talking to Charlie at home.

Although his grandmother surrounded Van with quiet affection, she and Charlie were both strict disciplinarians. Young Van was drilled in good manners, neatness of appearance, honesty, and respect for older people. As the lad matured, he was expected to take care of his own clothes, instilled with a keen sense of duty, and taught the importance of productive work. Charles could be severe with his son, and Van respected and admired as well as feared his father. "There was a rumor around," Charlie said later, "that I was a strict sourpuss father. I was strict about a few things, and one was [Van's] health. I never spanked him in my life. He was my buddy... and all it took was a hard look to straighten him out."

But the austere, unbending climate in which the boy was raised created an emotional distance between Van and his father. The child learned at an early age to restrain himself, to bridle his feelings, and not to act on impulse. Self-discipline, he was taught, meant that displays of joy, sorrow, or anger must be diverted into some less demonstrative behavior. For a sensitive, introverted child this led to inhibitions, fundamental insecurity, and repression. Despite the attention he was shown, Van could never be certain that he was loved.

Bessie Boone, a maiden lady in the neighborhood, helped mother the boy, and Van remembered her supervision as warm and kindly. Yet early in his life he became skilled at swallowing his emotions and withdrawing into a hidden world of self-absorption and fantasy. "I've often wished my childhood had been a little different," Van said early in his Hollywood career, and "that I had had a mother's guidance like other boys."

Sunday school and church were mandatory for young Van. Every Sunday morning the lad waited for Virginia Sullivan, a family friend, to pick him up and take him to Newport's old Trinity Church, a landmark in town since 1726. Charles believed in the Scriptures and insisted that his son know and revere the ways of God. "I learned enough to help me keep a balance and a sense of values," Van later maintained.

Charlie tried to be a comrade to the boy. One of Van's earliest memories was of going for a trolley ride with his father one Sunday afternoon and ending up on the Newport beach, where they shared a picnic lunch from a shoe box of food Grandma Johnson had prepared for them. Van and Charlie sometimes took the ferry to the other side of the bay and fed broken Necco wafers to the fish from the end of a stone pier. Charlie taught his son to swim, and the two swam together at Quigley's Beach almost the year around, even when snow covered the ground. "Dad was one of those guys who'd break ice to go swimming," Van recalled. "We spent a lot of time at the beach in the summer. In the winter we'd go swimming with nothing on but trunks."

Charlie had a passion for good music, and through his influence Van developed an interest in the classics. On Saturdays, Charlie tried to leave work early enough to listen to the opera on radio, and he made a note of all the symphony broadcasts for the week. Van often sat with his dad and drank Moxie, New England's equivalent of the South's Dr. Pepper, while they listened together to the broadcasts.

But much of the boy's early years was spent alone, and he passed endless hours entertaining himself in the backyard. The house on Ayrault Street was set close to the street, but there was a good-sized yard in back, and it became Van's haven. Years later, even though he thought of his boyhood as routine and unhappy, he would remember the smell of lilacs around the old house with fondness. Much of his childhood he claimed he could not recall. "I'm kind of soft about things I remember," Van told a reporter in 1945.

When he entered Cranston-Calvert Grammar School, Van made good grades but was considered a daydreamer by those who taught him. Miss King, Van's first-grade teacher, convinced the boy that it would be a great adventure to learn his letters since after a while he would be able to read exciting books about faraway places. "I think I must have been very fortunate in my teachers," Van said as an adult, "because they made me interested in what I was supposed to learn." But the redheaded, freckle-faced kid was bashful with girls and very much a loner. Neighbors remembered Van walking by himself though the leafy streets from school, wearing a knitted woolen cap to keep his head warm in the sharp salt air characteristic of Newport's winters.

For a special outing Charlie took Van to Providence one day to see a circus, driving through a storm in an old Ford to get there. Van would never forget the excitement of watching trapeze artists, a tightrope walker, a man shot from a cannon, and a pretty blond riding a horse bareback around the ring and jumping through hoops of fire. The excursion made him decide that he wanted to be in show business, preferably as a tightrope walker or a trapeze artist.

The lonely youth began doing odd jobs after school—shoveling snow, carrying out ashes, mowing lawns, delivering groceries, selling magazine subscriptions. "It wasn't that I loved work so much," Van said later, "but that I loved possessions more. Dad had one rule: I could have what I wanted if I earned the price of it myself." Van already was substituting possessions for affection and barricading himself behind a wall of defenses.

He bought a trapeze and rings, suspended them from a large tree limb in the backyard, and practiced on them for hours. Eventually Van, Betty Meikle, who lived across the street from the Johnsons, and a boy who lived next door to Betty put together an act. "We would work on that trapeze almost daily," the neighbor boy recalled. "Van was an inveterate circus buff. He, Betty, and I would practice some of the acts that he had seen." Van eventually became quite daring. When the three children staged an exhibition in a neighbor's barn, Van strung a wire from the top of the loft to the ground, where he placed an old mattress. With a leather band attached to a pulley around his head and under his chin, he performed a stunt billed as the "Sensational Slide for Life." Sticking out both arms, Van slid down the wire to the ground. "It's a wonder I didn't break my damned neck!" he reflected later.

When Van discovered silent movies, his interest in the world of entertainment broadened. *Galloping Fish* (1924) with Louise Fazenda and Chester Conklin was the first picture he remembered seeing, but he laughed so hard at the comedy that he made himself sick and had to be taken from the theater. He subsequently spent most of his Saturday afternoons and any evening he could get away from his studies at the movies. "Times when things weren't going so well, I'd buy a ticket to a picture show," Van recalled. He started reading fan magazines and cut out his favorite stars' pictures and pinned them to the walls of his room. "Van was stage-struck and had his room completely plastered with cutouts from magazines of Greta Garbo, his idol," a classmate remembered. Charles Johnson would walk into his son's room and say, "Must you clutter up the place like this?" but Van found delight in a mystical world he secretly longed to join. "I'd go home [from the theater] thinking how grand it must be to make other people feel good," he said, "but I didn't expect to get a chance to do it."

He wrote letters to Hollywood stars asking them for pictures and exchanged fan magazines with the girl next door. Whenever either of them finished an issue, he or she placed the magazine in the kitchen window to signal readiness to swap. The two children went to shows together, and it became clear to his schoolmates that Van had a desire to turn himself into a performer. By the time he was eight years old Dottie Sullivan, Rita McCarthy, and Van were putting on shows in the Johnson's backyard for the neighbors, charging a penny for admission. Charlie would snort, "Van, the only stage you'll ever be on will be a [house] painter's stage." But the rebuff fell on deaf ears. Entertaining people brought the boy the attention he so desperately needed.

As much as Van liked to show off, he was too shy to try out for school plays. The only serious encouragement he received for his ambition to entertain came from Professor Crosby, the Johnsons' landlord, who lived in an apartment upstairs with his cheery wife. But Van pretended a great deal as a boy, so much so in his daily routine that his lonely life was laced with make-believe. "Every day in every way I acted," he later admitted.

At age twelve Van suffered another emotional blow when his grandmother died. Without her sweetness and old-country decorum, the Johnson household turned empty. Distressed and numbed by her passing, Van withdrew into himself all the more. For a time he appeared inarticulate, puzzled, clearly mourning the loss of a vital component in his personal security. He suddenly had more responsibilities heaped on his shoulders, and there was less time for play. "My father and I did the cooking and I guess we weren't the best of cooks," Van said later. "When Mrs. Crosby brought us down some of her baked beans it was a big treat."

Aside from Saturday-night shopping trips and infrequent light moments together, father and son grew increasingly estranged. Laughter between them seemed uncomfortable, and they often spent evenings together with no exchange of words. Whereas Van reveled in glamour and lined his walls with movie-star pictures, Charles remained a staunch believer in physical culture and had a dozen pictures of his hero, Bernarr Macfadden, scattered about. Johnson decreed that he and his son should keep to a daily routine of exercises and follow a healthful diet. As Van became more the dreamer, his father's lack of ambition and simple existence bothered the boy. Charles was content merely to make a living and often warned his son that happiness did not come from chasing dollars or fame. Having enough to eat, a roof over his head, a pile of books, music, the sea, and a few friends was enough for Charles Johnson.

A short distance from the Johnsons' house on Ayrault Street were the palatial summer homes of the big spenders of the late nineteenth century—the Breakers and Marble House, both owned by the Vanderbilts; Chateau-Sur-Mer, designed by popular architect Richard M. Hunt; and the Breakwater, more commonly known as Lippitt's Castle. Van grew up watching the summer crowds that filled the boardwalks, the excursion steamers that brought visitors to Newport for a day, and the frivolity, clam bakes, and spending that took place along the beaches. As Van would remember, the wealthier summer people "came in floating chiffon and white flannel with the good weather and departed all tweeded up with the bad." He heard about the fabled dinners and the brilliant balls inside the mansions, the exclusive debuts and social weddings of the gilded-age aristocracy, and glimpsed the blue bloods who owned cabanas on Bailey's Beach, reputedly the most fashionable strip of sand in America. Although adolescent Van Johnson was not privy to the horse shows, the high teas, the concerts, and the backgammon games that the moneyed set enjoyed, he became aware that there was more to life than the restrictive parameters laid down by his father.

Resentment set in. As a successful adult Van could barely endure mention of either of his parents, and he vowed that he hated his father. If asked about his boyhood, he would usually make a face and decline comment. When his stepson, Ned Wynn, asked him about Charles, Van simply replied, "Horrible man, an awful man." About his mother he would say nothing. Van had little capacity as a child to understand his parents' unhappiness, and as an adolescent he failed to realize the extent of his father's unspoken feeling of rejection that Loretta had deserted them.

During Van's years at John Clarke Middle School, the boy attended whatever stage plays came to Newport and found them a welcome escape.

At the Casino Theater he saw Ruth Chatterton and Alice Brady in dramas, gaping down in ecstasy from the top gallery. An old showboat still tied up periodically at the town's wharf and, as Van later told a writer for *Photoplay,* the leading fan magazine, "where it docked, I docked, too." Once or twice his father took him to Boston to have dinner and see a show, but Van's obsession with show business was mainly an irritant to Charles, and he expected his son to outgrow it.

When Van enrolled himself in Dorothy Gladding's dancing school, his father was appalled. Odd jobs provided the three dollars a month the boy needed for dance lessons, and he soon showed a talent for tap, adagio, soft-shoe, and ballroom dancing. "I decided I wanted to be one of those people up there entertaining people," Van said. But every time he mentioned that he wanted to hoof for a living, his father winced and made some sarcastic remark, and the gulf between the two appeared to widen.

Every Thursday afternoon at five o'clock Van's dance class performed in a vaudeville show. "That's where I smelled my first greasepaint," the future movie star said. Before long, Van was performing with an amateur group at the Lions Club, the Rotary Club, the Knights of Columbus, church socials—any place that requested free entertainment. He had soon worked up a song-and-dance routine, with a straw hat and a cane like Broadway's Jack Donohue, performed in front of a line of girls. The act proved a big hit in the annual variety show at the Colonial Theater, Newport's principal vaudeville house. Van loved the attention he received and, in his mind, he showed enough promise that his career path was set. "I knew I had to get out of that small town," Van told a Hollywood reporter.

The unhappy lad somehow found time to take violin lessons, for he played in the orchestra at Rogers High School during his last three years there. The student ensemble performed for weekly assemblies under the direction of math teacher Louis Chase, whose daughter, Priscilla, played the piano. Van sat in the violin section next to his fellow trapeze participant from grammar-school days. Young Johnson was also in the Dramatic

Society during his freshman year, and while he tried out for play after play in high school, he never got a part. "I chewed up plenty of scenery at the tryouts," Van said, "but I could never make the grade." After repeated readings, the teacher in charge of school plays told him most emphatically, "You'll never make an actor."

Over six feet tall and nicknamed "Red," Van was miserable during his first two years of high school. His freckles caused him endless embarrassment, and the gangly youth appeared uncoordinated and unmanly. His was the innocent countenance that doting matrons often dub a "sweet child." Van felt the isolation. "I guess I always knew I was different," he later said. Hollywood fan magazines would make him out to have been a football and basketball player in Newport, but such was not the case. Van pursued a less academic, commercial course in high school, and his grades in bookkeeping, typing, and shorthand were nothing to brag about. He showed no interest in going to college, although his father talked idly about his son's attending Brown University in nearby Providence and studying law. Painting was the only class that Van truly enjoyed in high school, and the skills he discovered there would serve him well in his later life.

But Van was never part of the elite crowd during his early high school years. He did not date, and he was clearly a maladjusted boy. He found relief by losing himself in the fantasies he observed on the stage and screen. The neighborhood movie house, the Bijou, became Van's haunt, and he hunkered in a seat in the musty theater hour after hour, entranced by the beautiful people and fanciful stories that illuminated the darkness. "I sat through a picture two or three or four times," said Van. "I used to look around the audience, and I'd see the faces of people I knew very well, but they didn't look at all the same." Girls who were plain and uninteresting at school, men who were crabby and cranky on the streets, and women who looked tired and overworked when Van noticed them sitting on their front porches looked happier and more alive in the movie theater. "I could almost feel how they had forgotten their own lives and troubles and maybe the narrowness of existence," Van said, "how for a while they were carried out of themselves and could live so much more, so many more lives."

The boy decided that he had to be one of the people he watched on the screen. He wanted to make other people happy, and in his fancy he envisioned an escape from his own stifled condition. He had no notion of how to achieve such ends, how difficult a life in show business would be, for he knew little of anything beyond Newport. Yet a craving for fame and fortune was planted in his imagination as he became curious about the exciting life he imagined outside the island he came to view as his prison.

Van found his shorthand teacher, Winnie Tripp, attractive, since she was young and had the prettiest laugh he had ever heard. She exuded an ecstatic quality that Van found captivating. His bookkeeping teacher, Miss Phennenmiller, he regarded highly because she had traveled to big cities, spent summers in Europe, and visited Providence to hear lectures. What impressed Van most about Miss Phennenmiller was that she kept a notebook in which she recorded interesting tidbits about the places she had seen and the lectures she had heard to pass on to her classes. "I always thought it was swell of her to take all that trouble and make those notes so she'd have something to tell us," Van said. "Most of us never went anywhere and it made a lot of difference to me the way she told things."

During his high school days Van wrote three short stories for regional magazines, but they all came back with rejection notices attached to them. He wrote a piece on traveling for the *Red and Black,* the school periodical, posing as a far more cosmopolitan traveler than he actually was. "One of the first things I do when I know I'm going on a trip," he wrote, "is to make out a list of names of my friends to whom I want to send cards and letters." Van went on to state that he smoked and had been to New York City, but much of the article was sheer fabrication.

By the time Van became a junior at Rogers High School, he had shed some of his shyness and become more self-confident, mainly through the skill he demonstrated on the dance floor. He took his first girl to a dance that year and was soon invited to parties at the Newport Naval Base, where he met youngsters from all over the country. Dating was never the big preoccupation with Van that fan magazines later suggested, but he did become a popular partner at proms and social gatherings where records were played. "How the women did clamor to dance with Van!" the Rogers High School yearbook announced in 1934. "I knew Van Johnson well," said Juanita Gee, who took business classes with the future star. "I didn't date him, but I danced a lot with him."

Whether Van's sexual uncertainty was evident in Newport is a matter of conjecture. There were plenty of opportunities for homosexual experimentation in a port city. As a boy Van swept out the bathhouse at Quigley's Beach during summers, walked along the waterfront, swam, dug for clams, and encountered young sailors stationed at the naval base. He was a lonely boy, starved for affection, yet whatever sexual acts he engaged in doubtlessly came more from curiosity than an established preference. Van had been raised in an atmosphere of prudery and sexual repression. His father refused to talk about sex or any of the bodily functions. Van later manufactured a steady girlfriend in Newport for the benefit of Hollywood fan magazines, a tiny blond he called Mary who sent him a lacy valentine every year in grammar school and chose him for her escort when she was crowned May Day queen. "When we went to dances," Van apparently told a writer for *Photoplay* in 1945, "we saved the first and last dances for us, together. When we went to Rogers High, we became known as 'the best-known couple in school.' I don't believe we ever said so in so many words but we both believed that someday we would be married." But Mary probably was another fabrication.

Van graduated from Rogers High School in the spring of 1934. The class prophecy for him in the yearbook read:

> Van Johnson will be a dancer,
> For his snake hips he'll be known,
> You'll soon see him performing
> Before the English heir to the throne.

By the time Van left high school, Charles Johnson had advanced to a plumbing contractor, and he wanted his son to join him in the plumbing business. For a year after graduation Van did keep books for his father in a little office at 138 Broadway, doubling as a stenographer. "But I kept a pair of tap shoes in my closet," Van said. He found the work of an accountant dull, hated taking dictation and typing letters, and continued to dream, as he put it, of "something shadowy, dreamy, and dramatic."

Eager though he was to leave Newport, Van was reluctant to desert his father, who had no other family and would be all alone. Van felt an obligation to look after his dad. He tried to be a dutiful son, spent evenings playing games and checkers with his father, and listened to his dad's choice of music on the radio, but he was often miserable. Whenever Van mentioned taking a trip together, Charles would insist that a man's life happened in his mind, away from the crowd.

The movies remained Van's primary solace and source of excitement. He cried when he saw *Imitation of Life* (1934) at the Bijou and wrote ardent fan letters to the film's star, Claudette Colbert. Spencer Tracy became Van's favorite leading man, for he noted that Tracy had an ability most other movies actors did not. The star made acting look natural and easy. The musicals choreographed by Busby Berkeley and those featuring Ginger Rogers and Fred Astaire were so dazzling and thrilling to Van that he almost danced his way home after seeing them. But the boy could share none of these pleasures with his father, who dismissed such fluff as poppycock.

In the summer of 1935 Van took a job as a waiter and part-time cook at a clam house for tourists called the Barnacle. There he met Lois Sanborn, an attractive, redheaded girl of enormous vitality who had taken a summer job as assistant manager of the restaurant. Lois had been to Europe and graduated from Smith College, both of which impressed Van immensely. The girl's mother ran and owned the Newport weekly newspaper and was well known in the community. Lois was smart, ambitious, and courageous, and Van came to look up to her, even though she was not much older than himself. "She was so much the lady," he recalled, "she could have run a poolroom without losing caste."

Lois drove a brand-new Ford, and she and Van spent evenings after work driving around town in the car. Once they journeyed to Boston and dined at the princely Copley Hotel. They frequently went dancing together and ventured into deluxe places Van had never had nerve enough to walk into before. In the course of their summer friendship, the two spent hours talking about Van and his ambitions. Lois pulled no punches with the boy. She believed that people should try to fulfill their dreams; it was better to reach for a star and miss than not to grab for one at all. Van admitted that he was afraid to venture out of Newport. His father had always been the boss, and the boy saw no way of making a break. "A few people are born with some special gift for reaching the hearts of others," Lois told him. She felt that Van had that special gift.

Here was a young woman with brains and breeding telling an introverted young man what he most wanted to hear. "This girl knew so much more than I, and had seen so much more than I, and she believed in me!" Van said "It gave me a faith in myself I never could have attained otherwise." He suddenly began viewing life through Lois's eyes. At her house, overlooking Narragansett Bay, he saw a formal dinner table set for the first time, and he later ate there. When Lois found out that Irving Berlin's musical *As Thousands Cheer* was going to play in Boston, she suggested that they drive to the theater, buy tickets for seats in the balcony, see the show, and give Van a chance to inquire about how one went about getting a job in the theater. Since Lois was so persistent, Van gave in.

He waited outside the stage door in the rain for the show's star, Clifton Webb, before the show began. When Webb's limousine drew up to the curb and the actor got out, Van mustered his courage and approached the distinguished star. Tap shoes in hand, the nervous boy introduced himself and said that he would like some advice on how to get into show business. "What makes you think you want to go into the theater?" Webb said, as he swept past the callow youth and disappeared inside the theater to put on makeup for that night's performance. Van was crushed but later had fun reminding Webb of the incident when they became friends in Hollywood.

Lois's response to the rebuff was that it was time for her friend to strike out on his own. If show business was his ambition, then he must go to New York. Over the summer Van warmed to the idea. Although Hollywood was his dream, New York was closer. When the summer people began leaving Newport that fall, the Barnacle closed for the winter and Lois departed. Van told his father that he was going to try to find work on the stage and wanted to move to New York. Charles reluctantly agreed to let his son go but told him to come home when he had gotten his fill of such silly notions. As long as Van could support himself, he was free to live the life he wanted, his father said. Van bought a straw suitcase, packed it with an extra pair of brown pants, two changes of underwear, four pairs of socks, and a few ties and prepared to make his mark on New York.

He left home in September 1935, wearing a brown sports coat over white flannel pants and an old straw hat, with five dollars in his pocket. "That was my big snappy outfit," said Van. "There I was, a green kid who had never been fifty miles from home, on my way to New York to assault the town." He had just turned nineteen years old. Nine years later, before most of the great mansions in Newport were open to the public, tours of the city ended in front of the clapboard house at 16 Ayrault Street, where gawking tourists and busloads of screaming teenagers ogled Van Johnson's boyhood home. By then he was the most popular young star on the Metro-Goldwyn-Mayer lot.

CHAPTER 2

New York

An eager Van Johnson trudged up a ramp in Grand Central Station, carrying his straw suitcase, and stepped outside into a driving fall rainstorm. Since he owned no raincoat, there was nothing to do but let the battered straw hat he considered so smart protect his face from the downpour. People hurried all around him, ignoring his awkward appearance, shoving him, intent on their own destination. The intense looks on their faces seemed distant and unfriendly to the unsophisticated boy from Rhode Island. Since no one else was wearing a straw hat, Van's confidence plummeted. Within minutes he felt like a yokel from the provinces. Most young men his age were sporting felt hats, pulled down over one eye in natty fashion, despite the rain.

Van dug down into the pocket of his brown coat for his mother's address. Loretta had married Edward J. Neumann after her escape from Newport and had written to her son that he could stay with her and her new husband until he found his own quarters. The couple lived in a small apartment in the Sheepshead Bay district. Van had no idea where Sheepshead Bay was, but he managed to find his way there by subway and slept on the floor of his mother's living room for a few nights. He had not seen her in sixteen years, and the reunion brought more pain than pleasure.

The next five years were filled with uncertainty but would prove the most liberating period of Van's life. With a little additional money from his mother and stepfather, he took a small room in the Knickerbocker Hotel, where he shared a bath with a stranger, for nine dollars a week. He allowed himself fifteen cents a day for food. Most of the time Van ate at the hot dog and orange juice stands around Times Square, but lunch was often no more than a cup of coffee at Walgreen's drugstore. Before Van left Newport, his father had cautioned him always to wipe the silverware in any restaurant before using it and never to eat a rare hamburger.

Van's first step toward finding a job was to buy a newspaper and begin making the rounds of the theatrical offices. He ran into other kids doing the same thing and benefited from their experience. He learned that there was an office in the Astor Theater building where, for twenty-five cents a week, unemployed performers could sit in an outer room, read *Variety* to learn what new shows were in preparation, and listen to gossip about who was casting and where. Van tore names and addresses of agents out of the classified section of the Manhattan telephone directory and worked his way down the list alphabetically. The Broadway agencies seemed unimpressed by a redheaded, freckle-faced boy with little to distinguish himself except a New England twang in his speech. Van would walk into agents' offices and not an eyelash batted. "It wasn't that I didn't try," he said. "I tramped miles. I called in daily. I smiled. I hoofed. I sang." But no one seemed to want his brand of talent.

He grew discouraged yet seldom thought seriously of giving up and going home. It had taken Van a long time to make up his mind about pursuing the kind of career he wanted, and he had carefully weighed the options. No matter how lonely and scared he got in New York, he knew that returning to Newport would mark him a failure and that life there would be predictable and ordinary. The knowledge that his father expected him to fail was incentive enough to cause Van to try harder.

Besides, for a stagestruck youth from a northern port community, New York teemed with excitement. Van was awed by the beauty of Manhattan's architecture and marveled at the Art Deco skyscrapers recently constructed in the midtown area, particularly the soaring Empire State

Building, the gargoyled Chrysler Building, and the Rockefeller Center complex, with its cavernous Radio City Music Hall. He enjoyed the city's many art galleries and theaters. For a quarter he could manage a ticket in the top balcony to see almost any show on Broadway, many of them offering legendary stars Van had read about. He would occasionally glimpse an actor or an actress he recognized on the street, and his jaw would drop in astonishment. He loved riding the subways and, even with very little money, there was so much to do that Van basked in thrilling experiences—walking through Central Park, seeing the Statue of Liberty, and enjoying the company of would-be actors, singers, and dancers. He took menial jobs, and whenever he could afford to do so, he took dancing and singing lessons. He already realized that competition for jobs, in any aspect of professional entertainment, was fierce. America was just beginning to pull out of the worst of the Great Depression, but unemployment and privation still blighted much of the country's population. The 1929 stock market crash had taken a toll on show business, and Broadway was struggling to regain its patronage.

Van, who had always been given to moodiness, did succumb to periods of depression as the disappointments mounted. Within a few weeks of his arrival in Manhattan, the leaves fell from the trees, and winter soon set in. For months his prospects for employment as an entertainer remained bleak. Van had no letters of introduction and no contacts other than those he made through the network of hearsay among aspiring performers. At one point he was locked out of his hotel room for not paying his bill. Van later said that he was never exactly hungry during his early days in New York, but he was never exactly full either. He was almost ready to wire his father collect for money to return home when he received his first break.

Around six o'clock one evening in December, Van was walking toward the subway when he saw a light still on in an agent's window. He went inside and found the agent's wife waiting for her husband in an outer office. Van gave her the biggest smile he could muster. The woman showed him into her husband's office, where the agent, Murray Phillips, asked the youth what shows he had been in. Van lied and said that he had played juvenile leads in stock in Newport, done some understudying in New York, and was a seasoned song-and-dance man. Phillips was not fooled, but he told the callow boy to go the next morning to the Cherry Lane Theater in Greenwich Village, where the agent would be casting an intimate revue.

Van was so thrilled that he was awake before dawn the next day and began vocalizing and practicing dance steps. By the time he reached the theater, he was so nervous that he was sure his voice would crack when he sang. "There were no stage lights," Van said, "so nobody could see me trembling." He warbled "In My Solitude," sang it slow and easy, and somehow managed to sound casual. Somebody in the darkened theater said, "You're hired," and Van left Greenwich Village in a happy daze.

The show was called *Entre Nous,* and it lasted four weeks. Van moved into a dressing room that was being vacated by a young married couple, Robert Walker and a girl David Selznick would rename Jennifer Jones, both on their way to Hollywood. The Cherry Lane Theater was out of the way and small, yet audiences for *Entre Nous* seemed smaller. Van sang and danced in the revue, was one of eighteen young hopefuls who performed between sketches, and quickly felt like a professional. He demonstrated a nice baritone voice, showed aplomb as a dancer, and made fifteen dollars a week after rehearsals, but no one discovered him for the big time. Within a month Van was back on the pavement looking for work.

He began taking singing lessons at a studio next door to the famous Club 21. After class he often sat outside on the steps to cool off and watched for celebrities going in and coming out of the restaurant. To Van the clientele there were the beautiful people; they represented the ultimate in suave, and exuded the sophistication he longed to attain. Sometimes a group of fans congregated outside Club 21 to take snapshots and mob the stars for autographs, and Van would join the group. One afternoon a friendly doorman tipped Johnson off that Joan Crawford was inside. The boy managed to peek through a window of the club just as Crawford turned in his direction. The starstruck Van was so embarrassed that he made a funny face at her and ran away.

Exhilarated by his brush with the professional theater, Van moved into a furnished room in a midtown Manhattan brownstone with a bed, a chair, a bureau, a washbowl, and no clothes closet and continued to haunt the agents' offices. With a show to his credit he appeared more confident and started carrying a red leather notebook, found in a trash can, to jot down names and information that might lead to jobs. About the time his money was running out, he got an offer to tour as a substitute dancer with a troupe bound for New England. His salary would be twelve dollars a week, and the experience would lengthen his résumé. But Van would stay with the company only a short while.

Back in New York things really began to get tough. Van had managed to save half of his earnings on the road, but within a few weeks they were depleted. One day, on his way home from an audition for a dancing job he did not get, he heard a piano in a rehearsal hall and stepped inside to see what was going on. A man on the stage noticed Van standing around with his tap shoes and assumed that the young man had been sent by an agent in answer to a casting call. The man motioned for the lad to come forward and told him to get into his tap shoes and show what he could do. "I felt as if someone had run a blow torch up and down my spine," Van recalled. But he sensed that this was his big moment. He performed double time, triple time, and wing time. "Nobody had to give me a pep talk to make me knock myself out," Van said. "I was kicking through with everything I had."

The man in charge was the noted producer Leonard Sillman, who had already given an early career boost to actors Tyrone Power and Henry Fonda, comedienne Imogene Coca, and dancer and future Hollywood director Charles Walters. Sillman was currently in the second week of rehearsing *New Faces of 1936* and needed a replacement for a male dancer who had fallen and sprained an ankle. The experienced producer remembered Van as "a husky blond boy," so shy that he blushed and stammered when he talked. "He showed me some of his light fantastic stuff," Sillman recalled, "and he was unquestionably a brilliant hoofer." The producer hired the apt youngster on the spot and told Van to start learning the routines, which the boy did in quick order.

Sillman himself directed the revue's sketches. He was a comical man who usually began rehearsals with a joke. He liked young people, particularly attractive young males, and had an eye for blossoming talent. Van was ready for the challenge Sillman's revue presented. No matter how far back the show's dance director placed him, Van's shining countenance always seemed to be in the spotlight. He performed in the chorus of *New Faces of 1936* to music that was catchy and alive and impressed company members even though he was not singled out by the critics.

Mildred Burns, an actress known as Toddy to her friends, appeared in the revue's sketches and remembered Van as a lighthearted, happy boy with an outgoing personality. "Occasionally he was a little down," Toddy Burns recalled, "but mainly he was lots of fun. I knew Van would go on to bigger things, but I had no idea that he'd be the success he was. All he was doing in *New Faces* was shuffling his feet."

Toddy got to know Van well during the show's rehearsal period. The lad was so eager to learn that he stood in the wings and watched cast members as they went over their sketches. At the time Van and another young man in the show were living at a boardinghouse on West Fifty-fifth Street, where everyone on their floor shared the same bathroom. Toddy was then rooming with Judy Abbott, daughter of the great Broadway stage director and play doctor George Abbott. Van and his roommate frequently came over to the two girls' apartment for dinner. As time wore on, Judy and Toddy grew somewhat disgusted because the men never lifted a hand to help and expected the girls to prepare the meal and then clean up the mess.

Van always seemed to be "on" with his friends and seldom talked about Newport and never mentioned his family. Toddy had the impression that his childhood had been difficult. Cast members of *New Faces* wondered about Van's background yet were reluctant to ask him probing questions. Toddy Burns assumed that he was homosexual, which was accepted in the theatrical world. Van was a likable fellow who clearly had ability; to the young actors and chorus kids along Broadway, talent was what counted.

As the weeks of rehearsal went by, Van got to know future song-writer Ralph Blane, who was another chorus boy in *New Faces* and lived in the same boardinghouse as Van. During the run of the show Johnson met Keenan Wynn, a young actor and son of the famed comedian Ed Wynn. Soon he was introduced to Keenan's future wife, Evie, when Van accompanied Judy Abbott to the train station to see Keenan off for a try-out of one of George Abbott's shows in Boston. Van and the Wynns later became best friends. "Nobody could dislike this husky hunk of freckled health," Keenan wrote in his memoirs, "and we liked him very much. Compared with Van, most of us were worldly sophisticates."

Van had been hired for *New Faces of 1936* at twenty dollars a week, but when the revue went to Boston for tryouts, his pay leaped to thirty dollars a week. This second edition of *New Faces* featured the pixieish Imo-gene Coca, a holdover from Sillman's successful 1932 revue, and both the show and the comedienne received excellent notices. When *New Faces* opened at the Vanderbilt Theater in Manhattan on May 19, 1936, the *New York Times* reported, "With some good music and sketches that are not on the intellectual side, the latest of Leonard Sillman's cultural endeav-ors is a cheerful thing and unpretentious, amiable, and bustling with the zest that all new faces provide in the weary month of May."

Van stayed with the revue through its entire run, forty weeks, but socialized less with company members after the show opened. Toddy Burns remembered seeing him only at performances, since he had begun frater-nizing with a different crowd. Most of Van's extra money went for singing and dancing lessons, but now that he was earning a steady salary, he per-mitted himself to eat in better restaurants, although still nothing fancy. After performances he usually went out with friends, and he often spent his days reading. Van had given himself a year to make good when he left Newport, and within that time he had landed a job in a hit show and revealed a breezy, less inhibited side to his personality. But the old wounds from childhood still bled, and much of Van's effervescence was a facade to hide the reticent, morose nature that would be his the rest of his life.

When *New Faces of 1936* closed, the only job young Johnson could find was in the chorus of the Roxy Theater, one of New York's most majestic motion picture houses. His salary there was $23.70 a week, but he got to see all of the movies for free. The Roxy maintained a permanent line of girls called the Roxyettes and, when the need arose, the management hired a dozen or so boys to dance with the girls. Gae Foster, the theater's dance director, decided on the theme of each week's show, and her assistants worked out the details and rehearsed the chorus for the coming week while the movie was playing. "We'd just get up there and knock our brains out," said Dan Dailey, another of the Roxy's dancers who went to Hollywood about the same time that Van did.

The Roxy, like Manhattan's other great presentation houses (the Paramount, the Capitol, and Radio City Music Hall), offered five shows a day and sometimes seven on weekends, beginning at eleven o'clock in the morning and alternating live entertainment with a feature film, a newsreel, and an animated cartoon. The theater maintained an orchestra and an organist, and there was always the chance that one of the chorus kids would be tapped for something better. But the work there was grueling. "I didn't want to be an aging chorus boy," said Van, "or run a dance school in the Bronx." Yet the memory of hunkering over his dad's ledgers in Newport was sufficient incentive to keep him going.

One day acrobatic dancer Lucille Page, wife of comedian Buster West, came backstage at the Roxy and asked Van if he would like to work in a vaudeville act with her and Buster for seventy-five dollars a week plus expenses. The offer was too good to pass up, and for several months Van traveled with the team, performing in a dramatic sketch with them and standing in the wings holding Buster's shoes so the comedian could make a quick change. The act broke up when Lucille decided to take time off to have a baby, and Van returned to New York with no other prospects.

Between jobs he fell into moments of worry and melancholy. He pondered his future and the instability of the path that seemed to be his destiny. Much of the time he was lonesome; relief came in work. During the summer of 1938 Van entertained at resorts in the Catskills and enjoyed the demanding schedule and social life he found there. He sang, danced, served as master of ceremonies, played the violin, and did some acting. At the summer hotels on the so-called borscht circuit, he met an array of talented young performers, got slapped in the face as a comedy stooge, and earned a meager nine dollars a week besides room and board. But Van claimed his experience in the Catskills was "the finest all-around training ground since burlesque."

At Swan Lake, where Van's summer tour started, the hotel social staff put on a different show every evening in the resort's recreation room. One night the entertainment might be in a cabaret setting, whereas the next it might be a Gilbert and Sullivan operetta. Perhaps a concert followed the night after that, and the week might include a one-act play. "We were just a bunch of ambitious kids and loved the variety," said Van. Performers painted their own scenery, did their own laundry, ironed their own costumes, and rehearsed right up to time of the evening's performance. "I had a broken-down wardrobe that served many purposes," Van told a journalist later, but "the food was terrific."

After the night's show, Van danced with the wealthy matrons and their daughters and later said that the girdles he encircled with his arm were as hard as armor plate. He was popular with the guests, ate all of the lox and bagels he wanted, and enjoyed a social interaction that changed frequently enough that there was little chance of a relationship that became threatening. On his evenings off, Van usually went to movies.

At the end of the summer he hitchhiked back to New York and began making the rounds of agents' offices again. In January 1939 he joined a group called the Eight Men of Manhattan, which sang and danced with

Mary Martin in a midnight show in the swank Rainbow Room at Rockefeller Center, which had just opened. Martin had become the newest toast of Broadway that winter, singing a modestly naughty song titled "My Heart Belongs to Daddy" in Cole Porter's musical *Leave It to Me*. For eight weeks she did one show a night in the Rainbow Room after she had finished her performance in the theater. To back her, the Eight Men of Manhattan were decked out in white ties and tails, and Van was pleased to be part of such a well-dressed, classy act.

He and Martin became friends during the engagement, and she encouraged Van not to give up his ambitions. "You've got the stuff," Martin told him, and she was one of the first to urge him to try for a career in moving pictures. "Mary was a peach," said Van. "She never stopped boosting me. She had more faith in me than I did." One night Martin did her act on the Waldorf Hotel's Starlight Roof. The elegant atmosphere there invigorated Van, and he began to feel that he could do anything. Perhaps Hollywood was not an impossibility after all.

Later, for the fan magazines, Van would conjure up entanglements with girlfriends during his New York apprenticeship, but they were mainly friendships, not romances. He even feigned that he harbored a crush on Lois, the girl from Newport who had urged him to stretch his wings and see what Broadway had to offer in the way of employment. Van claimed that he once made plans to return home to see Lois, but before he got there he received a letter from her telling him that she was going to marry someone else. "I carried a torch for years," he said. "To call it heartbreak I went through is dramatizing it too much. I faced the truth. As my wife what chance would she have?" He often remarked that it was always the girls in his life who kept his spirits up and pushed him ahead at crucial moments.

What Van wanted for the time being was a speaking part in a Broadway musical. In the late summer of 1939 he tried out for a small role in Rodgers and Hart's *Too Many Girls,* but director George Abbott groaned when he listened to Van reading lines and put him in the chorus playing a

student, with no dialogue. The show starred Eddie Bracken, Richard Kollmar, and a twenty-two-year-old Cuban musician named Desi Arnaz. While
its plot was thin, the musical was fast paced and funny and included the
songs "I Didn't Know What Time It Was" and "You're Nearer," both of
which became standards. Arnaz was cast as a college football player from
South America and sang with a heavy accent, danced a conga, played a
bongo drum, strummed a guitar, and became a sensation with audiences.

Van's energy and charm so impressed Abbott during the show's rehearsal period that Johnson eventually became the understudy for all three
male leads. Stage manager Jerry White drilled the inexperienced actor in
the parts and taught him a great deal about delivering dialogue. But Abbott
taught Van about timing, how to make exits and entrances, and about the
need for discipline in the theater. As a member of the chorus Van made
forty dollars a week, but five dollars more was added once he became a
principal understudy.

"When we were in rehearsal, every one of us would be looking at
Van," said Bracken. "He had a charisma and a winning smile, and every
move he made was that of a great dancer. It was the first time in my life
that I saw a young chorus boy doing nothing but his work steal a show."
Future movie producer Martin Jurow, then the agent who represented
Bracken, Arnaz, and eventually Van himself for MCA, agreed with
Bracken's assessment. "Johnson was so attractive that he stood out," Jurow
said. "There was no one in the chorus that had the quality, the exuberance, and a kind of effulgence that Van did. He sang well and he danced
well, but that face in the chorus was simply fantastic."

During the show's weeks of preparation Van was surrounded by
homosexuals. Besides many of the boys in the chorus, choreographer
Robert Alton was known to be gay, as were lyricist Lorenz Hart and Hart's
friend and hanger-on, Milton G. "Doc" Bender. Hart frequented the cheap
bars around Eighth Avenue and Forty-fifth Street and was notorious for
his excesses and erratic behavior. Many felt that Doc Bender procured
whatever sexual partners the unattractive Hart enjoyed and orchestrated

the lyricist's late-night parties, which some say Van attended. Both Hart and Bender were reputed to be attracted to Arnaz, whom they had discovered working in a nightclub in Miami, but Arnaz, known even then as a wild character and a boozer, probably went no further in their escapades than joining them for an occasional drink.

Too Many Girls tried out in Boston and opened at the Imperial Theater in New York on October 18, 1939. Brooks Atkinson, reviewing the musical for the *New York Times*, called it "humorous, fresh, and exhilarating." Atkinson complimented Alton on the vivacious dances he had created for the show and said that there were "some likely young fry in the chief places."

During the production's seven-month run, Van's work seemed to improve as he grew more confident. He was feeling sick one afternoon from something he had eaten at the Automat when the telephone rang and White told Johnson that he would have to go on that night for Kollmar. Van pulled himself together, sang "I Didn't Know What Time It Was" with ingenue Marcy Westcott, and performed well as the athletic romantic lead. Van claimed that he was in such a dense fog that evening that he did not even remember walking on stage. When Eddie Bracken later went to California for a screen test, Van was called upon to play Bracken's comic role for two weeks.

"Everyone knew that Van would be a star," said Bracken. "It was a question of who was going to discover him and when would it be. We all felt that way. There could be twenty people on the stage, and the audience would look at Van. You'd meet people after the show, and they'd say, 'Who was that tall red-headed blond?' People would talk about him before they'd talk about the show."

Bracken, a married man who already had started a family, was not privy to Van's social life. Van seemed to associate mostly with the show's other chorus kids. They occasionally went bowling together, and Bracken was along one night when George Abbott joined the group with a date—luscious Betty Grable, who was performing on Broadway at the time in Cole Porter's *DuBarry Was a Lady*. "Betty was a great bowler," said Bracken, "and Van was there with the other guys from the chorus. He had a great sense of humor, and I liked him a lot." Bracken presumed that Van was homosexual, although he did not disclose that side of himself in public.

Jurow noticed that the other chorus boys seemed to look up to Van and maintained that the gay ones were eager to get their hands on the young strawberry blond. In Jurow's judgment, Van did not succumb to their advances. The agent had signed the promising chorus boy as a client and had no doubts that he could place Johnson with one of the major studios in Hollywood. But Jurow told Diosa Costello, another of his clients and one of the female leads in *Too Many Girls*, "I want to make sure that he'll be all boy, all man." Costello, a firebrand who exuded sexuality, said, "Leave him to me."

The star had a downstairs dressing room, and Van had to walk past Costello's quarters to get upstairs, where the chorus members made up and changed into their costumes. "As Van would attempt to pass," Jurow recalled, "Diosa would pluck him from the group. She worked him over and didn't stop. She loved him, and he loved her back. How far they went I don't know, but Van didn't recede, and he didn't leave until the last minute. The look in Diosa's eye afterwards told me, 'It all went well.'"

RKO bought the motion picture rights to *Too Many Girls,* and after the show closed on Broadway, Van left for California with Bracken, Arnaz, dancer Hal LeRoy, George Abbott, and other members of the show's chorus to make the film version. Many of the fans he had met outside Club 21 seeking autographs from celebrities had become friends by then, and some of them went to the train station to see Johnson off. They loaded him down with apples, lollipops, and books and showered him with good wishes. Van was thrilled at a chance to see Hollywood for the first time and eager to meet stars and test his appeal before a motion picture camera. When he boarded the train he was full of hope and vitality.

RKO contracted Van for $150 a week but gave him no billing in the picture. He found the studio "a dream place to work," with a congenial family atmosphere, flower gardens scattered about, and stars the caliber of Irene Dunne and Ginger Rogers. Richard Carlson replaced Kollmar in the movie version of *Too Many Girls*, Lucille Ball played Westcott's role, and Ann Miller took the Diosa Costello part. During the making of the picture, Ball was introduced to Arnaz. "We had lots of fun on the set," Bracken remembered, and "everybody loved each other."

But the film was not as good as the stage production. Abbott blamed the Hollywood censors. In the Broadway version of the show the virgins at Pottawatomie College, where the musical takes place, wore beanies. Since any mention of virginity or sexual intercourse was forbidden by the motion picture production code, the college girls who wore beanies in the movie were the ones who did not neck. Ball thought that Abbott's direction was the reason the film was not better. "Even at that time," Ball said, "I recognized that George Abbott was doing what I call shooting a picture with a Kodak in a hotel room. He was so used to that proscenium arch, and he used the camera as a fourth wall." That took away from the cinematic fluidity of the movie in Ball's opinion and gave *Too Many Girls* a static quality.

Van appears as a football player in the opening shot, and he is in the middle of the front row, smiling and singing. He appears in several scenes in the picture, usually dancing and singing in the background, but Abbott allowed Johnson to speak two quick lines. He obviously had spent many hours working out with weights and had matured into a handsome young man, and while basically still a chorus boy, he shows ability, exuberance, and an enchanting presence.

"I don't think anyone can tell what it is that makes a star," said Arnaz. "It's just somebody who jumps out of the screen at you. Van was a perfect example." Many of the cards turned in by preview audiences asked about the identity of the tall, redheaded fellow behind Arnaz, Ann Miller, or one of the other featured players. The viewers were referring to Van, for his radiance stood out even in crowd scenes.

Filming on *Too Many Girls* ended in September 1940. When Van's work on the picture was finished, he went to Chicago, where the stage version of the college musical was scheduled to open. By then Kollmar had married newspaper woman Dorothy Kilgallen, and Van took over his part while Kollmar went on a honeymoon. As a featured player Johnson earned $150 a week, but the show failed to catch on with Midwestern audiences and closed after a short run.

In the interim, George Abbott had returned to New York to begin preparations on Rodgers and Hart's new musical, *Pal Joey*, which Abbott was slated to direct. Based on some short stories by novelist John O'Hara that had appeared in the *New Yorker*, the show would prove a watershed musical, far ahead of its time in honesty and insight into human frailties. Joey, the central character, is an opportunist, a womanizer, and a consummate heel. "I looked upon Joey as an amoral character," said Gene Kelly, who created the role on Broadway. "He just didn't consider something right or wrong. He was completely self-centered, and everything was for him. He was brought up in an era in America when whatever you could do to get ahead, you did." O'Hara wrote with a bite, and Larry Hart heightened the author's sardonic book with his literate, scabrous lyrics. *Pal Joey* not only made a powerful social comment but also contained a brilliant score, tightly integrated into the plot, and contextual choreography devised by the dance director, Robert Alton.

At stage manager Jerry White's urging, Van received a short speaking role in addition to a place in the show's chorus. Having filled in for Kollmar and Bracken in *Too Many Girls*, he was disappointed that his part in *Joey* was not larger. "I was spoiled and I thought about tossing in the sponge and going back to Newport," he said. But after rehearsals began in November, Van seemed to be assigned more to do in the show every day. On one occasion Alton yelled at him, "Hey you—the guy with the freckles. Get off your rump and see if you can do a dance with June here. And make it a crazy one!" June was twenty-four-year-old June Havoc, the talented sister of stripper Gypsy Rose Lee, and she and Van made their dance together plenty crazy. Van ended up with a song and ten lines to speak in the final production. "By the time the show opened in Philly," he said, "I had a pretty decent part."

Kelly, under Alton's guidance, was perfecting his own special dance style, a combination of ballet, modern dance, and tap. "I like to think of [it] as a purely American style," said Kelly, and "it did have a streamlined look." The chorus needed to blend its work with Kelly's innovative approach, but the adjustments were as exciting as they were challenging. "I did things in *Pal Joey* that I never dreamed I was capable of," said Havoc. "I went in and did them and found out that I could. Robert Alton never took no for an answer. I think we were all pretty aware, even as brash kids, that this was not the usual dumb show."

In the chorus with Van was future Hollywood director Stanley Donen, then a sixteen-year-old boy fresh out of South Carolina. Donen lived in the same apartment building that Van did, along with aspiring songwriters Ralph Blane and Hugh Martin, who did the vocal arrangements for *Pal Joey*. Whenever Havoc and some of the chorus kids went out after rehearsals, Donen wanted to be included. "Stanley was our tagalong," said Havoc. "We didn't want to be seen with a kid that age, because we thought we were grown up." But Van befriended the awkward southern boy and invited him to join the group. "Everybody else was so mean and used to make fun of his accent," Van told Donen's biographer. "They thought he must be some kind of hayseed."

Later, when Donen's parents came to New York to see *Pal Joey,* they took their son and Johnson to dinner in the Starlight Room of the Waldorf-Astoria Hotel. "Thank God in those days I always wore a necktie to work," Van said. "Xavier Cugat and his band were playing, and I'll never forget going, because it was the first time in my life I ever ate lobster thermidor. It had real sherry in the sauce."

Since Kelly was the show's star and was a few years older than Johnson and Havoc, the star socialized with a more mature group. When *Pal Joey* tried out in Philadelphia, Kelly often accompanied O'Hara and Hart to after-hours drinking clubs around town. "I was too naive to go to bed early," said Kelly. "We'd drink till four or five in the morning, then I'd go back to the hotel and sleep." Rehearsals the next day started at ten o'clock, but Hart usually came in late, nursing a hangover. Havoc remembered

Kelly as "a brash, noisy, big-mouthed kid" who wanted to fight all the time. "He used to beat the devil out of the dancers onstage and yell at the orchestra," she said. Van often was intimidated by Kelly.

Kelly at the time was courting actress Betsy Blair, whom he later married. After Van was established in Hollywood, he claimed that Havoc and he, "went everywhere" with Kelly and Blair during *Pal Joey's* run on Broadway. But that was the kind of embellishment that studio publicists fed to fan magazines. In New York, Kelly and Johnson were casual acquaintances at best.

Even before the show opened in Manhattan, *Pal Joey* created argument. Audiences in Philadelphia complained that the musical made for an unpleasant evening, and women particularly found it difficult to accept a charming scoundrel as the hero. "Joey was a very hard-bitten, tough role for that time," said Kelly. "To have a young man living with an older woman and being in love with a young girl at the same time and also having affairs with every member of the chorus was quite revolutionary." The show was not so much dirty as it was earthy. But audiences in 1940 did not expect a frank slice of life in the musical theater.

To open such a bold show on Broadway on Christmas night was unwise. Atkinson, New York's most prestigious critic, gave *Pal Joey* a bad review; he called the story odious and said that the musical lacked moral taste. "Although *Pal Joey* is expertly done," Atkinson wrote, "can you draw sweet water from a foul well?" After the opening-night performance, the cast gathered at Hart's house to await the notices. Hart phoned a friend at the *New York Times* and had him read Atkinson's review as it rolled off the presses. "As Larry listened, he didn't say anything to us," Kelly recalled, "but he started to cry. He hung up and walked out of the room. Hart respected Brooks's opinion so much, as we all did, but the show puzzled reviewers."

The first-night audience seemed tremendously enthusiastic about *Pal Joey,* and a couple of newspaper critics liked the show and commented on its innovative aspects. One even mentioned the "blond and very personable Van Johnson," who, although handling only a few lines, "manages to project himself quite vividly." Van knew that people were beginning to notice him. When he was selected as Kelly's understudy in the show, Johnson was ecstatic, aware that Joey was a demanding and important role. "I was sailing on eggs," Johnson said. "I was in the chips—$150 a week. I had six suits."

Controversial though *Pal Joey* was, the production received much attention and created a great stir. There was no question that the impudent musical had been fashioned by some of Broadway's top talent. It was an expensive show—one hundred thousand dollars—and the cast was first-rate, headed by Vivienne Segal, the veteran star of many Rodgers and Hart musicals, in the role of the older woman. David O. Selznick, producer of *Gone with the Wind,* would soon sign Kelly to a Hollywood contract. Havoc also accepted a motion picture offer. Within a short time Donen would go to Metro-Goldwyn-Mayer as a dancer and later serve as Kelly's assistant. Van waited for his turn to come and was determined to be ready.

After the curtain fell at night on *Pal Joey,* Johnson usually grabbed something quick to eat and went to see a double feature at one of the off-Broadway movie houses. "He did that night after night," said Havoc, "to study Spencer Tracy and the other actors he admired. That's how he learned film acting. He taught himself. We knew that Van would turn into a movie star because he knew it."

Next door to the Ethel Barrymore Theater, where *Pal Joey* was playing, Ethel Merman was starring in the Cole Porter hit *Panama Hattie.* In the cast of the neighboring show was a young hopeful named June Allyson, who was understudying Betty Hutton in the Porter musical. Van met Allyson at the apartment of a mutual friend, and the two quickly became soul mates. On matinee days they often met for a hamburger between shows, and both were avid movie fans. Like Johnson, Allyson went to motion pictures more to learn than to be entertained. "Just like me and the other kids, Van had dreams of someday becoming an actor," she said. "We'd go to the movies and sit, not through a single showing, but three or four times." Whereas Van idolized Tracy, June thought Margaret Sulla-van was the screen's greatest actress and tried to emulate her. Sometimes in private the two young aspirants would act out scenes they had seen. Then they would critique each other's performances and try the scene again. "We kidded and talked about what we would do when we were motion picture celebrities," Allyson said, "how perhaps we'd even play in a picture together."

Both of them recognized that the stage offered the best training that a young actor could receive. They spent hours together discussing comedy pacing, motivation of character, and nuances of the craft. Van told June about the weeks he had spent in Hollywood making *Too Many Girls* and described the California sunshine and orange blossoms, but he confessed that he worried that he did not photograph well. "I reminded him that not all actors looked like Robert Taylor," Allyson said.

Pal Joey settled in for a nine-month run on Broadway, with audi-ences' reactions mixed. Wednesday matinees, which brought a large num-ber of women into town for shopping and a show, tended to be frigid to-ward the show. "In the eyes of the ladies from Westchester, the scenes we were playing were illicit," Kelly said. "They would sit there grimly and stare at us. There would hardly be a patter of applause. We dreaded doing the Wednesday matinee." But the Friday- and Saturday-night crowds were more receptive. "Those performances were a pleasure for us," said Kelly, "because then we got the swinging groups."

Jurow, the agent who represented Allyson as well as Johnson, was confident that he soon would be sending both of his young clients to Hol-lywood. "Van and June were my two pets," said Jurow. "I was sure that studio executives would see in them what I saw." While *Pal Joey* was still playing on Broadway, Columbia Pictures asked to make a screen test of Van. Richard Irving, another dancer in the show's chorus and later head of television at Universal, took over Johnson's part while Van flew to Cal-ifornia. Johnson spent less than a week on the West Coast, and the studio tested him opposite Janet Blair, one of its new stars. But Harry Cohn, Columbia's production head, was unimpressed with the results and decided not to sign Van to a contract.

The discouraged youth returned to New York and resumed his duties in *Pal Joey,* more fearful than ever that he did not come across well on film. When the Rodgers and Hart musical closed in September 1941, the disheartened chorus boy went home to Newport to visit his father. He ate clams, sat on the beach, and wondered whether his dreams were worth the effort. "I was beginning to be sick of Broadway," said Van, and Hollywood seemed unimpressed with him. Charlie Johnson assumed that Van's wanderlust was over and that he had come home to stay. Friends in Newport seemed to have changed, and Van quickly recognized that their lives had gone in different directions from his. Try as he might to find a common ground for conversation, there did not seem to be anything to say. Even the people he once knew best had no capacity to understand the ups and downs that an ambitious performer had experienced in the six years since he had been away from Rhode Island.

After Van had spent two days in Newport, the telephone rang. Jurow informed Van that Warner Bros. wanted to sign him to a six-month contract at three hundred dollars a week. "It was like asking a drowning man if he would consider being rescued by a yacht," Johnson said. "I was on that train before they could change their minds." Van rushed through New York, stopped long enough to buy a portable typewriter at Macy's and some fruit to eat on the trip, and arrived in Los Angeles four days later. Full of excitement, he got off the train only to discover that no one was at the station to meet him. Van called the studio, but no one there seemed to know who he was. Hollywood obviously would be no easier to conquer than Broadway had been.

CHAPTER 3

Early Hollywood

When Van stepped off the train in Los Angeles in late 1941, he was as excited as a schoolboy, eager to claim the laurels that awaited him in the film capital. But his spirits fell when Warner Bros. paid so little attention to him. He checked into a hotel and called the studio again the morning after he arrived. "Your six-months' contract entitles us to give you a six-weeks' layoff," a voice on the other end of the telephone said. "We are putting you on layoff starting today." So for six weeks Johnson went without salary. He moved into the Morrison apartments and waited for the studio's casting office to call.

To kill time he practiced dramatic expressions before a mirror and went to the beach. He took a sight-seeing tour of Los Angeles, during which he got his first glimpse of Grauman's Chinese Theater and a sampling of movie stars' homes, and visited Eddie Bracken, by then under contract to Paramount. Bracken took his former *Too Many Girls* colleague to lunch in the Paramount commissary, and Van was astonished when Dorothy Lamour, who was walking just ahead of him, reached back and held the door open for him. "Wow!" he said. "It was the greatest thrill of my life." Later he went to RKO to watch June Havoc work and tried to contact Gene Kelly, who was having frustrations of his own waiting for David O. Selznick to find a proper vehicle for the dancer's screen debut.

Van wondered what gracious phrases he should utter when executives at Warner Bros. finally found time to summon him to the studio. He bought himself a Ford roadster on credit and made trips to Palm Springs and Yosemite and fell in love with California. He spent evenings watching movies at the theaters along Hollywood Boulevard, but as the weeks of unemployment dragged on, he grew discouraged. "I just sat on my stern and drank orange juice," he later said.

When he visited the Warner Bros. lot in Burbank at last and innocently walked into the studio's Green Room for lunch, he was told by a waitress that those facilities were reserved for stars, directors, and producers only. Asked by a studio administrator who his favorite movie stars were, Van replied, "Greta Garbo and Spencer Tracy," both of whom were under contract to Metro-Goldwyn-Mayer. A secretary at Warner Bros. informed him that it would have been wiser to name Warner stars, perhaps Bette Davis and James Cagney. Van clearly had much to learn if he was successfully going to play the Hollywood game.

Executives at the studio liked his name, since Van Johnson runs together like a surname, but they disliked his sandy blond hair and dyed it black. "They told me blond men weren't star material," Van recalled. Publicists at Warner Bros. described him to the press as "a big fellow, boyish in type, and pleasant company either as an actor or a person." They claimed that he played football in high school and collected china elephants and first editions as a hobby. But it was evident that the studio did not know what to do with a strawberry blond with freckles who danced.

At the time Van was six feet, two inches tall and weighed 185 pounds, but his youthful looks and easy demeanor equipped him poorly for the tough kind of pictures about slums and gangsters that had been Warner's specialty. Producers at the studio favored rugged male stars like Humphrey Bogart, Errol Flynn, and John Garfield, not the soft, cute variety that Van Johnson represented.

With his six-month contract about to expire, Warner Bros. cast Van in an inexpensive programmer titled *Murder in the Big House*. Shooting began on the picture on January 13, 1942, five weeks after the United States entered World War II. With Hollywood adjusting to wartime priorities and restrictions and rampant fears of a possible Japanese bombing of the California coast, all of the studios were in an unsettled state. Jack Warner, production head at the Burbank studio, worried that Japanese aviators might mistake his sound stages for Lockheed aircraft plant and bomb them by mistake.

Van reported to the set of *Murder in the Big House* at nine o'clock in the morning on the Tuesday filming began, his hair and eyebrows blackened, ready to play a cub reporter just out of college. In the picture, a young journalist investigates and solves the mystery of the death of a condemned murderer sitting in his cell awaiting execution. In view of complaints from newspapermen that reporters were often portrayed in movies as drunkards, Hollywood's Production Code Administration urged the studio to modify the character Johnson played to avoid offense. In part for this reason, actor George Meeker had been taken out of the role and replaced with the more wholesome-looking Johnson.

B. Reeves Eason directed the fifty-nine-minute mystery, and Faye Emerson, whom the studio had put under contract as a potential cover for Bette Davis, was the picture's leading lady. In the movie, Van wore a black suit with white stripes that Dennis Morgan had worn in an earlier feature. Eason stayed within the two-week shooting schedule he had been allotted and finished *Murder in the Big House* on January 26. By early May the picture was in the theaters. *Variety* reported that Van handled his role "creditably," but the *New York Times* dismissed the movie as "potboiler fare." Most reviewers found the film routine, with little besides its title for marquee value. Van later commented that he looked far different on the screen than he had expected and claimed responsibility for giving what he considered a poor performance. "I simply didn't know how to act in front of a camera, and didn't know what to do with the role," he said. "I walked out of frames, waved my arms, and in general couldn't have been any worse."

During the time the picture was being shot, Van lived at 1755 Cold-water Canyon in Beverly Hills, but he spent a great deal of time at June Havoc's house on Alpine Drive. Havoc had rented the sizable place, bor-rowed furniture from the RKO prop department, and turned the home into a refuge for unemployed young actors. Eight or ten people lived there, paying whatever they could afford for boarding privileges. Most of them knew each other from shows they had done in New York, and the group formed a sort of extended family and mutual support system. Van was lonely and enjoyed the companionship he found there. He and Havoc oc-casionally went out on the town together, and she remembered how the dye that Warner Bros. put in Van's hair came off and ran down his face when they swam.

On February 28, 1942, Johnson received word that the studio was not picking up his option, which meant that his contract would not be re-newed. "After that," he said, "I figured I was all washed up." When Havoc got home from work that evening, she found Van sitting outside her house in his car. "In the back," she said, "I could see a battered suitcase and a corrugated carton filled with half-opened boxes of cornflakes and some moldy rolls. His face looked dismal." Van told her that he was finished at Warner Bros. and that he was driving back to New York. Havoc persuaded him to stay in California a while longer and invited him to live at her house. The next day Van moved in, bringing an unpainted bed he had bought for six dollars. Havoc loaned him some sheets and later wrote that the dye from his hair came off and ruined her pillowcases.

A few evenings after moving into the house on Alpine Drive, Van had dinner with Desi Arnaz and Lucille Ball, who had recently married. The three had become friends during the making of *Too Many Girls* at RKO, and Van had seen Ball again when she visited Arnaz during the musical's run in Chicago. Having heard that Van was about to leave Hollywood, the couple invited him to dine with them at Chasen's restaurant to say good-bye. Seated at the next table was Billy Grady, for many years head of tal-ent at Metro-Goldwyn-Mayer. Lucille had just signed a contract with that studio and, taking Van in tow, she walked over to Grady's table and told him Van's situation. "Look at this boy," Ball said to Grady. "Look at that smile." Van protested that he did not think that the picture business was for him. But Lucy pleaded, "Billy, don't let him say good-bye. Keep him here." Grady observed that the lad had a likable personality and sensed that he was eager and would be willing to work hard to master screen technique. The Metro talent head told Van to come to the Culver City studio the next day for a test.

Having been this route before, Van kept his hopes in check but showed up at Grady's office early the following morning. A few days later he tested opposite Donna Reed, a newly signed MGM player, and a contract was quickly negotiated for Van, with his salary starting at $350 a week. Grady told Benny Thau, the Metro executive in charge of contracts, that Johnson had been badly managed at Warner Bros. but explained that he now had some camera experience. "At MGM his spots would have to be handpicked," the studio's head of talent wrote in his memoirs. "It wasn't going to be easy." Roles would have to be carefully chosen to build a screen personality that fans—particularly younger fans—would find attractive.

But Grady did not know when he met Johnson that Lew Ayres, who had starred in the successful *Dr. Kildare* series, was leaving the studio to become a medic in the armed forces. Louis B. Mayer, MGM's boss, was eager to continue the series, since the Kildare pictures were almost as popular with audiences as the studio's Andy Hardy series had been. With Ayres out, a new twist would have to be concocted to give the movies continuity. Lionel Barrymore would continue to play Dr. Gillespie, Kildare's mentor, but another young doctor would need to be introduced.

Writer Carey Wilson remembered Grady coming into his office and saying, "Have you got a spare white coat? I've got a guy outside here that I think is star material, and I can get him under contract to the studio, but only if there's a specific part for him to play." Grady thought Van might be added as an extra intern in the next Kildare picture, unaware that a script was in preparation with no Ayres to play Kildare. "I think you'll be glad to meet this boy," Grady told Wilson, and the talent head opened the door and said, "Come on in, Red."

Van walked in—tall, freckled, redheaded—and the team of writers working on the Kildare script eyed one another and knew that Grady's discovery was the embodiment of a new character they had invented for their medical series, a young doctor named Dr. Randall Adams. "We talked to this young chap, who was shy and embarrassed but very impressive," Wilson recalled, and the writers urged that he be offered a contract. They agreed to cast Johnson as Dr. Red Adams, Dr. Gillespie's new assistant.

While the Gillespie script was being finalized, Van went to classes. Metro-Goldwyn-Mayer, the largest and most prestigious of Hollywood's big studios, was a well-oiled factory whose stars were manufactured and trained in an almost assembly-line fashion. Young contract players took fencing lessons, horseback riding lessons, and singing and dancing lessons and learned whatever they might need to know for various pictures. Van was sent to Gertrude Fogler for speech and diction lessons, and once he was handed a script he worked with Lillian Burns, the studio's respected drama coach. Burns believed that a young star must develop a persona, and she worked with each new player to create a unique, appealing personality. To sustain a career, MGM performers needed to know about decor, about music, about culture, Burns maintained. "If Ava Gardner didn't know how to hold a champagne glass," the coach said, "she had to learn." Lillie, as Mayer called Burns, was a powerful force at Metro, known for her honesty and toughness yet feared by many who studied with her. Burns could make or break a career, but she also coaxed deepened performances out of beginning actors that often surprised the novices themselves. Aware of how much he had to learn, Van liked and trusted Burns immediately and later recalled the "good vibrations" between them.

Van also cooperated with the studio's publicity department, headed by the efficient Howard Strickling, and went along with the buildup Strickling's staff devised for him. When MGM publicists elevated Johnson's father from a plumber to a real estate agent, the dutiful new contract player voiced no objection. If the studio wanted him to be a robust athlete, he would assume that pose. At the time Van was signed by Metro, the major concern expressed by Benny Thau, MGM's head of personnel, was the possibility that Van might be homosexual. "Do we have a situation here?" Thau tactfully asked Martin Jurow. Van's agent replied that as far as he knew, there was "no situation" and no cause for concern. Despite his masculine demeanor, Johnson possessed an androgynous quality that continued to raise doubts among studio executives.

In the golden age of Hollywood, not only did motion pictures offer audiences entertainment and relief from troubled times, but movie producers were also major curators of the national imagination. American filmmakers of the 1930s and 1940s created an idealistic world in which shop girls wore designer clothes, heroes were valiant and conquered all obstacles, and even married couples slept in twin beds. MGM stars, as depicted in the fan magazines, did not drink liquor in excess, smoke cigarettes, or engage in sexual dalliances, much less indulge in alternative sex, and even babies for properly wedded couples came as blessings from heaven and not from biological couplings. The studio's publicity office made sure that this fantasy was preserved.

Having created a dream world for himself in childhood, Van had little difficulty accepting Metro-Goldwyn-Mayer's expanded version. "As soon as I walked through those gates, I knew I was home," Johnson said. Ever the starstruck kid, Van wandered around the studio's sixty-five acres of standing sets and was enthralled by what he saw. A city within a city, Metro in 1942 had more than five thousand people on its payroll and the biggest contract list of any motion picture company in town. Its streets and soundstages were awhirl with activity, and Van basked in the excitement.

When not busy with classes, interviews, and gallery sittings, Van scurried from set to set with his autograph book in hand. He later claimed that Hedy Lamarr had him thrown off the soundstage when she was filming *White Cargo* because of his persistence and said that Ingrid Bergman was ready to scream at his constant presence on her sets. Van stood mesmerized as he watched such stars as Spencer Tracy, Katharine Hepburn, and Clark Gable go about the business of creating motion picture magic. Johnson realized how much he had to learn about screen technique, about camera angles, and about makeup. He mainly needed to know how to scale down a performance for the benefit of the camera, which Lillian Burns called the truth machine. "In moving pictures," the drama coach was fond of saying, "you cannot say 'dog' and think 'cat' because 'meow' will come out if you do."

During those early weeks on the MGM lot, Van assisted with a few screen tests but again grew discouraged, not understanding that the studio was grooming him for roles and did not want to place too taxing a load on him at the outset. Van sometimes dropped by Billy Grady's home in Beverly Hills, where Mrs. Grady consoled him and reassured him about how much her husband believed in him. Yet Van feared a repeat of what had happened at Warner Bros. Within six months Metro would have the option of either raising his salary and keeping him under contract or terminating their agreement and letting him go. He needed to prove his worth before that time came.

The studio first cast Johnson in a *Crime Does Not Pay* short in which he played an FBI agent tracking down Nazi-Japanese agents in South America. Van's freckles were covered up with makeup, he was given a black mustache, and once again his reddish blond hair was turned dark. "Each morning I'd report to makeup and they'd spray me into a brunette," Van said, "and each night I'd wash me back into being a redhead again. All went well until we had to work in a rainstorm."

One day Van dashed into June Havoc's house shouting, "Joan Crawford has asked me to play tennis with her!" The assemblage living there scrambled to find him an appropriate outfit to wear, and Van went off to play tennis in borrowed clothes except for his own dancing belt, which he wore under his shorts to hold his stomach in. "We thought he looked sublime," said Havoc. When Van returned to the house that afternoon, he announced that Crawford had invited him to her home for dinner that night. Again the gang at Havoc's place contributed clothing and decked him out in an acceptable manner.

When Van returned that night, he was serious and reflective. "You know, that's the way to live," he said. "Everything in that house is proper and right." Then he surprised Havoc by saying, "June, I'm going to be a big star. I have to live in an expensive house and have a wife who can entertain graciously and who can speak to the press properly. Why don't we get married? You have the down payment for a house like that, and the FHA would trust me for the rest because I've got my Metro contract." Havoc wisely ignored the proposal.

When Billy Grady and Louis B. Mayer found out that Van was living with Havoc, they demanded that he move out. Rumors had reached Grady's office that Van had fallen in love and that Johnson and Havoc planned to elope. "I heard about it and stepped in," said Grady. "Johnson and his lady friend were as opposite as day and night. He was an introvert, she the boisterous extrovert. They came together in adversity. When it cleared up, there had to be misunderstanding and tragedy." Van accepted studio executives' dictates, much as he had his father's. He was accustomed to taking orders and would devote the next twelve years of his life to trying to be L. B. Mayer's obedient child.

"Van Johnson is one of the nicest boys who ever lived," Lucille Ball said, "and Hollywood hasn't spoiled him. Nothing ever will. He's just as honest and sunny-dispositioned as he looks." Such was Van's image, and he played the role to perfection. By nature he was the introvert Grady mentioned, yet Van's comfort with fantasy distorted his concept of reality. He was grateful for the buildup Metro was giving him, and as long as the studio's demands and hyperbole pointed him toward stardom, he was willing to abide by the wishes of the executives in charge and repress any behavior that might blemish his public image, no matter what inner stresses resulted.

The studio's casting mill mentioned Van for an unbilled part in *Cairo*, and he tested for the Jeanette MacDonald vehicle sporting a mustache and a pipe between his teeth. The actress who tested opposite him had once been a star, and Johnson was stunned when he met her, since he re-called how beautiful she had been when he watched her movies in New-port. "I saw what bad health and bad luck can do to a girl like that," he said. Neither of them got the roles, but Van grasped an important lesson. "I had learned, by shock," he said, "that a career must be guarded every minute."

The front office soon called Van and told him that he had been as-signed to *Somewhere I'll Find You,* an A picture starring Clark Gable and Lana Turner. "It was a mediocre movie," producer Pandro Berman admit-ted, "but it did a hell of a business because of the popularity of Gable and Turner as a team." The stars played two war correspondents and on-again, off-again lovers sent to Indochina in the weeks before the Japanese bomb-ing of Pearl Harbor. Gable's character saw the war coming and made a strong stand against his newspaper's endorsement of appeasement. By December 7, 1941, Turner and Gable's characters were both in the Philip-pines and remained there to cover the final days of fighting on Bataan. Van appears during the last twenty minutes of the film as an army lieu-tenant who is killed along with most of the men serving under him. Van looks uncomfortable in his brief scenes, his face coated with makeup, and he admitted to being nervous, particularly in his exchange with Gable. "I blew my lines and the director blew his top," Johnson said. "I did the scene again and again, with [the director, Wesley Ruggles] getting madder and madder." Van said that Gable always terrified him, even though the two men played poker on subsequent occasions. "Gable did not have much humor," said Van, "and was always fighting a weight problem."

Somewhere I'll Find You was also Keenan Wynn's first movie, although neither Keenan nor Van was billed in the main titles. Keenan kept Van laughing in private, and the two MGM newcomers began spending a great deal of time together. "We were working in the same backyard," said Wynn, "and our friendship really got into gear." Fan magazines reported the two men to be best friends and portrayed Van, Keenan, and Evie Wynn as a convivial threesome, going everywhere together.

Keenan seemed to be everything Van was not—brash, outwardly

funny, loud, a daredevil with an obsession for speed. While he was work-ing in New York, the bold young Wynn established a speedboat record, racing around Manhattan Island in thirty-nine minutes flat. Born in 1916, the same year as Van, Keenan was the only son of Jewish vaudeville star Ed Wynn. His grandfather, Frank Keenan, was a celebrated Shakespearean actor who made his stage debut in 1876. Keenan had grown up surrounded by members of the theatrical profession. Ethel Barrymore was his "Auntie B," and he was accustomed to associating with stars of the top rank and to romping with their children.

Whereas Van Johnson yearned for a prominent place in the galaxy of show business, Keenan Wynn resented what he knew to be the price of stardom and preferred acceptance as a regular fellow. "I am the product of the worst parents," Wynn said, "and at a very young age I went to boarding school. I was raised by housekeepers and chauffeurs and yacht captains." Work and career were the center of Ed Wynn's life, and the co-median seemed happy only when he was on the stage or before a camera. At home he was crotchety and cold. "Ed was a principal client of mine," said Martin Jurow, "and I knew him well. He wouldn't let anything inter-fere with his stardom, including his son."

As a boy Keenan had no intention of going into show business. He dropped out of high school and, knowing no other means of earning a living, made his stage debut as a teenager. He claimed that he appeared in twenty-two flops on Broadway or headed for New York, performed on radio, and acted in numerous summer-stock productions. Young Wynn demonstrated genuine talent, but he was far from the happy person he seemed on the surface. "His feeling seemed to be that the world was pres-suring him in some puzzling and eminently unfair way," wrote Keenan's older son, Ned. "He seemed to feel that he could never satisfy the myriad demands that were crushing him." So Keenan raced boats and cars, rode motorcycles, and became known as a prankster and wit around Broad-way and later Hollywood.

In 1939 Keenan was in Boston for the tryout of a show when Ed Wynn called Jurow at a Shubert theater in Philadelphia. "Something terrible is happening in Boston," the elder Wynn told his agent. "Keenan is going to jump off the ledge of a hotel." Ed asked Jurow to go to Boston and look into the situation. "The father didn't go up there himself," said Jurow, "because Ed didn't have the nerve to go." The agent drove to Boston, found Keenan still on the ledge with his head down and refusing to talk to anyone. After much pleading, Jurow finally coaxed the despondent actor back inside. "You'll never know what it meant to Keenan not to feel important," the agent said, "when he had been raised with someone who was important."

Keenan met Eve Abbott when they were both appearing in *The Star Wagon* with Lillian Gish, Burgess Meredith, and Mildred Natwick. Eve was a vivacious, statuesque brunette from Buffalo, New York, and had made her Broadway debut in 1935 in a production of *Romeo and Juliet* that starred Katharine Cornell. Eve's father operated theaters and, caught up in the theatrical world since childhood, the ambitious girl was as eager as Van Johnson to try her luck on the stage in New York. After serving an apprenticeship with Cornell and Guthrie McClintic's stock company, Eve moved in with an aunt in Brooklyn and made the rounds of producers' offices. She acted in *Hamlet* with John Gielgud, Lillian Gish, and Judith Anderson; *Key Largo* with Paul Muni and José Ferrer; and *The American Way* with Fredric March and Florence Eldridge. During the time Abbott performed in *Romeo and Juliet* with Cornell, she dated future matinee idol Tyrone Power. "Ty was too beautiful," Eve said later. "I knew he would never settle down with one person."

When she married Keenan Wynn in 1939, Eve gave up acting to ser.e as her husband's unofficial agent and business manager. She recognized Keenan's talent and potential. "You know," Eve told him, "you'd be a fine actor if you took yourself seriously and stopped wasting your time." But Keenan showed little willingness to give up his frivolous, erratic ways, and tension quickly developed in the marriage. "I was Evie's hobby more than her hubby," said Wynn. "Before long we began to realize that the only thing we had in common was my career, and even that bond was disappearing."

To the reticent, unsophisticated Johnson, Keenan and Evie Wynn seemed to be experienced, worldly-wise professionals who knew their way around the entertainment business and could handle Hollywood's social demands with ease and aplomb. Van, conversely, was nervous at parties and formal dinners. He was thrilled when Ginger Rogers invited him to a gathering at her house shortly after he had been signed by MGM, but making conversation once he arrived there was difficult and painful for him. "I'd be almost sick with trying to think of something to say," Van said. The Jack Bennys hosted Johnson's first Hollywood sit-down dinner, but Van knew no one there and was miserable. "It was the longest hour I've ever spent in my life," he said. "I died a thousand deaths before the evening was over." Van began wearing red socks, hoping they might spark a casual banter that would help him relax and feel comfortable at social gatherings. Later, no matter what the rest of his outfit was, Van usually had on a pair of bright-red socks. He made them his trademark.

When Keenan and Eve arrived in Hollywood, they were immediately accepted as part of the town's inner circle. Evie loved giving parties, met people easily, and soon became enthralled with the California lifestyle. Keenan drank too much, but he was charming and amusing and had ready access to important people in the picture business. With Keenan and Evie, Van felt protected and safe. He could follow their lead, emulate them, and learn from them. He liked being with the couple, and he shared interests with Evie that Keenan found a bore. When Eve bought a new dress, Van noticed it. He was alert to a change in drapery or wallpaper and enjoyed going on shopping trips with Evie. She became his buddy and emotional support in ways different from Keenan.

Keenan hated the insignificant roles that Metro gave him and felt that most of what he did there was a waste of his talent. He always seemed to play the leading man's best friend. "They gave me junk," Wynn said, and the actor maintained a negative attitude throughout the years he spent under contract to the studio. "Keenan was an unhappy, melancholy person," said Eddie Bracken, who lived across the street from the Wynns when they first came to Hollywood. "He'd be negative about anything. I'm sure Keenan gave MGM an awful lot of trouble."

Van was distressed much of the time, too, since the studio seemed determined to hide his freckles and red hair and turn him into a pale imitation of the screen's established war heroes. Then came *The War against Mrs. Hadley,* and the film's juvenile role was ideal for Johnson. The part of a young, Irish-faced soldier was the kind of part with which Grady had hoped to start Johnson, and the talent director went to George Oppenheimer, the writer and coproducer of the movie, and argued Van's cause. Grady pointed out that the budding actor's lack of experience was exactly what the role needed. Since many of Hollywood's young featured players had been called to the armed forces, Oppenheimer agreed to test Johnson for the picture. "He came through with flying colors," said Grady, and "his joy at the news was heartwarming."

In *The War against Mrs. Hadley* (released in November 1942) Van was permitted to go before the cameras with minimal makeup. For the first time in movies he looked natural and relaxed. His well-scrubbed appearance took on a radiance, and his smile proved captivating. Fay Bainter, the veteran actress who played the title role, was kind and helpful to the newcomer, so that making the picture was a pleasure for Van. "Thank God for *Mrs. Hadley,* " he said; "that was the beginning. . . . Then I began to roll."

The story was typical wartime fare, aimed at armchair isolationists and at persuading the American public to accept the sacrifices necessary in total war. Mrs. Hadley's birthday dinner is interrupted by the news that Pearl Harbor has been bombed. Although the wealthy Washington socialite thinks of herself as a patriot, she fails to adjust her lifestyle to the conditions at hand. When her daughter goes to work in a servicemen's canteen, falls in love with a private she meets there, and marries the boy, Mrs. Hadley disowns her.

Van played the private—his first chance at a romantic role. He and Jean Rogers made a winsome couple in the picture, and one scene had

Van holding the girl's hand under some dishwater. Critics said that he made the most of his slight part, but fans took notice and began writing him letters. "Van Johnson is an extremely attractive youth," wrote Louella Parsons, Hollywood's premier gossip columnist, "and as the Irish soldier in *The War against Mrs. Hadley* he impresses me as being a lad who will go far."

Hollywood suddenly was buzzing with talk about the redheaded kid with the freckles over at Metro, and studio executives were made to realize that they had material for a juvenile star in their ranks. With the release of *Mrs. Hadley,* Van sent Billy Grady a silver cigarette case as a token of his gratitude. "Now he had to be kept alive with more roles," said Grady. "His name must always be up for consideration." The talent head instructed his staff to be on the lookout for suitable roles for this young comer who clearly had a future.

By the time *The War against Mrs. Hadley* was finished, *Dr. Gillespie's New Assistant* was ready to go before the cameras, with Van tagged to play Dr. Red Adams. The series had an established audience, and Metro's method of building promising performers was to put them in starring roles in budget pictures and alternate those assignments with smaller parts in big productions that profited from the presence of seasoned stars. Dr. Gillespie, as played by the crusty, wheelchair-bound character actor Lionel Barrymore, was a lovable curmudgeon. In this episode he put three young surgeons to the test in an effort to find a replacement for Dr. Kildare, with Red Adams winning the position. Van handled the part admirably, although he did not become identified with the series the way Lew Ayres did.

Van's boyish grin, blue eyes, and snub-nosed face soon began appearing in the Hollywood fan magazines. Journalists concentrated on his warm, open, easygoing personality, overlooking the sensitive, reclusive, morose quality hidden beneath the surface. Through MGM's training program, Van had developed a breezy way of expressing himself, and he came across in interviews as affable, eager to please, and boyishly regular. He was quoted as saying that he looked shorter than he was "because I'm a chronic sloucher." He said that he could not believe that he was working on the same lot as Norma Shearer, Joan Crawford, Hedy Lamarr, Lana Turner, and Greer Garson and frequently asked himself, "What are you doing here, you schnook?" Van was reported to play tennis, swim, and ride horses for exercise and collect autographed pictures of movie stars as a hobby. He liked hot dogs, ice cream cones, and candy but hated hillbilly music and snobs. Gossip columnist Hedda Hopper was impressed with the energetic youth when she met him but "never dreamed that Van would become the greatest bobby-sox idol in the country."

What impressed colleagues at MGM most was Johnson's drive, his willingness to accommodate, and his capacity for work. "That boy will get some place," one actor on the lot commented. "Anyone with that much enthusiasm just has to." Having been poor in his youth, Van was motivated to move ahead. He sensed after his recognition in *Mrs. Hadley* that his moment had come. The opportunities that Metro began handing him pointed to fame and fortune, and nothing was going to stand in the way of Van achieving the goal he had dreamed about since childhood. "I couldn't wait to get to work in the morning," Johnson said. "What a kick it was to drive through those MGM gates in the smog every morning and see that big Leo the Lion looking down at me."

Much of his bravado was an attempt to cover up an inferiority complex, and Van sometimes surprised himself with the confidence he exuded. He was in awe of his surroundings, agog at the talent he met and worked with on the Culver City lot, and resolved to turn himself into a multitalented performer. He saw an average of five movies a week in the studio's projection rooms, where he studied the great screen achievements of the past and present. He watched the work of his favorite actors in batches—all of Garbo's films, then all of Tracy's, Crawford's, and Shearer's, learning by osmosis film technique and how to scale down his performance for the camera.

When not busy on a production, Van participated in Friday-afternoon sessions in Lillian Burns's office, where young actors presented scenes on which they had been working. Burns conducted the meetings as if they were rehearsals with herself as director, although those in attendance were permitted to ask questions and make comments. Gathered in her outer office on various Fridays might be Ava Gardner, Barry Nelson, Marilyn Maxwell, Robert Sterling, and June Allyson, all of whom were striving to master the craft of motion picture acting. If Spencer Tracy was working and the youngsters had nothing else to do, they often went to their idol's set and stood in a group behind the camera to study Tracy's concentration and method of reacting. "It was a great learning experience," said Allyson.

By early 1943 Van was working steadily in pictures. He appeared as another army private in *The Human Comedy,* a film that received much critical attention because it was based on a story by William Saroyan. Produced and directed by the experienced Clarence Brown, the movie starred Mickey Rooney as Van's adolescent brother and benefited from a strong supporting cast that included brief appearances by Robert Mitchum, Barry Nelson, and Don DeFore as three soldiers on furlough. Van's performance showed vast improvement over his awkward efforts in *Somewhere I'll Find You,* and he demonstrated in his short but meaty role that he could effectively handle comedy, musical scenes, and serious drama. Toward the end of the story, notification comes by telegraph that Van's character has been killed in action, but the death of American servicemen is viewed as the price of healing international differences and preserving civilized values. With the United States in its second year of war, *The Human Comedy* touched audiences' hearts with its sentiment, its moving view of small-town life, and its call for strength and moral courage in a time of duress. Although the script was episodic, *The Human Comedy* made probing comments about the human condition, and its ensemble performances gave the movie a timeless quality.

Pilot No. 5, Van's next assignment, dealt with a Huey Long counterpart and was a sharp indictment of fascism in the United States. Van supported Franchot Tone and Gene Kelly in the picture, and the film garnered excellent reviews and did well at the box office. "We used a kind of avant garde way of telling a story in *Pilot No. 5,*" director George Sidney said of the movie's flashback development, "and it was an exciting experience." The production also gave Kelly and Johnson a chance to do some serious acting, although Kelly's role was far meatier than Van's.

Even before shooting on Sidney's movie was completed, Van was back in the role of Dr. Red Adams, this time working on *Dr. Gillespie's Criminal Case*. The medical series followed a tested formula, mixed fun with tragedy, and was peopled with likable characters. In Johnson's second Gillespie picture the elderly doctor, again played by Barrymore, unravels a murder for which an innocent man has been sent to prison. Van performed his duties in the programmer well, but the demands on his talent were slight.

In 1943's *Madame Curie* he played the brief role of a novice newspaper reporter, but the film gave him an opportunity to appear in a token scene with Greer Garson, a star of the first magnitude. *Madame Curie* was an important production and served as Van's introduction to a more sophisticated audience. In casting him in the picture, the studio intended to lift his status by pairing him in a short sequence with the reigning queen of the Metro lot in the hope that Garson's audience would notice the budding star and watch for him in future pictures. Before the segment was shot, Garson asked director Mervyn LeRoy who was to play the reporter sent to interview Marie Curie after her discovery of radium. LeRoy told her, "A young song-and-dance man named Van Johnson." When Van arrived on the set, the star was struck by his "shining schoolboy face and ingenuous blue eyes" and remembered how much the production company liked him. "Since he had to play a rather ingenuous young man," the actress said, "it was nice casting."

Film crews worked six days a week in the early 1940s, so Sunday was often Van's only time off. He spent evenings studying scripts and reading, sometimes practiced the fiddle when he was alone, and called his father in Newport once or twice a month. Most of the busy young actor's free time was spent with Keenan and Evie Wynn, and he was a constant visitor to their home in Brentwood. Eddie Bracken then lived across the street from the Wynns on Saltair Avenue, near where Gary Cooper, Tyrone Power, and Fred MacMurray owned homes, and Bracken frequently saw Van out on the lawn with Keenan and Eve.

One day a sightseeing bus came down the street, causing the neighborhood of celebrities to run for cover. Bracken suggested that the stars instead give the tourists a show by forming a human pyramid, with Bracken on top, Johnson, Cooper, and MacMurray on bottom, and Power and Wynn in the middle. "We had a lot of fun," said Bracken, and the busload of fans went wild watching six laughing movie stars fall into a heap.

Rumors were rife in Hollywood that Van and Keenan were more than friends, that theirs was a homosexual liaison. Eve later stated categorically that such allegations were untrue, yet the rumors persist to the present day. For sure, the relationship among Van, Keenan, and Evie was not altogether harmonious. "Sometimes the loudness of their arguments was ferocious," Bracken recalled.

The Wynns already had a son, Ned, born in 1941. The bosses at Metro-Goldwyn-Mayer were grateful when Ned was born and made certain that he was frequently photographed with his father to dispel invidious rumors. "A child was a useful commercial asset for an actor like me," Keenan Wynn wrote in his memoirs, "because this was the era of Happy Families." By the time they came to Hollywood, Keenan and Eve's relationship was far from happy. "Our marriage had followed the inevitable, sad course of marriages in decline," the actor said. "We had gone from coolness to bickering and then to open disputes. We had nothing in common, no shared interest except our son Ned."

Keenan found solace in a motorcycle gang that gathered every Sunday morning at Hog Canyon, spent an hour or so polishing the machines, then took off for a couple more hours of cruising through the hills and slopes off Mulholland Drive and down into the San Fernando Valley. Wearing leather gear and calling themselves the Moraga Spit and Polish Club, the group sometimes numbered as many as twenty cyclists, among whom were Clark Gable; character actors Ward Bond and Andy Devine; directors

Howard Hawks, Victor Fleming, and William Wellman; stuntman Cary Loften; test pilot Vance Breeze; and aviation innovator Bill Lear. The assemblage crossed fixed social lines, but all of them were macho types who delighted in discussing gaskets and cylinders and roaring through canyons at a decibel level almost certain to cause deafness, which it ultimately did with Keenan Wynn. After their morning excursions the group members either convened at Howard Hawks's house for a hearty lunch or adjourned to Andy Devine's ranch to drink beer and swap stories about their exploits.

Van bought himself a Harley and occasionally accompanied Keenan on these Sunday outings, but he was never comfortable with the virile gathering of cyclists and hated their noisy braggadocio. Keenan remembered his best friend's "plugging along, enjoying himself, and leaving the hell-for-leather stuff to hotter heads than his." Wynn would be rearing to go but felt compelled to hold down his speed, since Van was new to the sport and reluctant to take the firebreaks at top speed.

Whereas Keenan found motorcycling a "wonderful refreshment of spirit," Van preferred the Sunday-afternoon volleyball games at Gene Kelly's house attended by members of the theatrical crowd Kelly had met in New York, such as Phil Silvers, June Allyson, Ralph Blane, Nancy Walker, Betty Comden, and Adolph Green. Louis B. Mayer did not approve of Keenan's haphazard and dangerous activities away from the studio, and Van had no intention of displeasing Mayer with similar activities now that the Johnson career was beginning to take off. Keenan might consider it cool to pal around with ordinary guys in grease pits and seedy watering holes, but Van harbored more refined tastes. He had seen the MGM publicity department coddle the studio's stars, and Van longed for that kind of treatment. He had lived the life of a blue-collar worker in Newport; what he wanted from Hollywood and sensed was within his grasp was stardom and all the exclusivity and perks that celebrity entailed.

In February 1943 Metro announced that Johnson would play Ted Randall, the juvenile lead, in *A Guy Named Joe,* a big-budget film that starred two of Van's idols, Spencer Tracy and Irene Dunne. Robert Young had been slated for the role of the young pilot who eventually woos Dunne's character, but studio executives decided to put Van in the part instead to attract a bigger teenage audience. Johnson knew that this was his big break and reported to work on the picture excited but scared. Since he would have love scenes with Irene Dunne, he had to make a test with the regal actress, and Van at first was convinced that she did not want a new-comer, fifteen years her junior, playing opposite her. Nor did he feel that director Victor Fleming was pleased to have a novice in such a central role. Fleming had directed *Gone With the Wind* and was among MGM's most respected craftsmen, while Dunne ranked in the superstar category. When the director introduced Van to his leading lady, he said, "Miss Dunne, this is Mr. Van Warren." Johnson found the gaffe revealing: "He didn't even have my name straight!" Van complained.

Dunne saw how nervous the young actor was and helped put John-son at ease for the test by pretending to be nervous herself. "I stood there, my face against the beautiful face of a star miles above me," Van said. But when Dunne made believe that she too was having trouble remembering her lines and improvised words when Van faltered, the neophyte forgot his uneasiness and began responding to the gracious woman seated next to him. "Five minutes later making love to her was no strain," he said. Dunne remained supportive throughout the long shooting schedule. If Van rattled off lines without the proper inflection or failed to match his words with his actions, she took him aside for a pep talk. "She gave me confidence in myself," Van said.

Virtually every actor in Hollywood viewed Tracy as the master of his craft, and Van marveled at the way his hero listened to other performers and did not answer their questions right away but thought about them and then reacted. "That's true acting," said Keenan Wynn, who would name his second son Tracy. Thrilled though Johnson was to be working with an actor of such skill and integrity, he said that he was "sweating gumdrops" at the prospect of playing scenes with Tracy. When not needed in front of the camera, Van observed the two leads' casual manner of delivering lines, their matchless timing, and their general deportment on the set. Tracy did not favor extensive rehearsal, preferring to give a spontaneous performance, but his technique was flawless.

Fleming remained an aloof director who catered to Tracy's wishes. With his silver mane and rugged features, Fleming looked more severe than he was, and Van found his direction precise and meaningful. Having been a dancer, Johnson brought a well-developed sense of rhythm to his acting and revealed an instinct for timing. He had been taught to revere—and even fear—choreographers and therefore took direction without question. Fleming appreciated the young man's willingness and began paying more attention to him, convinced that Van was turning in a solid performance.

Two weeks into the shooting of *A Guy Named Joe*, Van, Keenan and Evie Wynn, and two servicemen friends were in Johnson's DeSoto convertible driving to the MGM lot for a special screening of the Spencer Tracy–Katharine Hepburn film *Keeper of the Flame*. They had just entered the intersection of Venice Boulevard and Clarington Street, near the studio, when another car ran a red light and smashed into the side of Van's convertible and sent it rolling on its side. "Like a jerk," Van said, "I put my head forward to brace myself. I remember trying to turn off the ignition to cut down the danger of fire, but I turned on the radio and windshield wiper instead." He clung to the steering wheel, and on impact his head struck the clamp in the middle of the windshield frame that locked the convertible top when it was up. The car had been open at the time of the crash, and Van was thrown from the wreckage and into a gutter, where his head hit a curb. Gasping, he tried to stand up but fell. "My face was wet," he said, "and I thought it was raining, but it was blood."

The other driver escaped unharmed, Eve suffered a back injury, and Keenan and the two servicemen riding with them were badly shaken but little more. Van received a fractured skull and severe facial injuries as glass slashed across his face and neck, and the back of his head was peeled off and his brain was pierced by fragments of bone. An artery in his neck

was severed, and he lost three quarts of blood before an ambulance arrived to rush him to a hospital. As he lay waiting, Van remembered hearing a woman whisper, "He's dead."

The wreck happened on the border between the city of Los Angeles
and Culver City. Because of a zoning ordinance, a Los Angeles policeman
could not aid an accident victim who lay on the Culver City side of the
street. While Van bled profusely, a cop came over to him and said that he
would have to send for the Culver City police, since the car had thrown
his body to the wrong side of the street. "Tell me where the right side is,"
Van said, "and I'll crawl there." He instead waited in the gutter for forty-five
minutes until the proper ambulance came. By that time Whitey Hendry,
MGM's chief of police, had arrived on the scene and taken charge.

Van was wheeled into an operating room at the Hollywood Presbyterian Hospital, where a surgeon closed up the bleeding artery, sewed his
scalp back on, and went to work on the cavity in his skull. "They tell me I
was almost decapitated, but I never once lost consciousness," Van said.
"My nose was up against my eyes, and my scalp had come unstuck. They
lifted it up like a flap and poured in handfuls of sulfa." Van remembered
lying in a hospital bed, gripping its sides from pain, and feeling as though
his head would explode. From what seemed like a great distance, he heard
a doctor's voice say, "It's a question whether he can pull through." Van
had lost so much blood that his pulse wavered.

Keenan Wynn stayed at the hospital that night to keep watch over
his friend. The doctors kept saying, "He'll never work in movies again.
He'll be lucky if he lives through this." In his lucid moments Van worried
less about the possibility of damaging scars than about what would happen
when he did not show up for work on *A Guy Named Joe.* "I haven't got
time to be sick," he kept thinking, "I've got a picture to make."

The next morning Van awoke to find Eddie Mannix, Metro's general
manager, and some of the studio's other executives standing over his bed.
Their faces were ashen. He heard someone outside in the corridor say, "Too

bad about Van's accident. That's the end of his career." A beautiful rhodo-dendron plant soon arrived from Joan Crawford. Spencer Tracy showed up at the hospital and offered his own blood for the transfusions Van needed, and Victor Fleming arrived to express his concern.

Louis B. Mayer and Benny Thau considered replacing Johnson in *A Guy Named Joe* with either John Hodiak or Peter Lawford, but when Tracy found out about the proposed change, the actor insisted that if Van were dropped from the picture, neither star would shoot another scene. Irene Dunne and Tracy did not have the easiest relationship off screen, but Dunne agreed with her costar that removing Johnson from the movie was un-thinkable. Fleming returned to the hospital a few days later and told Van that Tracy and Dunne had been so relentless in their support of him that Mayer and Thau had agreed not to resume work on *A Guy Named Joe* until Johnson was well. Fortunately for the production schedule, Van did not appear in the first half of the movie.

The accident had taken place on March 30, 1943, and Van was out of commission for the next three months. Several operations were required to patch him together, and there was fear of possible brain damage. A metal plate five inches long was put into the left side of Van's head, and another operation was performed to remove pressure on his brain. Surgeons ex-tracted muscle tissue from his right arm and used it to rebuild his gashed forehead. During the weeks Van was in Hollywood Presbyterian Hospital, he was deluged with flowers, fruit, books, letters, cards, and telephone messages. Dunne and Tracy both came to see him at least three times a week. At the end of two months the Keenan Wynns took the ailing actor to their house for further convalescence. When Van left the hospital, the prediction was that he would not be able to work for a year.

Against doctor's orders, Johnson returned to the studio in late June to complete *A Guy Named Joe*. His forehead was deeply scarred, requiring intricate makeup to prepare him for the camera, and he suffered severe headaches almost every afternoon. His right arm was weak, and he tired easily. Yet Van was so grateful that he had not been replaced on the picture that he tried to appear a dynamo of energy and enthusiasm. "Things like that you never forget," he said. "I'm a man with a debt to pay."

Some observers thought that Van returned to work after the accident a deeper, more serious person. Others disagreed. "I felt sure that, in the face of death, that immaturity of his would disappear," a friend reported. "But it didn't. Not then anyway. When he left the hospital and went back to the picture, he was his usual bumbling, trusting self. His very charm, the endearing quality that helped to make him a star, was preventing him from becoming a mature, well-rounded human being." Some colleagues even claimed that following the accident Van seemed more boyish and dependent than ever.

During the months of recuperation Van had done a lot of thinking, and the accident sharpened his religious beliefs. He thanked God for saving his life and believed that his recovery had been a miracle. He began attending Episcopalian Church services on Sundays and spent less time with the roughhouse group that met on Sunday mornings to cycle through the canyons off Mulholland. "People tell me that accident changed me," said Van. "But I think it only intensified the kind of guy I am. Until then I'd been a little shy about admitting how much I like to stay home alone, reading, listening to records, mapping out the years ahead. Now I'm not."

Swimmer Esther Williams first met Van after he returned to the set of *A Guy Named Joe* and noticed the large scar he was sporting. Tapping the side of his head, Van told her, "I've got service for twelve in here. And its sterling, not silver plate. Only the best for MGM." Williams danced with Van in the picture and observed that he had a unique quality—"part strong man, part eager boy." The two stars would eventually make five pictures together.

A Guy Named Joe marked Van's entrance into MGM's major league and gave his career an important boost toward stardom. Yet Irene Dunne remembered the film as perhaps the most difficult she ever made, even before Johnson's accident interrupted shooting. "It was winter," she said, "it was dark and raining and the whole set was gloomy." While waiting for the injured actor's recovery, Dunne started work on *The White Cliffs of Dover* at the same studio, so there were times when the actress was rushing back and forth between the two assignments. Altogether, production on *A Guy Named Joe* dragged on for more than six months. Victor Fleming was not well at the time, there had to be a change of cameramen, and the picture was physically difficult for the actors. "All of those things made filming not run smoothly," said Dunne. "I liked the movie when it was finished, but physically we had a lot of problems."

Wartime audiences flocked to see *A Guy Named Joe* and were enchanted by its characters and poetic sentiment. Most also reassessed Van Johnson's charm and found him an appealing new personality. Dalton Trumbo's script fit the period's mood. In the story a cocky, foolhardy Air Corps combat pilot (Tracy) is killed while sinking a Nazi aircraft carrier, but he comes back as an apparition to oversee the final training of a nervous, rich young cadet (Johnson) and instill courage into the woman he loves (Dunne), who also happens to be a pilot. Tracy's ghost accompanies Johnson to New Guinea, where the baby-faced pilot meets Dunne's character and Tracy's spirit has trouble accepting the romance that develops between the two. The picture is an engaging fantasy, with strong performances from all three of its leads. Trumbo's message is that no man is truly dead unless he breaks with the future, and the script reinforces why the war is being fought. *A Guy Named Joe* earned more than four million dollars during its initial run, ranked in the top ten films of 1943–44, and was remade by Steven Spielberg in 1989 as *Always,* with Richard Dreyfuss and Holly Hunter in the starring roles.

By the time *A Guy Named Joe* was released in December 1943, Van's accident had been covered at length by the major newspapers and movie-fan magazines. Although makeup had been applied to conceal the worst of Van's head injuries, Fleming had insisted that it was better "for the scars to show than to wipe out the boy's personality." So Van appeared on the screen in military uniform with visible blemishes that not only disclosed his own victory over death but somehow made him an acceptable war hero to vast segments of the American public. Women particularly responded to his wounded good looks as never before, and during early showings of *A Guy Named Joe* teenagers began to swoon and shriek, displays that would reach thunderous proportions in the months ahead.

More than any single factor, his automobile accident boosted Van Johnson to fame and major stardom. His determination and effervescent screen personality had laid the groundwork, but the public embraced him as a fighter, a survivor, and a sex symbol only after reading detailed reports of his near-fatal car wreck. Adolescent girls, wrapped in wartime patriotism, yearned for a hero who was brave, lovable, wholesome, and vulnerable, and Van's freckled face and strawberry blond good looks gave him the demeanor of the perennial boy next door. He was attractive, cute, and bouncy but not reckless or threatening. Van exuded an air of naive helplessness that made older women want to pamper him. Mothers who had lost sons or had boys fighting overseas could make Johnson a safe and acceptable substitute to love and revere. Since the grim inflictions he had suffered in the auto crash disqualified Van for military service, men in the armed forces and on the home front could see his films and watch him play war heroes without rancor or undue suspicion that the young actor was evading a duty to his country in private. For millions, Johnson became the boy who went to war and came home a man. His acceptance as a war hero is ironic yet points out public confusion over reality and fantasy not unlike what John Wayne experienced at the time and Ronald Reagan did later. Surviving the car wreck won Van mass sympathy similar to what Reagan garnered after surviving an attempted assassination.

The critical consensus was that Van had delivered a relaxed, sensitive performance in *A Guy Named Joe,* but the headlines that splashed his name across newspapers and magazines from coast to coast encouraged the nation to take this personable, hurt youth to its heart. For the next decade Van would play soldiers, sailors, and fliers and was rarely seen on the screen out of uniform. He became the symbol of the affable American, a composite of the young men who were actually in the trenches and the cockpits, dodging bullets and all too often dying for the preservation of democracy.

Within two years Johnson was among Hollywood's top five box-office stars and one of MGM's most valuable properties. He ranked with Frank Sinatra as the heartthrob of teenage girls across war-torn America, creating a sensation that only Elvis Presley and the Beatles would later match. Fans began hanging around the studio gate to catch a glimpse of Van as he left work at night and shoved autograph books at him wherever he went. Any time a new movie of his was previewed, audiences cheered and applauded the boy who had faced death and managed to live. The crooked scar that ran down his forehead became a badge of courage, his mark of acceptability, and a ticket to popularity. "I've never seen anybody do what Van did," said Martin Jurow. "Within four years he went to the top and became the highest moneymaker for MGM. He was a sensation."

CHAPTER 4

Heartthrob

Early in 1944 Van Johnson was living in a small rented house in Brentwood and earning $750 a week. A maid came in three times a week, but as Van's fame grew, the more insulated and internalized he became. At the studio he seemed the gregarious, charming young star on the rise, yet he appeared to withdraw into a solitary world once he left the MGM lot. Fundamentally shy, sober minded, and often gloomy, Van jealously guarded his right to quiet and kept his private life private. Secret about any sex life, he seemed to lack strong sexual drives. Without a high degree of psychological self-awareness, Van was willing to be what people expected him to be. His basic emotional nature remained sealed, even from himself, and his preoccupation with work allowed him to keep a fundamental part of himself locked.

Still nervous in gatherings of people he did not know, Van admitted that he sometimes drove around the block three or four times before mustering sufficient courage to go into a party. Once there he would agonize at having to walk into a crowded room by himself and attempt a conversation. He continued to wear bright red socks as his badge of distinction, and fan-magazine writers linked the eccentricity to his red hair and adolescent demeanor, although Van knew better. "They were a crutch," he said later. His attitude in public gatherings was amiable yet cautious. Johnson quickly became a master at superficial finesse without revealing a great deal about himself. Metro-Goldwyn-Mayer created an image for him, and Van saw that the image was projected at all times.

Even though he was legitimately disqualified from the draft after his automobile accident, Van was sensitive about not serving in the armed forces, particularly since Jimmy Stewart, Tyrone Power, Gene Autry, Robert Taylor, and so many others were in uniform. Johnson tried to stay out of nightclubs, feeling that the guys overseas would resent his having fun while they were fighting and facing death in far off war zones. He also kept away from the Hollywood Canteen, sensing that the servicemen there would not understand a big fellow like him not being in some branch of the military. To compensate, Van made frequent visits to military hospitals but invariably came away from them shaken. Seeing the injured boys there "makes you feel so helpless," he told friends.

As a result of his accident, Van still suffered throbbing headaches, which he described as the "granddaddies of all headaches," although those, like his scars, slowly began to diminish. To strengthen the muscles in his right arm, Van worked out with a hundred-pound barbell, and even though he hated exercise, he found physical activity necessary to keep his weight below two hundred pounds. He swam, played tennis, rode horses, and was often pictured in the fan magazines with a rifle or an ax in his hand or engaged in some form of home repair. "He's really a 100 percent outdoor man!" *Movieland* reported in 1944. "Van has warmth and sincerity of personality," wrote Hedda Hopper; he is "a husky, typically American kid."

Soon to be twenty-eight years old, Van saw his growing success as a miracle. "You've had nothing but luck, fellow," he told himself time and again. In interviews he assumed a cheery, informal attitude that fans mistook for his true identity. "Boy, what a wonderful day," he supposedly told a *Photoplay* writer a few months after *A Guy Named Joe* was released, "blue sky, California sun, a swell breakfast just shoved away—and look at that orange tree reaching out into a rash of blossoms over there! Days like this a fellow feels it's good to be alive—especially when he knows that all over the world guys who like the sun and the sky as much as he does are getting their last look at it." There was little hint of Van's dark moods or cloistered self in what his public read.

Keenan and Evie Wynn understood that there were two Van Johnsons. One was the feigned extrovert, given to smart talk and cute remarks; the other was the silent introvert who found getting close to anyone difficult and shared his most intimate thoughts with practically no one. The real Van was restless, fearful of reality, and dwelled in a world of make-believe. Stardom and Metro publicists contributed to the tendency. "I hated to leave MGM at night to go home," Van said, "because I didn't want to go out into the real world. What I was leaving was the real world." Yet sudden success weighed on him, overshadowed his fragile personal identity, and further retarded his emotional development. "Things happened with a rush for me in the beginning," said Van, and "caught me off guard."

The former chorus boy was being asked by reporters what he thought about international diplomacy and whether he believed Franklin Roosevelt should run for a fourth term in the White House, and Van was not prepared to answer such questions. The MGM publicity department provided him with acceptable responses and created a persona for him that was consistent with what the public expected, but this facade had little to do with his real person. Van was tutored in simplistic observations about life and handed a list of puerile habits to claim as his own, most of them idiotic but safe. Van, according to the fan magazines, liked to chew gum and sometimes placed a wad behind his ear before going in front of a camera. He enjoyed an occasional beer, slept in the nude with his bedroom windows open, and tended to pull his pants legs up around his knees when he sat down to talk. He was too impatient to play golf but loved to dance and listen to big-band music. He liked silly jokes and ate candy kisses before breakfast. *Life* magazine claimed that his "Johnsonisms" mixed metaphors as no one except producer Samuel Goldwyn could. According to the reports, Van once said, "Come on, we're wasting high time," unaware of the garbling. To emphasize a point he sometimes declared, "That's like carrying oil to Newcastle." But Van never claimed to be a worldly person.

The young star was up every morning at 6:00, arrived at the studio by 8:30, worked until 6:00 that evening, ate dinner, learned his lines for the next day, and went to bed on weeknights by 9:00. When not working, he was likely to stay home and wash windows or wax floors. Different from the many New Yorkers who considered Hollywood a wasteland, Van loved the glamour of the film colony and enjoyed the special treatment he was beginning to receive in restaurants.

The touchiest point in his publicity interviews was how to explain why he had no special girlfriend. Until 1945 Van's name was never linked seriously with any of the Hollywood beauties. "I'm married to MGM," he said. "I have one love and it's pictures." He denied that he hated women and remarked that any guy who did was "a fellow who's sour on life." When asked to describe his ideal woman, Van said, "I guess the most important thing is that she can swing a tennis racket or throw a straight ball," since he maintained that he preferred the outdoor type.

Of screen actresses, Johnson claimed to favor veterans like Katharine Hepburn, Bette Davis, Irene Dunne, and Rosalind Russell. "I think the greatest of all was Garbo and Norma Shearer," he said. He admired great ladies and the heavy emotional–type actresses. "Nobody could cry on the screen better than Norma," said Van.

His deportment still made him seem much younger than he was, so the absence of romance in Van's life did not become an issue until later. In the meantime he could ooze charm and personal magnetism and allow his female fans to covet him for their own. Early in his Hollywood career Van learned the art of ingratiating himself. Although he was serious about developing his talent, he knew that an unctuous smile could win favor with studio executives and serve him well when he had to go on public display.

Johnson's sudden surge in box-office appeal came as such a surprise to MGM that the studio's casting office was caught unprepared. Before *A*

Guy Named Joe was released, the studio gave Van a small role in Irene Dunne's next picture, *The White Cliffs of Dover.* Johnson and Dunne worked well together, but he only had two short scenes in the second film with her. *The White Cliffs of Dover* was largely Dunne's movie, with Van a supporting player. Set in England and based on Alice Duer Miller's poem "The White Cliffs," the film is a wartime romance meant to strengthen the common bond between England and the United States. Dunne plays an American girl who falls in love with a British aristocrat, marries him on the eve of World War I, and lives the rest of her life in England. The courageous bride endures the death of her husband in combat and is a head nurse when her son is returned home critically wounded from fighting along the French coast in World War II. The movie's message is summed up in Dunne's final line: "God will never forgive us if we break faith with our dead again." Glossy and mawkish, *The White Cliffs of Dover* was done with great style and proved a box-office winner. "Sidney Franklin, the producer, was disappointed," Dunne recalled, "because he thought our picture was going to be another *Mrs. Miniver,* but it didn't quite achieve that."

Van's next assignment was *Three Men in White,* the third of his Dr. Gillespie pictures. This time the cantankerous old doctor felt the need to test the character and integrity of his young intern and see if Dr. Red Adams could resist the temptations of the pretty young nurses and patients he encountered. Ava Gardner and Marilyn Maxwell were selected from Metro's starlet pool as seductresses capable of enticing Adams into compromising his professionalism. "I had to pretend to be a sexy clinging lush who was still sober enough to make a pass at Van in the emergency room," Gardner remembered. But the young doctor disregarded all such efforts to lure him into bed and measured up to Dr. Gillespie's expectations. *Three Men in White,* Gardner wrote in her memoirs, was "a really silly story, but Hollywood was awash with quick, silly stories in those war years."

When the movie previewed in Inglewood, California, teenage girls in the audience set up an uproar of squeals, howls, and applause when the main titles flashed on the screen. "At first I thought Frank Sinatra had come in the back of the theater," said writer Carey Wilson. But the manager of the theater explained that Van Johnson had built up a following and was an important personality to these youngsters. *Three Men in White* grossed double what its predecessors in the Gillespie series had.

Van was most popular with girls below the age of consent—bobbysoxers, as the teenage girls of the 1940s who followed current fads were known because of the ankle socks they wore. Overnight he was described as the "voiceless Sinatra," and his sunny smile and unruly sandy hair began to appear on the covers of leading fan magazines. Gossip columnists soon referred to the commotion that surrounded him as a bobby-soxer blitz, and the examples were endless. Van came out of a barbershop one day and found fifty kids waiting for him beside his car. Within a few months fans mobbed him wherever he went. Young people scaled fences and scrambled over automobiles to get at him. They ripped his clothes, tore off buttons, and smeared his face with lipstick. Admirers sent him gifts, baked bread for him, and inundated the awestruck actor with candy and mint-flavored gum, which they had heard was his favorite. One teenage girl saved her allowance and bought him a pair of initialed gold cuff links. By the end of 1944 nearly all of Van's moves and utterances were lightning rods for publicity. Somehow the insecure, introverted lad from Rhode Island had become America's favorite boy.

Fan magazines and amusement writers worked overtime to inflate the Johnson myth that the public wanted so desperately to believe. Journalists depicted him as a modest, ebullient boy, much like the youngsters who used to swipe apples from their neighbors' trees. "He's a hunk of Americana," said Hollywood columnist Sidney Skolsky. "He is as American as ice cream, as masculine as a briar pipe, and as cleanly, unaffectedly appealing as a sea breeze in July," Edward Thompson wrote in the *Los Angeles Times*.

Van's attitude toward his sudden fame was equal parts joy and bewilderment. "I can't pick my nose in public any more," he said. Yet he got a terrific kick out of having fans behave toward him in a manner similar to the way he had responded to more established stars. "I loved it all," he later said. "It was crazy a lot of the time, but it was fun. Everything happened so fast I didn't have time to worry. My head was up in the clouds. I thought making pictures was the most exciting work in the world."

With Van rapidly becoming America's sweetheart, Metro executives decided to cast him in *Two Girls and a Sailor* opposite June Allyson and Gloria DeHaven. If Johnson represented the boy next door to a war-torn nation, Allyson became the adored girl next door. On the screen she and Van proved a winsome combination, and they would eventually make five pictures together. Louis B. Mayer thought the two should date, particularly since they had been friends in New York, and he tried to stir up an offscreen romance between them. Fans also came to favor a Johnson-Allyson courtship and went so far as to suggest names for the couple's first child once they were married. Johnson did squire Allyson to a series of premieres and official studio functions, and they later shared fan clubs, but no love match ever developed.

Allyson remembered coming out of the studio with Van one evening to find hundreds of admirers waiting for them. "I had my first taste of mass hysteria," she wrote. "Some nights were so bad we didn't dare leave the studio. There was that kind of unruly crowd outside the gates at Culver City. Every bobby-soxer in America was swooning over Van Johnson."

Van played a wealthy sailor in *Two Girls and a Sailor,* his first time as the leading man in an A picture. The script originally had his character living in the luxury of his family's mansion, but the Navy Department requested that the studio change the story so that he was on sick leave or simply on leave from a ship at sea: "It would probably make him a more acceptable character to the public," a Navy official wrote, "and certainly would be more true to life." But realism was not the mood that producer Joe Pasternak intended. *Two Girls and a Sailor* is a musical and pure escapism, featuring band leaders Harry James and Xavier Cugat, pianist José Iturbi, singer Lena Horne, and comedians Jimmy Durante and Gracie Allen. Allyson and DeHaven play the daughters of vaudevillians, determined to enter big-time show business. After performing their club act, they entertain servicemen with nightly parties in their home, until a rich sailor (Johnson) enables them to open a palatial canteen with lavish entertainment presented free to members of the armed forces.

Van's scars are more visible in the film, since MGM had become aware that his accident had helped propel him to popularity, and he participates in a short musical number. He serves primarily as the romantic lead, attracted first to DeHaven but switching his affections to Allyson by the final reel. Both sisters are in love with the generous sailor, one for his sixty million dollars and the other for himself. True love wins out, but not until rivalry between the army and navy has been resolved, a style show of women's fashions has been staged, and the assembled talent has had an opportunity to perform at least one specialty number apiece.

Van enjoyed making *Two Girls and a Sailor,* aware that the black-and-white musical marked a big step forward in his career. Since the accident, producers had been afraid to use him in rough-and-tumble pictures, but the part of the sailor was masculine yet sweet and sedate without being simpering. Johnson and Allyson renewed their friendship during the production and occasionally ate evening meals together in fancy restaurants, sharing the expense, as they had done at the Automat when they were struggling bit players on Broadway. On the set Van was a tease. He called DeHaven the "Comb," since she was forever fixing her hair and worried that the slightest strand might be out of place. Johnson relished his work and proved to be a dedicated professional. He always knew his lines, made notes all over the margins of his script, and was dutiful about watching each day's rushes once he no longer was needed before the camera.

Metro was certain that *Two Girls and a Sailor* would be a blockbuster at the box office and sent Allyson and contract player Nancy Walker on a personal-appearance tour with the picture, although most fans would have preferred seeing Van. The *Los Angeles Times* reported that the movie "packs such a load of entertainment that the actual plot doesn't matter." The reviewer found Johnson a "special attraction" and said, "He has the audiences applauding these days almost before he is seen on the screen."

With the June 1944 release of *Two Girls and a Sailor,* the frenzy over Van Johnson reached a new high. Whenever he was spotted, teenage girls shrieked his name in a crescendo of hysteria: "VaaaAAN JOHNSON!" If he opened his door at home in the morning to bring in a bottle of milk, he ran the risk of finding a young person in bobby socks waiting outside, eager to meet him. When he took part in radio shows, a police escort was necessary to hold back the crowd that gathered at the station. "One night when I was coming out of a broadcast on which Van Johnson had appeared," Hearst journalist Adela Rogers St. Johns wrote, "I saw about 5,000 people waiting in a crowd to get a glimpse of him. Fathers were holding up little children, old ladies were shoving for a better view, service men were grinning." By the end of the year Van's fan mail tallied eight thousand letters a week, the highest of any star in Hollywood. He had to have his car painted every month or so because he constantly found soap or lipstick messages written on it.

"He's my dream man," sighed twenty-year-old Louise Tapler. "He's not a glamour boy. He's a typical American." Inez DeCicco admired Van's shoulders. "And he's just an ordinary fellow, not conceited—the kind of guy you'd like to come home to," DeCicco effused. Another member of Van's swoon sisterhood said, "He's my boy. He can't sing, but aside from that he's got everything."

Dana Welborne was a preteen girl in Texas during the last years of World War II, and like most of her classmates, she collected movie-star pictures and pinned them to the wall of her room. "Van Johnson was my major love," Welborne said. "For many years my preference in boys was redheads or blondes, usually with freckles. I blame Van. He was so cuddly and manly. He played so many war heroes, and I fantasized that I was the girl waiting for him at home."

With Johnson's popularity on the ascent, every studio in Hollywood went on watch for a Van Johnson look-alike. Paramount had Sonny Tufts, Twentieth Century–Fox had Lon McAllister and William Eythe, RKO had Bill Williams, Universal had Donald O'Connor, and Selznick had Guy Madison. MGM groomed Tom Drake, Robert Walker, Peter Lawford, and James Craig as possible replacements should anything happen to their freckled dream boat. But none had quite Van's fresh-faced, clean-cut naïveté or his combination of vigor, charm, and vulnerability. "We like personality," a teenage girl told Louella Parsons. "Van has so much personality, and he's the type we would like to have for our dates."

Over and over journalists wrote that Johnson had become an idealized version of all the boys fighting overseas. "Perhaps he fills the empty place in our hearts," Adela Rogers St. Johns said in *Photoplay*. "He has created so much love in human hearts so badly in need of love." Van's explanation for his popularity was less saccharine. "I'm such an average punk I remind them of somebody," he said. "I've played so many soldiers that everyone thinks of me as the kid in uniform, their kid in uniform." He hoped that the craze would last, even though the adulation he received could be bothersome at times.

Many of Van's fans worried about his health in the months after his accident. Was there permanent damage to their idol? "There isn't anything more to be done for him, no further operations, no treatment," William E. Branch, Johnson's doctor, declared. "Time is the only thing he needs to be 100% okay again." Toward the end of 1944 rumors spread that Van had died on an operating table. Johnson himself heard the news when Gene Kelly burst into his dressing room at MGM waving a telegram and asking, "You aren't dead or anything are you, fellow?" Metro star Lana Turner was eating lunch at Romanoff's when she learned of the report. "I had dinner with him last night," the blond actress told the press. "He was looking extremely healthy then." But phone calls, wires, and messages from every part of the United States poured into Metro-Goldwyn-Mayer before the gossip was squelched.

So great was the fervor of his fans that Van was persuaded to move from the home he had rented in Brentwood. Admirers camped on his doorstep to get a look at him, awakened him by throwing pebbles at his bedroom window in the middle of the night, and begged for an opportunity to clean his quarters and cook dinner for him. On one occasion two teenage girls sneaked into the house and barricaded themselves in the bathroom. After a few months of such shenanigans, the beleaguered star moved into the Bel Air Hotel, where tightened security insured his privacy. Yet the isolation he experienced there sometimes became almost unbearable, even for an introvert. While the outside world viewed Johnson's success as a fulfillment of the American dream, in private the bobby-soxers' darling was still the insecure, lonely boy he had always been. "I kept telling myself that [fame] couldn't last," he said, "and I got more and more scared."

Keenan and Evie Wynn served as Van's major supports, and he found refuge in their home and delighted in being part of their family. The Wynns' two boys looked on him as Uncle Van, and he took pleasure in romping with the kids, playing games with them, and buying them presents. Keenan and Van engaged in their own horseplay, sometimes carrying on like children, much to Evie's disgust. Keenan might suddenly jump on Van, wrestle him to the ground, and rub his knuckles into his friend's head.

When Keenan went on a fifty-five-thousand-mile USO tour to army camps in China, India, and Burma in 1944, Van escorted Evie to several Hollywood functions. If Keenan was busy with work or absorbed in his outdoor recreations, Van took Evie to dinner at fashionable restaurants and did the things with her that her husband hated. "Theirs was a truly platonic friendship, corny as it sounds," Keenan said. "I [was] selfish and I was doing exactly what I wanted to do."

Wynn's own film career had begun to click when he played the sentimental gangster in *Lost Angel* with child star Margaret O'Brien. He followed that role with the chiseling Private Mulvehill in *See Here, Private Hargrove,* a highly successful wartime comedy. But the happy-go-lucky actor played only supporting roles, and his billing was always "with," "and," or "also." Worse still, Louis B. Mayer admitted that he had signed Keenan to a contract as a favor to his family. "To have a job under those circumstances is a kiss of death," Wynn said, "no producer on the lot wanted to cast me in a good part. Everyone automatically assumed I had no talent." Since Ed Wynn was a comic, the assumption was that his son was a comedian as well, even though the younger Wynn had Broadway experience and longed to prove his worth as a serious actor. "When I did get a job, the cast hated me before they met me," Keenan said. "They were sure my dad had bought my way in and that I would be a conceited pup."

So while Van's movie career was skyrocketing, Keenan's was held in check, thereby adding pressure to the Wynns' already strained marriage. Absorbed in his personal agonies, Keenan showed no interest in home-making, a point that Evie found increasingly objectionable. The press commended the way Keenan and Evie had taken Van under their protection and reported the triad in friendly terms. The threesome appeared insepa-rable, and fan magazines depicted Keenan as the faithful pal of America's redheaded hero, while Evie was Van's nurse and comforter. Questions later circulated about the nature of this ménage à trois, but not until John-son had reached the pinnacle of his success. Many Hollywood insiders as-sumed or became convinced that Van's relationship with Keenan had a sexual component.

Metro elevated Van to the next level of stardom by awarding him the lead in *Thirty Seconds over Tokyo*, a major production and by far John-son's biggest break yet. While recuperating in the hospital, Van had read Captain Ted Lawson's best-seller about the first American bombing raid on Japan in April 1942, and he immediately wished to play a role—any role—in the movie. With his surge in popularity after the release of *A Guy Named Joe*, the studio decided that Van was ready for the demanding lead in *Thirty Seconds over Tokyo*. Johnson would play the book's author, an army flier whose crew crash-landed on the coast of Japanese-occupied China. With the aid of Chinese resistance fighters, the badly injured Lawson es-caped the encroaching enemy, eventually received medical care, and re-turned to the United States, where he wrote his account of the mission.

Veteran screenwriter Dalton Trumbo followed the actual happenings closely in his script, with relatively few Hollywood touches added. The dia-logue contains enough grit that the heroics of the story become believable. The film dwells on the airmen's rigorous training for the daring, secret assignment, meant to bolster American morale by letting folks on the home front know that the heart of Japan had been bombed only four months after the attack on Pearl Harbor. The B-25 bombers' dangerous takeoffs from the deck of the aircraft carrier *Hornet* are shown, with no hope of the planes returning since their fuel supply was limited. The movie builds effectively to the assault on Tokyo, which occurs about two-thirds of the way through the film. Lawson's leg is split open when his plane crashes before reaching the designated landing strip in China, and the pilot has to be carried hundreds of miles on a litter by bands of Chinese guerrillas before he receives medical attention. Lawson loses his leg when gangrene develops, but after a period of mental anguish, he is reunited with his adoring, pregnant wife in Walter Reed Hospital. When she walks through the door of his room, the overjoyed airman forgets his amputated leg, stands up from his wheelchair, and falls. *Time* called the scene the "most shocking and piteous moment any American war film has yet dared to exhibit."

Because of his own accident and its accompanying publicity, Van was an ideal choice to play the movie's central role. Images of the wounded Lawson were reminiscent of the young actor's brush with death, and the full extent of Johnson's wounds from the car accident is visible in the latter part of the picture, adding to the film's realism. Van admirably handled his largest and most serious acting challenge to date, giving a three-dimensional portrayal. Bosley Crowther of the *New York Times* wrote than Johnson turned in a "warm and brave performance and managed quite well to achieve a moving tenderness in love scenes and rigid strength in the action field." *Time*'s reviewer said that Van played the part with "unusual heart and simplicity," and Pete Martin wrote in the *Saturday Evening Post* that "a few more opportunities like that and he may take the same grip on the grown-up public that he now has on the wearers of beanies, friendship rings, and charm bracelets."

Thirty Seconds over Tokyo was not an easy film to make. Van still suffered from recurrent headaches, had to be careful about his diet, and went to bed early every night to be rested enough to face the cameras the next day. The company worked in Florida for weeks, living in barracks at the Naval Air Station near Pensacola. At times bad weather held up production, and for days the actors and crew shivered in the cold, even though they were wearing fur coats and fur hats. Back in California, director Mervyn LeRoy found a spot near Malibu where a landlocked aircraft carrier could be made to look as if it were far out at sea. But seagulls were attracted to the vessel and, since there are no seagulls in the middle of the ocean, the ship had to be abandoned and a simulation built on MGM's stage 15, the studio's largest soundstage. Some B-25s were brought onto the set, and the fumes that came off their huge engines soon grew oppressive to the film's crew. Metro's back lot served for the sequences in China, with the buildings, towering gates, and a segment of the Great Wall that Cedric Gibbons had designed for *The Good Earth* (1937) substituting for the Japanese-controlled Chinese mainland.

Lawson himself served as the film's technical adviser, although Colonel James H. Doolittle, commander of the bombing raid on Japan, was present for some of the shooting, as was General Hap Arnold. Spencer Tracy played Doolittle in the movie and was granted special billing in the main titles for what was an important and well-delineated supporting role.

Van Johnson's name heads the cast, but he is paired with Robert Walker in the credits, followed by Robert Mitchum and Don DeFore. Phyllis Thaxter, who had acted with Lunt and Fontanne and played the title role in *Claudia* for two years on the stage, made her screen debut as Van's wife. Thaxter tested with Johnson before getting the part, and the two of them are convincing in the picture's overwritten love scenes. "I was a little nervous," the actress said about working with Johnson, but "right away something clicked between us. I felt at ease."

Released five months after *A Guy Named Joe*, *Thirty Seconds over Tokyo* did enormous business and continues to hold up well among Hollywood's spate of war movies. The film's aerial shots are impressive for the time, and its action is presented with greater tension and more authenticity than usual. Johnson's performance is by no means negligible. Taking Tracy as his model, Van achieved a convincing naturalism in the role. "That kind of acting is the finest and the hardest," Johnson said. "To appear so completely natural that the audience becomes engrossed in the characterization and forgets the actor is the essence of acting." Van felt close to Lawson, "even if my own injuries came from just an accident," he said, "and not from serving my country like he did."

With his sincere portrayal in *Thirty Seconds over Tokyo*, Van's appeal spread beyond his teenage following. Older women more frequently told him, "You remind me of my son so much," often adding, "He was killed in the war." Yet Van's well-scrubbed look and awkward charm continued to set bobby-soxers' hearts aflutter. Part of his popularity stemmed from an absence of established Hollywood stars, since many of them were serving overseas in the armed forces. Altogether, the movie industry temporarily lost approximately two thousand actors during the war. Yet for younger audiences who wanted their own heroes, Van seemed like the perfect guy to carry a girl into a rainbowed stratosphere and turn her life into eternal bliss. "On the screen Van was so good-looking and well built and had such a nice personality," said Anne Dimery, one of Johnson's acquaintances in Newport. "He had an air of innocence about him which we found comforting during the Second World War. So many of our brothers and classmates were away in the service."

Teenage girls then, as now, were addicted to love stories. "I used to go to the library and take out romances," said Mary Rodgers, daughter of composer Richard Rodgers. "I was madly in love with the war and very angry that I was too young for it. I wanted to have a husband who was like Van Johnson in *Thirty Seconds over Tokyo*." Millions of other American girls harbored similar fantasies.

Part of Van's allure for the bobby-sox brigade hinged on his remaining a bachelor. Time and again his fan mail contained such lines as, "Don't get married; wait for me to grow up." Johnson's stance in interviews was that he would not think of marrying until he was thirty years old. "Right now," he said, "I'm too busy. After making love all day in front of the camera, I haven't got enough energy to keep it up at night. One career at a time is enough."

To fill his leisure hours Van became more serious about painting, as did a number of other Hollywood stars. He collected old movie magazines, bathed two or three times a day, loved to play practical jokes, and liked to rumba. He occasionally drove down to the beach at Laguna and loved to eat fattening foods, although he had to watch his weight to stay trim for the camera. On Saturday nights he usually joined the gang that met at Gene Kelly's house to play charades and eat beans, frankfurters, and brown bread.

When working on a picture, Johnson normally took his lunch in a pail to the studio and ate in his dressing room. "This way I get a chance for a short nap before returning to the set," he said. Metro assigned him a knotty-pine dressing room that had a sitting room, heavy chairs, copper lamps, and brightly colored accessories. Among his colleagues Van could be lively company, loved to talk shop, and was clearly fired with ambition. Even with a group of friends he always seemed "on," talking fast and using his hands in animated conversation. He had a knack for sensing who was important or was on the way up and made little secret of his intent to be among the most successful.

Hollywood's social strata were well defined during the golden era, and Van longed to enter the elite rank. He wanted to be included in the gala affairs and to hobnob with Tinseltown's kings and queens. "There was such ruthlessness in Hollywood," Martin Jurow said, "and some foolish things commanded people's attention." Jules Stein, one of the town's most powerful agents, supposedly had a toothbrush for every day of the week on a rack that rotated. Stein could push a button in the bathroom of his Beverly Hills mansion and the next brush came around. "Jules's tooth-brushes were a topic of conversation," said Jurow. "People were curious about whether anyone had seen them."

Toward the end of 1944, Van knew that he was going to be big in Hollywood. Not only did MGM control the largest pool of talent of any studio in town, but its minions pampered the company's stars and took care of most routine tasks for them. "They treated you like you were a mixture of a jewel and a retarded child," said Fernando Lamas, who enjoyed stardom for a while at Metro. "They kept you in cotton. If you had a headache, three doctors came on the set with three pills and three shots. If you needed a driver's license, some inspector from the Department of Motor Vehicles came to the studio; you never went any place." Van later admitted that he was spoiled by MGM and that part of his helplessness came as a result of the studio's coddling.

In the grooming process at Metro, Van not only learned the technique of motion picture acting but also mastered the role of playing Van Johnson. He worked hard to achieve a place in the MGM galaxy, and as his dollar value to the studio rose, so did his effrontery. With Van's advance in stature, the men in Metro's casting office saw less and less of the freckled-faced fellow who had once pestered them for roles. Talent head Billy Grady thought that Johnson turned his back on the people who had helped push him to the top. "The only elite he knew in the bygone days were the casting office staff," said Grady. But by the time Van had finished *Thirty Seconds over Tokyo,* the eligible young bachelor was invited everywhere and courted by the important people, and he no longer seemed to have time for the little ones. "I didn't speak to Van for several years," said Grady, "although my staff and I kept him in picture after picture."

While Johnson was a workhorse and dedicated to his craft, he also loved being treated as a star and began to get testy about the parts he accepted. "The studio and staffs were good enough at the beginning," Grady said, "but now our man was an authority on what was good and what he thought was not. Suffice to say he was overruled." Van changed agents, and while he remained grateful for all MGM had done for him, he became difficult with underlings—"just what you expect when you elevate a newcomer to star level," Grady said.

Van certainly did not want to make *Between Two Women,* the last film in which he played Red Adams in the Dr. Gillespie series. The picture was tedious and uninspired, but the bobby-soxers turned out in full squeal for it, and the movie grossed more than two million dollars in the United States alone. When the run of the picture was extended in Los Angeles, advertisements in the local press read: "That Man Van . . . Stays for a Second (Bobby) Sockeroo Week!" Johnson's performance in *Between Two Women* reveals the ability that had made him a star, and the series' producer was notified by MGM executives when shooting ended that Van would no longer be available for budget productions. Relieved to be free of such small-time obligations, Johnson complained, "Another one like *Between Two Women* and I'll be on the skids."

But MGM had no intention of letting such a catastrophe happen. The studio next put their golden boy in the Technicolor musical *Thrill of a Romance,* opposite swimmer Esther Williams, by then a popular leading lady. The picture had little plot, but audiences responded enthusiastically to the chemistry Johnson and Williams engendered. "We were a sweetheart couple who had that MGM look that was so 'American,' with no ethnic traces whatsoever," Esther Williams wrote in her memoirs. She teaches Johnson to swim in the picture and would later claim that when they did the backstroke together, she had to put her hand under her costar's body to keep him afloat. Van portrays an air force hero on furlough in the movie, and his easy manner proved tailor-made for light comedy. Director Richard Thorpe was noted for finishing his pictures on schedule and under budget and, with no heavy drama involved, Thorpe got most of his scenes in one take.

Johnson and Williams developed a close relationship on the set, but they did not spend much time together in private life. The studio tried to convince the two attractive stars to go out on dates, but no romantic sparks

ever developed between them off camera. "There was no cuter human being in the world at that time," Williams said of Johnson, yet the two went
their separate ways after work. When someone asked Van why he and
Esther did not socialize together, he quipped, "Because I'm afraid she can't
get her webbed feet into a pair of evening sandals."

The Office of War Information voiced concern that *Thrill of a Romance*,
a lush production set in an elegant resort, would pose problems in overseas
distribution. "We have discovered," a memo from the government agency
stated, "that films boasting of American opulence or showing an abundance of food or other material goods during wartime are apt to be seriously resented by our less fortunate allies who are closer to the fighting
front." Yet *Thrill of a Romance* reflected Hollywood opulence at its flashiest
and was intended as strictly escapist entertainment. It contained the song
"I Should Care," by Sammy Cahn, Axel Stordahl, and Paul Weston, music
by Metropolitan Opera tenor Lauritz Melchior and Tommy Dorsey's orchestra, and light comedy in a romantic atmosphere far removed from the
ravages of war.

The picture wrapped on October 1, 1944, and was previewed in a
neighborhood theater outside Los Angeles. Cards filled out by the audience included such comments as "Van is a darling," "He's my man," and
"I love that boy. . . . I love him more than Frankie." The following July,
Thrill of a Romance premiered at the Egyptian Theater in Hollywood, with
proceeds going to the war wounded. Grandstands were erected on both
sides of Hollywood Boulevard for the occasion, and they were filled by
early afternoon with bobby-soxers, mature women, and even elderly grand-
mothers waiting to catch a glimpse of Van. The star arrived with a fancy
handkerchief in his coat pocket and a flower in his buttonhole. Shrieking
females grabbed the handkerchief, the flower, and the buttons from his
shirt after the movie. They yanked at his tie, tore his collar, got a fistful of
his red hair, and left his scalp bleeding. "He emerged looking like the
runner-up in a commando raid," *Liberty* magazine reported. By then Van's
fan letters had swollen to a record forty-nine thousand a month.

The reviewer for the *Los Angeles Times* wrote, "*Thrill of a Romance* is all bright colors but the luster is only glaze deep. But its gaudiness will carry it through, especially with the fans." When the film opened at the Capitol Theater in Manhattan, the critic said in the *New York Herald Tribune* that Johnson gave "the type of performance that has endeared him to the younger set. He is the antithesis of the 'wolf' . . . clean cut, amiable, a little shy, and needing aid and comfort."

Having worked in films steadily for two years, Van went on a short vacation to Mexico after *Thrill of a Romance* was finished. He went fishing and enjoyed walking through the streets of Mexican villages without being mobbed. "When I came back and the crowd in the airport recognized me," he said, "I got a great kick out of it." At times his life seemed to contain as much fantasy as did Metro's escapist movies.

Before leaving for Mexico, Johnson had dated MGM starlets Frances Rafferty and Kay Williams, who later married Clark Gable. He and Kay Williams had been seen together at Ciro's, which caused a great stir, but Williams claimed that she herself read Louella Parsons's column every day to find out how her romance with Van was coming along. Johnson told reporters that he had learned to be careful and not date the same girl twice, since if he did, gossip columnists had them engaged. Van remained an idealist about women and said that his model for a serious relationship was Irene Dunne, although he claimed he would prefer not to marry an actress. "I adore women," he said, but "what really counts is what is in the head and heart." He loathed dumb types who lay around all day and complained about imaginary illnesses. *Silver Screen* quoted him as saying, "Somebody should start a school for brides to teach them how to be the best wives—a cook in the kitchen, a lovely hostess in the living room, a perfect mother, and an exciting woman at other times." Van maintained that he hoped to marry, have at least five children, and wanted to build a New England–style house, which he planned to fill with the fundamental values that he had learned as a boy—independence, free thought, hard work, and friendliness. "That's my dream," he told an interviewer. "Darned if I know what is going on in this country, with all this talk about mixing careers and marriage. It just can't be done with any measure of success in either field. One must suffer and it's usually the marriage."

Van repeatedly claimed that he was currently too busy and had too many things he wanted to do to develop serious romantic notions. "I've always wanted a dog, a baby, and a home," he said, "but I'm too fickle to have all my eggs in one basket. I want to save my little pot and travel round the world. I want that old steamship ticket and that trunk."

Outwardly, America's favorite heartthrob seemed to have changed very little since achieving success in Hollywood. He appeared amazingly modest in interviews, disclosed good manners, showed an interest in what happened to other people, listened politely to his elders, and exuded a zest for life. "There is nothing spoiled about Van Johnson," Adela Rogers St. Johns wrote, and her comment reflected the consensus among Hollywood reporters. Many writers remarked about how honest and direct Van was, but others noted that he appeared to answer questions with utmost frankness yet gave no hint of what was locked inside him. Overriding everything else was his subconscious need to discard anything that might prove detrimental to his career.

Van's ambition was fired by the same insecurities that had hounded him since childhood. His overwhelming determination to earn fame and distinction left a vacuum in his personal development. Beneath his buoyant exterior, a band of iron was wrapped around Van's emotions, so tightly that his growth was impeded. Like the adolescent boy in his hometown, he avoided realistically dealing with his problems. The hallucinatory world of MGM became Van's sanctuary, with his movie-star image protecting the doubts and vulnerability locked inside. For the most part he was the same withdrawn person who had walked alone on the streets of Newport, the same boy who had recoiled in the darkness of his local movie palace. But the years were beginning to catch up with him, and there were sexual urges that did not fit the facade he had fabricated.

On the surface, Metro's golden boy was the blissful beneficiary of Hollywood's grooming and promotion. Again and again he told fan-magazine columnists, "I look at myself every morning when I'm shaving and I say to myself, "Johnson, you are a lucky stiff." But with sudden fame came the fear of losing what he had gained so unexpectedly and the need to confirm his worth. "You feel just like yourself inside," he said, "except you begin to get scared part of the time and excited and triumphant the rest of it." He tried to hide the frightened portion of himself, the downcast part, and keep his worrying secret. But the mask occasionally slipped. "I'm the original Wailing Wall," Van admitted. "I'm the bleeding heart. I fret all the time." The tension inside him was building.

Adding to the snarl of his slow emotional growth was the uprooted nature of his youth. His formative years in Rhode Island seemed so distant that Van Johnson, the international movie star, had trouble connecting his origins with his present station. There was no consistent or continuous identity. After he arrived in Hollywood, Van liked to say that it gave him a warm feeling to know that the house where he and his father had spent so many years together was still there. Yet as an MGM star he never encouraged his father to move to California, and Charles Johnson showed no interest in leaving the island he considered home until his death. Van did invite his dad to visit him in Los Angeles on one occasion and, to show Charlie a good time, took him to Dave Chasen's restaurant, which was known for its New York steaks and high prices. While the elder Johnson sat looking at the menu, tight-lipped and dour, Van told his father to order whatever he wanted. When the old man asked for a tuna fish sandwich, Van was shattered. Charlie's attitude was that simple food was good enough for a workingman, and he made it clear that he wanted no part of the Hollywood high life. Van felt that his father had rejected him and cast doubt on his celebrity, which hurt him deeply.

Charlie continued to live on alone in the old-fashioned house in Newport where Van had been raised. He ate breakfast and lunch every day at the same restaurant, a little hole in the wall that served good food, and walked around town by himself chatting with people he knew. Van eventually bought his father a Ford car, and Charlie drove it down to Ruth White's Clover Farm Store and took the men gathered out front of the store for a ride. But he had difficulty voicing his pride to Van.

Before long even Charles Johnson began getting letters from his son's admirers, sometimes several dozen a day. Charlie was proud of his boy, and neighbors remembered him sitting in the back row of the Strand Theater in Newport and watching Van's movies over and over. When asked about his son's success, Charlie always replied that he was tickled to death. "It's just like a Cinderella or fairy story you'd read in a book," he said.

Three weeks after *Thrill of a Romance* wrapped, shooting began on Van's next picture, *Weekend at the Waldorf.* A remake of MGM's *Grand Hotel* (1932), the updated version of Vicki Baum's novel has Van playing a wounded airman threatened with an early death from a shrapnel fragment lodged near his heart. What the character needs most is the will to live, but the flyer is lonely and depressed. He has no home and no family, and he mourns a buddy who was shot down over Formosa. At the famous Waldorf-Astoria Hotel in Manhattan, he meets a public stenographer, played by Lana Turner, Metro's hottest glamour girl, who eventually becomes his reason for living.

The production glitters with an all-star cast that includes Ginger Rogers as a movie star, Walter Pidgeon as a war correspondent, and Keenan Wynn in a supporting role as a bumbling cub reporter. Portions of the Waldorf Hotel were reproduced in exact detail for the cameras, and the film radiates MGM glamour in all departments—sets, costumes, hairstyles, performances, musical selections.

Van was excited about working with the voluptuous Turner and found the blond star "dynamite" as a performer. "People don't know what a great actress she is," he said. "They notice her beauty and don't realize she can act." He had no scenes with Ginger Rogers in the picture, but ate lunch with the versatile actress one day in the studio's commissary, where he behaved like the incurable fan that he still was.

When *Weekend at the Waldorf* opened in New York in October 1945, the movie broke all records at Radio City Music Hall for nine weeks. Critics judged Johnson's portrayal of the young army captain "boyishly appealing." Although the picture is slick, pleasant entertainment, it suffers in comparison with the original screen version, which starred Greta Garbo, John Barrymore, Joan Crawford, and Wallace Beery.

Shortly after finishing work on *Weekend at the Waldorf,* Van was invited up to San Simeon, the William Randolph Hearst castle on the California coast near San Luis Obispo. An invitation to San Simeon was a sure sign that a member of the movie colony had gained importance, since Hearst and his mistress, screen actress Marion Davies, had been social arbiters in the film world since the 1920s. Van counted the weekend he spent at the Hearst ranch, with some thirty other guests, among his fondest memories. "I was up before everybody," he recalled, "and rode over all those 300,000 acres."

In January 1945, Keenan Wynn decided to join the U.S. Navy, and he and Eve agreed to separate legally. On the day before he was to report for duty, Keenan was critically injured when his motorcycle crashed into an automobile at the corner of Sunset Boulevard and Hilgard, not far from the hotel where Johnson was living. Wynn suffered a fractured jaw, a severe concussion, a back injury, and lacerations above the left eye. For eleven days he lay in a coma, while Van and actors Peter Lawford and Paul Stewart kept watch over him. "The results were a lot more serious than most people knew," Wynn said later, "so Evie wouldn't leave me." After Keenan was released from the hospital, he was warned not to drink liquor because of his head injury. "I ignored it," he said, "and had unfortunate results." But Eve stayed with her husband and took care of him.

The accident occurred while Keenan and Van were making *Easy to Wed,* Van's third picture with Esther Williams. A Technicolor remake of

MGM's *Libeled Lady* (1936), the film cast Johnson and Williams in the roles William Powell and Myrna Loy had played earlier and Wynn and Lucille Ball in the parts created by Spencer Tracy and Jean Harlow. *Easy to Wed* proved an unashamedly fatuous movie, but it was carefully crafted and its stars guaranteed box-office success.

"Van and I matched," said Williams. "It looked like we belonged together as a couple. He was as much the all-American boy as I was the all-American girl. As World War II drew to a close, we . . . became icons, in a way, symbolizing the virtues that people loved best about America. Van represented all the young men who had gone off to war for their country, and I represented the girls they were fighting to come home to." In *Easy to Wed* Van proved surprisingly adept at farce. In an eight-minute duck-hunting scene he is hilarious, causing critics to hail a new Van Johnson and refer to him as a master at the pratfall. While Van might not be maturing emotionally, it was clear that he was mastering his craft.

Director Edward Buzzell, an old song-and-dance man who came to Hollywood by way of the Orpheum vaudeville circuit, kept the tone of the movie light and chose to demonstrate what he wanted actors to do for the camera. "I gave them the feel of a scene," said Buzzell. "It went faster that way." Johnson and Williams had to sing a duet in Portuguese in the movie, and since neither of them knew a word of the language, the studio hired a musician from Brazilian performer Carmen Miranda's band to teach the stars the lyric.

Van and Metro contract player Jean Porter worked for weeks on a number called "Tell Ya What I'm Gonna Do," which dance director Jack Donohue choreographed for them. With John Green, head of the studio's music department, the two performers prerecorded the song, and they rehearsed and rehearsed it to the playback. "We ended up with a really good number," said Porter, "but it was cut out because the film was too long." Such disappointments were not uncommon.

Lucille Ball and Keenan Wynn contributed much of the humor to *Easy to Wed,* and the two played off one another effectively. Ball's performance as Gladys reveals the embryo of her Lucy Ricardo role in the later *I Love Lucy* television series, and Wynn's role is meatier than Metro normally granted him. Keenan had his mouth wired shut after the motorcycle accident and had to talk between his teeth. Although Wynn's speech improved with practice, finishing *Easy to Wed* was an ordeal for the actor. "I walked out of a door in one scene at 183 pounds," he said, "and I walked through the door on the other side at 153. I lost thirty pounds in four weeks."

Despite the difficulties involved with its production and its vacuous nature, the picture received excellent notices. "Mr. Johnson," a reviewer for *Harper's* magazine wrote, "is fairly typical of the dream boys that Hollywood likes to set up as representative American youths, and as such he is an interesting phenomenon. Johnson avoids the forthright tactics that used to propel ladies into old fashioned heroes' brawny arms. Instead he is inclined to blush and stammer his way along, assuming in moments of high ardor the look of a water spaniel."

Photoplay named Van the magazine's favorite beefcake pinup of 1945, even though his physique was nothing striking. The Gallup poll reported that Van Johnson was the fastest-rising male star in the country, and the year ended with Van occupying second place among the top ten moneymakers in Hollywood. Nearly every incoming train brought to the movie capital another load of wholesome-looking young men who hoped to become the next Van Johnson, but Van remained unique, a product of circumstances and the moment.

For the next few years the hysteria around the strawberry blond star continued. Wherever Van went he was mobbed, and MGM publicity men and uniformed cops had to run interference for him in crowds. One night a group of screeching girls rushed toward their idol in a theater lobby and knocked over a metal candy machine a few inches from where Van had been shoved against a wall. Even messenger girls at the studio were not immune from his spell, and he was constantly approached by girls delivering phony memos to his dressing room and those who dropped in on him by "mistake." Anywhere he looked he was likely to see teenagers with eyes fixed adoringly on him, yearning for some word from him that signaled recognition.

Metro had to hire extra people to handle Johnson's fan mail. Most of the letters he received came from girls between the ages of twelve and eighteen, although some were signed by several hundred fans in the hope that numbers would produce an answer. Others contained poetry such as:

> For Van we Live,
> For Van we Die,
> This Man we Love,
> For Him we Sigh.

Throughout America, sidewalks and walls were scribbled with hearts and arrows bearing Van's initials. Fan magazines tried to satisfy their readers' appetite for stories and photographs of filmland's most adored male, but there were constant pleas for more. In issue after issue, Van was pictured wearing fancy sweaters or posing bare chested, with freckles over his face, shoulders, and front. "They're my living," he said of his freckles, fully aware that almost every teenage girl in the country dreamed of having a date with him. Psychologists referred to Johnson's older fans as mental bobby-soxers. "All of these facts point to the conclusion that American women are tired of being chased and caught and taken care of by a know-it-all male," *Life* magazine reported in 1945. "The kind of man that most of them want . . . is Van Johnson."

All Van had to do, it seemed, was inhale, exhale, and be charming. "I had a terrific crush on him," said Jack Benny's daughter, Joan. "He looked outdoorish, sporty, and always wore red socks." Young Joan liked Van because he talked to her at parties about his art and listened to her opinions. When he gave her one of his paintings, she hung it over her bed. "Everyone loves Van," said actress Greer Garson. "I've always thought of Van as a sort of big and burly Shirley Temple." Somehow Johnson seemed to convey sexual virility without being threatening.

Van undoubtedly remained in many ways a child. Fame and isolation had stifled him, in contrast to the rebellion and career frustration that had perpetuated an adolescent streak in Keenan Wynn. Mrs. Verner Maloney, the woman Keenan's motorcycle had hit in the recent accident, sued Wynn for eighty thousand dollars, although the actor claimed that she had been "negligent and careless." Keenan and Eve continued to live at 212 North Saltair, where Van remained their constant companion. "I'm the man who came to dinner," Johnson said. "They can't get rid of me." Keenan called his friend V.J., and Evie looked on her husband's best friend as her kindred spirit. Unlike Keenan, who wasted his talent and squandered money, Van had a purpose and planned for the future. Whereas her husband had a habit of getting involved in dubious business endeavors, Van was sensible and cautious about money. "What she most objected to about Dad," Ned Wynn wrote, "were his drinking, his motorcycles, and his low-crotch friends." Van had turned his back on the Sunday biker crowd and their grease-pit inclinations. He aimed for bigger things, which included a suaver lifestyle.

Although Van liked to say that he was simply a starstruck kid lucky enough to have made it over the MGM gate, he began to feel, as his success grew, that life's rules were different for the famous. Keenan had been raised with that attitude, and Evie quickly adopted her own sense of entitlement. All three viewed themselves, in different ways, as standing above the common herd, free from ordinary restrictions. Van was eager for more of Hollywood's euphoria. During the war, quick success and unimagined material rewards had been enough for him. He had gone from chorus boy to fame beyond his wildest dreams and in record time had become one of the most famous young men in the world. What he faced in the years ahead was the challenge of keeping the prize he had won and accepting himself, with all of his uncertainties and contradictions.

CHAPTER 5

Trouble in Paradise

At the end of World War II, Metro-Goldwyn-Mayer had reached its zenith. Considered the Tiffany's of Hollywood studios, MGM was a finely tuned operation bristling with tremendous energy. Its pictures were glossy and expensive, its actors and actresses talented and beautiful. Louis B. Mayer, the studio's administrative head, was a man of intelligence who understood popular tastes and settled for nothing less than the best. A shrewd showman, Mayer referred to Metro employees as his children, but he ruled them with a combination of love and intimidation. MGM stars ranked among Hollywood's petted elite, but they also did what they were told.

Fear of losing favor with the studio kept the press from printing damaging stories about the company's methods and personnel. Newspapers and magazines depicted all of Hollywood as a happy nirvana peopled by celestial creatures who led pristine lives in the elysian fields of Beverly Hills, Bel Air, and Malibu. For reporters to do otherwise threatened a loss of movie advertising, and Metro in particular was a major account. Fan magazines understood that much of their livelihood depended on the largesse of major film companies, and it was in the magazines' best interest to underscore the fanciful images that studio publicists concocted for publication.

Van Johnson had benefited from this arrangement, and he accepted it unconditionally. "We were a big happy family," Van said of MGM. "Louis B.

Mayer was always looking for a son, and I think he found that in me. I adored him. He was my father." Mayer had seen to it that Johnson was assigned roles that were carefully tailored for him—winsomely romantic parts in which Van could appear debonair and well groomed and prime the reveries of his growing horde of aficionados. The former chorus boy was making more money that he had ever dreamed possible. He was on Tinseltown's most desired invitation lists and adored by millions from coast to coast. He had no reason to question the system that had tutored him and propelled him to such eminence.

Within a year after the war ended, Mayer's empire would begin to come crumbling down. Older stars returned from the service ready to resume their place in Hollywood's cosmos. When handsome Robert Taylor was released from the navy, Metro assigned him a dressing room next to Johnson's, proof of their comparative rank. Clark Gable came back from the air force and was greeted by a standing ovation when he walked into the MGM commissary on the day of his return. Before long new sex symbols such as John Derek and Rock Hudson appeared on the Hollywood scene, and fan magazines speculated that their appeal might mean a finish to the Van Johnson boom.

The movie industry itself was changing. In the fall of 1945, with the wartime no-strike pledge no longer in effect, the Conference of Studio Unions called a walkout of Hollywood painters, carpenters, electricians, office workers, readers, and other members of the craft unions that had been organized during the 1930s. The strike, led by Herb Sorrell of the Painters Union, who was widely considered a political radical, quickly turned angry. At first the strikers concentrated their efforts against Warner Bros., where more than a thousand pickets massed in front of the studio's main gate on October 5, 1945, but the turmoil continued for nearly eight months and soon spread to other studios.

At the height of the violence, strikers torched a car outside MGM's walls. Van Johnson and Keenan Wynn were finishing *No Leave, No Love* when the strike began. Van faced the wrath of union members each morning by crossing the picket lines and going to work as usual. Throughout his tenure at Metro, Johnson would be known as a loyal company man, essentially untouched by the social and political issues of the time. He reported to the set letter-perfect in his lines and seldom gave directors any trouble. Whatever problems he had with the studio were focused on lesser bureaucrats.

No Love, No Leave was a light comedy sprinkled with music and romance, well below producer Joe Pasternak's standards. Van plays a marine who falls in love with a radio singer in the picture, while Keenan handles most of the humor. "Van Johnson is still such a solid draw," the *Hollywood Reporter* said, "that any picture which has him will do business, big business." But *No Love, No Leave* was mediocre, and its star was well aware that the movie was little more than filler for the company's chain of theaters.

Van next got a much-desired chance to do his first song-and-dance routine on film. The movie was *Till the Clouds Roll By,* a syrupy screen biography of songwriter Jerome Kern, who had recently died. Johnson's partner in the Technicolor musical was Lucille Bremer, a personal favorite of producer Arthur Freed and a fine dancer. The two performed a sprightly rendition of Kern's "I Won't Dance" from the Broadway show *Roberta* that was sure to win favor with audiences. The number reunited Van with dance director Robert Alton, whom Johnson had impressed on Broadway. Robert Walker played Jerome Kern in *Till the Clouds Roll By,* and Van simply appeared as one of the film's many guest stars.

Although Johnson still considered himself a dancer more than a serious actor, he panicked as time neared for him to sing for the sound camera. Kay Thompson, a respected member of Freed's musical staff, was sent to coach him, as she did for many performers. "She came in wearing a lynx coat and just sat there and smiled, and I sang to her," Van recalled. "That was it. I got over my fright."

Johnson's popularity by then had stretched well beyond the bobby-soxer set. When he showed up at the Shrine Auditorium in November 1945 to hear a San Francisco Opera production of Wagner's *Tristan und*

Isolde that featured Lauritz Melchior and Helen Traubel, he was pursued by two autograph seekers as he walked down the aisle before the curtain rose on the third act. The commotion caught the attention of the audience seated on the lower floor, and they stood almost en masse to give Van an ovation. He accepted the plaudits graciously, beaming with pride that he had been recognized by the cultured crowd.

Between movie assignments the busy actor went to Lake Arrowhead to water ski, which he enjoyed, and in February 1946 Metro sent him to New York for the first time since he had left Manhattan nearly five years earlier. With his fans so rambunctious and aggressive, the studio had been afraid to let its fair-haired boy go east on a personal-appearance tour, and Johnson claimed that not until this first trip back to New York did he truly become scared of being mobbed. The streets he had once walked every day without being recognized were no longer safe for him. "It was pretty frightening to realize what the power of pictures could do to a guy like me," Van said.

As he neared the age of thirty, Johnson admitted that he was tiring of life in the public eye. There were times when the constant threat of having his privacy invaded by swooning fans turned his life into a hazardous farce. Celebrity had separated him from old friends and added to his isolation. "If you talk about your life in Hollywood, you're afraid people will think you are bragging," Van said. "If you don't talk about Hollywood, they think you're stuck up and aloof. If you reminisce, you feel as if you're being patronizing." Johnson admitted in 1946 that he was feeling "damned lonely" and that he would like nothing better than to find someone to share his success. He was growing uneasy about life as a bachelor and hungered for companionship.

In the fall of 1945 Van met ice skater Sonja Henie at a party at Jules Stein's house. Both stars were ambitious, both were of Scandinavian descent, and both appreciated the value of favorable publicity. Although Henie's movie career was on the wane, she had turned live ice shows into a big business. Each of her tours had grossed about $2.5 million, and the skater was known to be a tough lady where her career and money were concerned. Sonja was three years older than Van and still married to Dan Topping, owner of the New York Yankees, when they met. But Van made a habit of calling her regularly after they had been introduced, and when Henie opened her *Ice Revue* in Indianapolis, he sent orchids to her dressing room.

In December the skater took her ice show to Chicago, and Van surprised her by phoning from the lobby of the hotel where she was staying. "I have a week's holiday," he announced. "Not a soul knows I'm here." The two ended up spending the Christmas holiday together, although both claimed that there was nothing serious about their relationship and that they were strictly good friends. MGM was not pleased about the alliance, fearing that an entanglement, particularly with an older woman, might jeopardize Van's standing with his fans. The studio's publicity department quickly issued the statement: "Sonja is a nice girl, but her friendship with Mr. Johnson could not possibly be construed as a romance." To lure Van away from Henie and protect the studio's investment, Metro hastily arranged the personal-appearance tour to New York in February 1946, preceded by a trip to Washington, D.C., where Van participated in a memorial birthday ball for the late President Franklin Roosevelt to benefit a fund for infantile paralysis.

When Mayer learned that Henie was returning to California, he manipulated Van's schedule so that his star was in Florida when the skater arrived home. Sonja kept rumors of a romance with Johnson flying when she told reporters, "I only met Van a couple of months ago, and who knows what might happen?" Meanwhile, Hollywood gossip columnists were calling Johnson's hotel rooms wherever he went for an update.

Van continued to see Henie when he returned to Los Angeles, despite Mayer's protests. He attended a dinner party at her house for visiting Norwegian royalty and saw Sonja's ice show in Westwood. Johnson began wearing a small pair of silver skates in his lapel, and reporters maintained that when the two stars were together they beamed with a telltale glow.

But their romance, regardless of how real the attraction may have been, was doomed from the outset. "Whether Van Johnson marries Sonja Henie depends in the long run on his studio," columnist Sheilah Graham wrote in March 1946. "Van is ambitious first and in love second. And I don't think that Metro will allow his admiration for Sonja to blossom into orange blossoms."

The love affair with Henie proved a mirage, both for the media and for the stars themselves. Henie needed publicity, and dating Johnson assured her of headlines. Van knew by then, no matter how hard he tried to repress the instinct, that he was either homosexual or bisexual. Mayer later regretted that he had gone to such lengths to squelch talk of a romance between Johnson and the popular ice skater, for Mayer's boy wonder soon put the studio and himself in a far more embarrassing situation.

Nothing posed as great a threat to the spotless image studio publicists worked to create as homosexuality. As far as the media were concerned, homosexual actors did not exist in the film colony. Mayer did not want to hear the word. In the 1940s any star who was gay knew that his or her career depended on keeping an alternative sexual orientation secret, even among close friends. "Any hint of homosexuality and an actor's prominence would go," said Martin Jurow's wife, Erin-Jo. "We didn't talk about such matters with anybody. We shut the door and that was it." Given the temper of the times, it would have been a near impossibility for a young gay star to advance toward a major career in Hollywood and explore his or her true sexual impulses in a sensible and responsible manner.

More adventurous types—Tyrone Power and Errol Flynn, Danny Kaye and Laurence Olivier, Cary Grant and Randolph Scott, if one believes the abiding rumors—may have experimented with homoerotic relationships but were cautious enough to keep such dalliances from the public until later. Metro's silent picture star William Haines was a known homosexual during the 1920s and had sustained a gay relationship that lasted longer than most marriages in the film community. But when Haines was discovered with a young sailor on his cot at a local YMCA in 1933, his screen career was finished. Mayer made certain that the scandal did not reach the press, but he fired Haines, who subsequently became one of Tinseltown's most sought-after interior decorators.

Haines had a penchant for men in uniform, whom he frequently met in Pershing Square in downtown Los Angeles. On the occasion in question, Haines had taken a sailor to his room on the seventh floor of a nearby YMCA, where a house detective and members of the vice squad burst in and handcuffed both men. In an interview years later, Haines claimed that a similar incident happened in the 1940s to an actor who had "the same initials as one of the celebrations of the end of the war," clearly a reference to V-J Day. Haines said that MGM bailed out the star in question and kept his arrest from the newspapers because the actor's pictures were still making a great deal of money.

Playwright Arthur Laurents, an acknowledged homosexual, was working in Hollywood shortly after World War II ended. In his autobiography, Laurents maintained that everyone in the film colony "knew who was gay and who was lesbian, whose marriage was arranged and who arranged gang bangs, who rented tricks, male and female, but they all pretended gracefully that they didn't. The hypocrisy was considered sensible, even admirable." Image in 1940s Hollywood was everything.

That Van Johnson had homosexual tendencies seems to have been well known in the film capital, yet his sexual proclivities were seldom discussed. "Van is thirty years old and has never come close to marrying," Louella Parsons confessed in a moment of partial candor, "regardless of what has been written about his 'romances.'" Most members of the film colony looked on another person's sexual preferences as none of their business—at least until scandal occurred. Homosexuality and bisexuality were widespread in Hollywood and throughout the theater world, but sophisticates in the profession accepted that fact and winked on all but the most outrageous behavior.

Yet Louis B. Mayer was shattered by the thought that the nation's sweetheart, his boy Van, might in fact be gay. The threat that possibility posed to the studio's investment in Johnson was too calamitous for Papa Mayer even to contemplate. With the company's theaters about to be snatched away as a result of antitrust decrees, Mayer felt that his life's work was in danger. The mogul suddenly seemed distrustful of everyone.

Because of their friendships with Johnson, Mayer suspected that Keenan Wynn and Peter Lawford might also be gay. Lawford's mother, who created more than her share of trouble for MGM, came home one day to find Van and Keenan and Evie Wynn sitting in the drawing room with Peter. Lady Lawford promptly left the room and instructed the servants never to admit the threesome into her house again. "Peter was quite upset at me for storming out and refusing them further admittance," she said. But Lawford told her son, "I don't want homosexuals in our drawing room. If you want them here, then notify me and I will leave while they are here."

Desperate to keep Van's image from being tarnished by rumors, Mayer sent the star to England early in the summer of 1946. Johnson returned from his trip abroad full of remorse that he had not fought in the war. By then Van seemed to carry a plethora of guilt about many things—his sexual ambivalence, his poor relationship with his father, the unlikelihood of ever having a normal home and family, the gap between his public image and his private life, and his lack of a war record. "I wish I could be like that guy up there on the screen," Johnson said. "I feel like I'm on such a pedestal with some of those kids that I can't do anything human. It's not easy. Everyone in Hollywood is so damned scared all the time."

Van himself seemed to grow increasingly frightened, aware that at any minute stardom could be snatched away from him. On the surface he remained the cute, nice guy—casual, bashful, and inexperienced enough in worldly matters to encourage mothering yet relaxed enough to laugh at himself. Inside an attractive exterior was a gnawing fear and unhappiness. Van was tired of living in hotel rooms and longed for a permanent relationship, although he tended to dismiss his darker sexual urges as little more than a postadolescent desire to experiment. His elevated status and a heightened sense of self-importance were at odds with a carnal nature of any sort.

With the war over, Johnson had doubts that his days in the limelight would last much longer. "I've still got some good years ahead of me," he said during his relationship with Sonja Henie. "I've still got a chance. A man just gets to his beautiful period when he's forty. He's grown up then and he knows what to do and how to do it." But such statements were largely wishful thinking. Johnson knew that his future in films was precarious as the national mood began to change.

What Van knew how to do best was work. On the set he was surrounded by nurturing colleagues with common goals. He was told what to do, and he gladly obliged. Johnson had no sooner returned from England than the studio put him to work on *High Barbaree,* a sentimental and sometimes tearful story based on a novel by Charles Nordhoff and James Norman Hall, the authors of *Mutiny on the Bounty.* In the picture Van plays yet another flyer, shot down this time in the South Pacific. June Allyson, his love interest in the movie, is a navy nurse who senses that her childhood sweetheart is in danger, even though they are separated by the war. As the downed pilot lies adrift in the ocean, he reviews his life and thinks of the mythic island he had heard about as a boy. MGM felt the need to give the film a happy ending, contrary to the original plot, and had its writers emphasize pleasant reveries and romance. The outcome was so puzzling that both Johnson and Allyson could not make complete sense of the muddled screenplay and later admitted their confusion. The joke around the studio at the time was that the only missions Johnson had flown in the war were over Allyson's dressing room.

Part of *High Barbaree* was shot along the beach in Coronado, California, and the production wrapped on August 14, 1946. When the film was released the following summer, *Newsweek* said, "It would be unfair to criticize *High Barbaree* for not accomplishing much, because the picture gives no evidence of trying to accomplish anything." Yet Van's role was his most demanding since *Thirty Seconds over Tokyo,* and he handled it with more authority than conviction.

Ten days after finishing *High Barbaree,* a studio car picked Johnson up at his hotel and took him to the train station, where a Metro crew left for Santa Cruz, California, and location shooting on *The Romance of Rosy Ridge.* The story of *Rosy Ridge,* based on a novella by McKinlay Kantor, was set in the mountains of Missouri. Van plays a Union soldier who returns from the Civil War to find that neighbors in the border state are still emotionally caught up in the sectional conflict. Johnson was by no means screenwriter Lester Cole's choice for the male lead in the picture, which called for a kindly but robust young he-man who could acquit himself well in a knockdown fight. "He didn't look like a man who had spent four rough years on the front lines of the Civil War," Cole said. But Mayer felt that the time had come to give Van the "virile" treatment and insisted that Johnson be given the role. Under the skilled direction of Roy Rowland, Van rendered an excellent portrayal and even looks convincing in a fistfight with brawny actor Jim Davis.

Van's leading lady in the picture was neophyte Janet Leigh, a masterful choice to play the naive mountain girl torn between a gruff, unreconstructed father and the Union veteran she comes to love. A sweet, unaffected young woman, Leigh quickly became a favorite with the production crew, and she responded to their support by turning in an able performance. "I've acted with a lot of girls," Johnson said, "but I've never known a newcomer to do as well as Janet Leigh." The actress claimed that Van thought up her screen name, changed from Jeanette Morrison, and said that she learned from him how to handle herself on a set. Early in the shoot, Leigh accidentally blocked her costar from the camera's view during a scene. When filming stopped, Leigh panicked, knowing that she had done something wrong. "Honey, don't worry about that," Van told her. "The camera will find me. If not, we'll do it again."

Away from studio interference, *Rosy Ridge*'s cast and crew were freed from the tensions and infighting that existed in Culver City. "We were a unified, happy family, working toward our mutual goal," Leigh recalled. On a few occasions, various members of the company cooked spaghetti for the group in Van's hotel suite, since he could not go to restaurants without running the risk of being mobbed. "Van Johnson became my favorite leading man," said Leigh, who eventually made three pictures with him. "He was always a joy—no tantrums, no ego. A young girl starting out couldn't ask for any better than Van. Without his patience, I never would have gotten through my first picture."

Unit publicists saw to it that representatives from *Photoplay* and other fan magazines made the trek to Santa Cruz to do stories about the production, and most of the writers concentrated on Van. An ice cream parlor in the California community began featuring a Van Johnson sundae, and one of the local barbers announced a Van Johnson haircut. A restaurant added a Van Johnson stew to its menu, and one of the town's clothing stores advertised a Van Johnson tie. Two nearby theaters did a lively business by booking Van's earlier pictures for a repeat showing. "All that remains," a resident wit remarked, "is for them to change the name of the town to Vantown or Johnson City."

A few days of work on *Rosy Ridge* were lost when Van ran into poison oak during a chase scene through heavy brush. "How he suffered," Leigh recalled. The young actress detected that Johnson was going through a difficult period personally. "He was a bit moody and seemed troubled," she reflected, "although that never showed in his work." Already Van evidenced a nostalgia for his youth, which he knew was slipping away and feared was his major asset. "When I was a kid," he told ten-year-old actor Dean Stockwell on the set one day, "I looked like you."

In October the company departed for Sonora, near Yosemite National Park, where location work was completed. Accommodations there were rustic, but the setting was beautiful. *The Romance of Rosy Ridge* was finished in early December and was released in September 1947. The picture marked a departure for Johnson, for it was a message film about healing the wounds of war and making friends of former enemies. The screenplay by Lester Cole, one of the Hollywood Ten who eventually went to prison for contempt of Congress during the McCarthy era, was literate and honest, and the movie received critical acclaim and did good business when it opened in theaters. But the movie was not the usual Van Johnson block-buster at the box office, which worried both the star and his studio.

By the time Van returned from location filming on *Rosy Ridge,* Keenan and Eve Wynn had been separated for two months. Their marriage had been on-again, off-again for two years, and Evie had left Keenan twice before. Once she had fled to Las Vegas, where she planned to file for divorce, taking their son Ned with her. When Eve discovered that she was pregnant with Tracy, she decided to give the marriage another chance for the sake of the children. But the situation got no better. The couple quarreled constantly, often in the presence of their children. In October 1946 Evie went to Sun Valley, Idaho, intending to divorce her husband there. "For me to say I will change my ways is a ridiculous assumption," Keenan said. "Nothing can be solved by talk. . . . As a husband I am cold."

At the end of 1946, the big question focused on Eve's possible marriage to Van Johnson once her divorce from Keenan Wynn became final. Both Louella Parsons and Hedda Hopper thought she would, although Eve declined to comment on the possibility. When Parsons phoned and asked Evie point-blank about the chances of her marrying Van, Eve replied, "Oh, let's not talk about that now. I really feel badly about breaking up my marriage of eight years with Keenan. . . . But I think he'll be happier alone."

Rumors grew thicker when it was discovered that Johnson would be in Sun Valley during the time Evie was there. "Van is just going on a vacation," Eve said. "I'm going to join the Gary Coopers there." But when asked in December 1946 if she might one day marry Johnson, Evie answered, "Who knows?" These reports created much stir in the fan magazines and prompted negative discussion among Van's female following.

Meanwhile, Keenan told the press that neither Van nor Hollywood had anything to do with his wife's decision to divorce him. "I owe her a lot," Wynn said. "She sparked my early career, stuck with me when I was hurt, and stood by during a subsequent mental sickness, when I tried to corner the highball market and came close to botching everything I had worked for."

The previous year had been a perplexing time for Keenan, Evie, Van, and their public. One night the Wynns would be seen out together, and a few evenings later Evie would be spotted in a nightclub with Van. The next night she might be with Keenan again. Even Ed Wynn, Keenan's father, was bewildered. "I can't keep them straight," the elder Wynn said at a New Year's Eve party in 1946. "Evie loves Keenan. Keenan loves Evie. Van loves Evie. Evie loves Van. Van loves Keenan. Keenan loves Van." Eve left Sun Valley to spend the holidays with her husband and sons in Los Angeles, but then Keenan put her on a train for Idaho to join Van and get a divorce. The day after Evie returned to Sun Valley, Van left for Hollywood. Within a few days she too was back in California.

One circumspect moviegoer wrote to Hedda Hopper, asking, "Now the $64 question I want to know is, will Van Johnson become the second Mrs. Keenan Wynn?" It was curious phrasing, to be sure. And in response to Hopper's contention that Van might marry Evie, another fan wrote the gossip columnist, "Come on, Hedda!"

With the finish of *The Romance of Rosy Ridge,* Van borrowed money from MGM to buy a house—not just any house, but the former mansion that set designer Cedric Gibbons had built for his wife, actress Delores Del Rio. Johnson paid one hundred thousand dollars for the estate, located in Santa Monica Canyon and overlooking the ocean. Constructed on several levels, the art deco house had a modern spiral staircase, a projection room, a bar, a compact kitchen on each floor, and a children's wing off to one side. The sprawling grounds contained a sunken tennis court, a swimming pool with cabana, servants' quarters, and a playhouse. Van at last would have a nest.

With tongues wagging all over town about the Wynn-Johnson affair, Van showed up at his friend Lucille Ball's house one night and announced that he was in love with Evie and could not live without her. Lucy said, "Evie who?" Van replied, "Evie Wynn." Ball could not believe that he was serious and from that point on had mixed feelings about Johnson. "I liked Van," Lucy told a friend years later, "but I thought he was a very selfish man. He had turned from a sweet kid into an egomaniac. . . . I spoke to him after that, but I didn't think much of him." Like Billy Grady, Ball seemed to feel that Johnson had changed, had become consumed with his celebrity, and was willing to go to any lengths to protect it.

Four hours after Eve Wynn obtained a Mexican divorce from Keenan, she and Van Johnson were married in Juarez by civil judge Raoul Orozco. "It was all rather sudden," Johnson said. "We just made up our minds and did it." Eve had flown to El Paso the day before under an assumed name, carrying in her purse Keenan's power of attorney so that she could obtain a divorce by proxy and remarry the same day. Van followed her to the border town on the morning of January 25, 1947, and they were married that afternoon, with Metro publicist Morgan Hudgins in attendance. The newlyweds left El Paso by chartered plane and flew to Burbank immediately after the ceremony.

Keenan kept the two Wynn boys, aged five and two, while their mother went on a honeymoon to Sun Valley, although Eve was granted permanent custody of the children. Ned Wynn remembered his father coming into the kitchen with a small radio under his arm the night his mother married Van. Keenan set the radio down on a table, plugged it into a wall socket, and turned it on. Walter Winchell's voice was coming over the airwaves, and Ned heard his mother's name. Winchell said that Eve Wynn, former wife of actor Keenan Wynn, had married bobby-soxer idol Van Johnson. "Sorry all you heartsick gals," the newscaster said, "better luck next time." In this impersonal way, Ned found out that his parents were divorced and that his mother had remarried.

Ned recalled that learning of his mother's marriage to his Uncle Van was like the spankings he got as a child. "At first there's no pain," he recounted in 1990. "Then it dawns on me that something bad has happened. I start to cry. My father comes over. His face has a crumpled look, lopsided, full of anguish. He takes my hand and places a dollar bill in it." Keenan then unplugged the radio and walked out of the room with it, while Ned stared at the dollar in his fist. Soon Maria, Ned's nurse, came in, picked up the boy, and started toward the stairs. Over his shoulder Ned could see his father sitting in a chair in the living room. Keenan watched as Maria carried the child upstairs to his room. Just before he disappeared from view, Ned waved the dollar bill at his dad. "I suddenly remember my mother will not be home," Ned recalled. "She has gone somewhere. I forget. Somewhere with Uncle Van. But why?"

Despite the earlier rumors, Hollywood and movie fans alike were shocked by Van's marriage. Insiders predicted that matrimony would cause Johnson to lose his enormous following, and sure enough a storm of protests erupted from fans all over the country. A telephone operator in Peoria, Illinois, said, "The moment Van got married, I crossed him off my list." A theater cashier in Sacramento wrote, "I don't think he should've married his best friend's wife." Two coeds at the University of Texas in Austin protested, "We used to think of Van Johnson as the nice boy-next-door. But when he got married to Evie Wynn and became stepfather to a couple of kids, he lost all his glamour for us."

For many of his admirers, America's sweetheart had turned into a menace and a home wrecker. Some objected to his marrying a sophisticated woman, the wife of his dear friend, who looked older than Van although she was actually a year younger. In addition, he would now be in part responsible for the raising of two small children, destroying the illusion of his eternal innocence. Most of his younger fans expected Metro's surrogate war hero to find a younger, more strikingly beautiful girl, somebody they could identify with personally and one who had not been married before.

In 1946 Van Johnson had taken a step down at the box office but still ranked third among Hollywood's top moneymakers and even surpassed Clark Gable in popularity. Bobby-soxers continued to squeal at the sight of Van on the screen—to the point that a manager of a theater in Inglewood, California, had to stop a film one night and admonish teenagers to keep quiet. But in the weeks after Van and Evie's wedding, that tumult came to a halt. A joke circulated around the country that when underage girls learned that Van Johnson had married, they wore their bobby-socks at half-mast. But the bereavement seemed short-lived. Where it had once been rumored that a girls' basketball team had lost a game when its opponents reported that Van Johnson had died, now the perfidious golden boy was spoken of in villainous terms. MGM was deluged with ugly letters, some from fans swearing that they would never see another of Van's films. Others enclosed photographs of their former idol ripped to shreds. "I think that the marriage was the beginning of the end of Van's career," studio publicist Morgan Hudgins later said.

Fan magazines also turned hostile, insinuating that Van's marriage had cost him his career, although a few writers speculated that his decline in popularity was only temporary. "Is Van Johnson dead at the box office?" *Screen Guide* asked in early 1948. Always supportive of harmony within the motion picture industry, Louella Parsons, the queen of Hollywood gossip, attempted to still criticism by stating that whatever difficulties had arisen between Van Johnson and Keenan Wynn, the two buddies had "settled it all beautifully."

Van felt betrayed by the same publications that only recently had courted his favor. One movie magazine alone had run his picture six times on its cover during his rise to popularity. He could not understand the magazines' sudden disapproving attitude or imagine what he had done wrong by marrying Evie. He was a prince, and royalty should be forgiven everything.

Many insiders blamed Eve, arguing that she was an aggressive woman who wanted to carve out a position of importance for herself and snatched Van as her entrée into the top rung of Hollywood's social circle. Some viewed her as the bossy sort who had failed to achieve her goal with Keenan Wynn and saw Van as a much more successful and malleable match that would gain her the goals she desired.

But the reasons behind the marriage were darker than the public realized. Eve later claimed that Louis B. Mayer instigated the union to put a stop to gossip about Van's homosexuality. "For my money Mayer was

the worst of the lot, a dictator with the ethics and morals of a cockroach,"
Evie told author David Heymann. "Mayer decided that unless I married
Van Johnson . . . , he wouldn't renew Keenan's contract. I was young and
stupid enough to let Mayer manipulate me. I divorced Keenan, married
Van Johnson, and thus became another of L.B.'s little victims." In 1999
Eve wrote, "I have been reduced to near poverty and went bankrupt some
years ago thanks to Van's [lack of] appreciation of what I did for him by
being pressured to marry him by MGM (Mr. Mayer). They needed their
'Big Star' to be married to quell rumors about his sexual preferences, and
unfortunately I was 'It!'—the only woman he would marry."

In his autobiography, Arthur Laurents gave a Hollywood insider's
explanation for Johnson's sudden marriage. "A sunny male star caught
performing in public urinals once too often was ordered by his studio to
get married. His best friends, a young comedian and his wife, divorced so
he could marry the wife."

Keenan maintained that Evie and Mayer spoke the same language.
The mogul admired her spirit, and Eve apparently had passed along reports
to her first husband of talks she and Mayer had in his office. "Where I
was concerned," Wynn said, "she'd become a kind of stage mother, with
great ambition for me as a star." Keenan acknowledged that Eve had gotten him one of the best deals in the business as a supporting player at
Metro—a contract paying him $2,500 a week for forty weeks.

While the controversy over Van Johnson's marriage raged, the beleaguered star claimed that he had never been happier. "All my life I have
lived in hotels and restaurants," he said. "Now Evie is making a wonderful
home for me." What he wanted, Van said, was a wholesome life, a wife
and family of his own, and the warmth and cheer of having children around
him. He longed for the tranquillity and peace of mind to develop into a
truly fine actor. "If two people are companionable and share each other's
likes and dislikes," he said, "it must help make an ideally happy marriage."

Van envisioned that the gregarious Eve would be his hostess, his social arbiter, and his front. She was tough and businesslike, thoroughly ca-

pable of supervising his finances and handling details of his career in which Van had no interest. Evie's drive and determination should make her the ideal person to negotiate with agents and studio executives. How she would work with the press was more problematic. One acquaintance said, "Van seemed totally unable to think for himself, and he hated dissension. Evie did battle for him. He's soft, and Evie was the strong one. She thought she was doing the best she could for him, but it's obvious her judgment was pretty faulty."

Keenan denied that he was a victim. He gave Eve almost everything in their divorce, but the loss mattered more to Ed Wynn than to Keenan. "All I want is Evie's happiness," Keenan said. "If she is happy with Van, that's all right with me." Keenan's main concern was that the boys be looked after properly, and Eve assured him that he could see his sons whenever he wished. "There were some pangs in this parting," Keenan admitted, "but I imagined I'd get over them. I kept my books and my phonograph records."

Yet Keenan was hurt by the divorce. As Ned Wynn remembered, "My father walks heavily every night now. His face is red and big. He gets up at noon and doesn't speak to me until two or three. He drinks black coffee and eats burned toast for breakfast. He doesn't know it, but at night I see him in the living room in the chair. He sits and stares and drinks from a bottle he keeps by him on the floor." Keenan began spending more time with members of his motorcycle gang, but his life was filled with tension and loneliness. "We wanted a little dignity about the end of our marriage," Keenan said, "but it wasn't to be that way."

Ed Wynn, who never seemed reliable support for his son, remained furious over the divorce settlement. "You are giving away your house, your furniture, your shirt studs and cuff links," he told Keenan. "And to whom? To your wife and your best friend!" Van persistently denied that he had broken up his friends' marriage. "If a marriage is any good, no one can do that," he said. "Evie and Keenan's marriage was finished long before I arrived on the scene."

Johnson later admitted that his own marriage to Eve was over before it really got started. With hindsight Evie insisted that Van was a "misogynist beyond compare," and she attributed his hatred of women to his mother's desertion. Johnson refused to talk about his mother, who represented nothing but grief for him, and he would have preferred to think that she did not exist.

But in 1946, shortly before Van and Evie married, Loretta Newman showed up in Hollywood and began making demands on her son. When Van refused to see her, Loretta went to Louella Parsons and asked the powerful columnist to help arrange a meeting between her and her famous offspring. Van continued to avoid his mother, indicating that he did so out of fear of hurting his father. He also felt that Loretta was trying to exploit him, which was probably true. But Van had a tendency to think that all women wanted something from him, even his fans.

In May 1947, Van, Evie, and the Wynn boys moved into the palatial new home he had bought in Santa Monica, and the couple quickly became a hub of Hollywood's social whirl. The wives of the big agents were fond of Van, liked to coddle him, and invited him to all of their big gatherings. He in turn was delighted to have a proper place to entertain his friends in a manner he could now afford.

Janet Leigh remembered going to visit Van and Eve shortly after finishing *The Romance of Rosy Ridge*. It was the first time the young actress had seen a private tennis court or watched a movie in a home. Evie's closet "looked like a department store," recalled Leigh, who was still living in a small apartment with a pull-down table in the kitchen. When Leigh was invited to a lawn party at Atwater Kent's mansion, where there was to be dancing to a live orchestra, she rushed to the Johnsons' house for advice on the proper dress for the evening. "Van and Evie dug their invitation out of the waste basket," Leigh said, "and Evie took me upstairs and found a black evening skirt and top for me to wear." Van loaned a tux to Leigh's husband at the time, and the Johnsons went to the party with the inexperienced couple so that the newcomers would feel more comfortable.

"It was like a dream," Leigh said, "exactly what I'd read about in movie magazines."

Ned Wynn remembered life in the Johnson house in Santa Monica as one of affluence, although the people inside were "familiar but not familiar." Evie soon bought a new fur coat and wore Balenciaga gowns, Givenchy cocktail sheaths, and jewelry from Tiffany and Cartier. Van drove a 1947 midnight-blue Cadillac convertible with a tan top and sported cashmere sweaters and a camel-hair overcoat, which he usually wore open. MGM renegotiated Johnson's contract soon after his marriage, which not only brought Van's salary up to five thousand dollars a week but assured him of a bonus at the completion of each picture.

In March 1947, at the annual Academy Awards ceremony in Shrine Auditorium, Van presented the Oscar for best song of the year to Harry Warren and Johnny Mercer for "On the Atchison, Topeka, and the Santa Fe." A year earlier, he and his agent had been dining together when they heard on the radio that Joan Crawford had won the best actress award for *Mildred Pierce.* Since Johnson's agent was also Crawford's, the two men drove to the ailing star's house to congratulate her. By 1947 Van had been admitted into the Academy's select circle, and he came to look on himself as a member of the Hollywood establishment. Friends recall how he entered a room with an attitude, almost as if the king had arrived. "There was nothing malicious," Eddie Bracken maintained. "Van simply enjoyed his stardom."

Yet with his marriage to Eve, Johnson's career slowed to a walk for more than two years. Not only did his fan mail subside, but the uproar over his marriage continued in the movie magazines and blackened his image. At one point Van became so exasperated with the bad publicity that he refused to grant interviews. Although Johnson declared that he was tired of boyish parts and wanted to become a serious dramatic actor, his youthful looks made the transition difficult. Studio executives were not sure how to cast him. At thirty-one Van was too old to play teenagers and needed to broaden his audience. MGM decided to put him in supporting roles in important pictures and alternate the challenging smaller assignments with the lighter parts that his fans had come to expect.

First up for Van in 1947 was *State of the Union,* based on the Pulitzer Prize–winning play by Howard Lindsay and Russel Crouse. The studio played safe by billing Johnson third after Spencer Tracy and Katharine Hepburn. "That couldn't have happened a year ago," Sheilah Graham said of his lesser billing. In the picture, Tracy is an idealistic airplane manufacturer turned political candidate, while Van plays his disillusioned, smart-talking aide. *State of the Union* was a witty yet knowing look at contemporary American politics, filmed at a time when the motion picture industry was torn with infighting over questions of political radicalism and national loyalty. The movie's director was the gifted Frank Capra, a champion of Americanism, while his cast ran the gamut from the politically liberal Hepburn to the reactionary Adolphe Menjou. But the ensemble worked well together and turned out a solid film. Capra claimed that his hardest job was to keep Johnson and Menjou, along with Angela Lansbury and veteran character actor Lewis Stone, from stealing too many scenes from his two luminaries, Tracy and Hepburn.

"I'm in good company," Van acknowledged when shooting began on *State of the Union.* The characterization he gives in the picture differs from anything he had done before and shows subtlety and skill. The only reminder of his heartthrob days comes when homely character actress Margaret Hamilton ogles him in a couple of scenes. "I knew to survive I had to begin and build my future as a mature actor," Van said. "All I want now is to have more solid roles like this—and as simple a life as the complications of moviemaking allow."

But his next picture, *The Bride Goes Wild,* was reminiscent of the fluff in which he had so often been cast. In the comedy Van plays Uncle Bumps, an immature author of children's books who hates kids, and much of what Johnson was called on to do proved downright silly. To insure the movie's appeal at the box office, the studio again paired Van with June

Allyson. Director Norman Taurog, who had thirty-five years of experience with the kind of humor *The Bride Goes Wild* offers, drew on the old Mack Sennett approach in silent pictures for laughs—pies flung in the face, people getting kicked in the pants or having their shins whacked, and other crude acts of physical annoyance and embarrassment. "Evidently this is still a good formula," a critic for *Cue* magazine wrote. "Metro-Goldwyn-Mayer here, however, gave pioneer Sennett one better. They have added glamour to slapstick."

After finishing *The Bride Goes Wild,* Johnson was consigned to a stellar supporting role in *Command Decision,* which again reveals his potential as an earnest actor in a film of distinction. Although the movie is not as forceful as the stage hit on which it was based, *Command Decision* is nonetheless an effective questioning of the human cost that was necessary to win the air war against Nazi Germany. Johnson plays a breezy technical sergeant with a reputation as a ladies' man. His is a small part, but Van acquits himself well in a seasoned cast that includes Clark Gable, Walter Pidgeon, Brian Donlevy, Charles Bickford, and John Hodiak. Although a gripping film, *Command Decision* is static and talky, some of which may be the fault of director Sam Wood, who was getting along in years. "Wood at that time was almost senile," said actor Marshall Thompson, who worked on the picture, "at least that's what we all felt. He was very slow, and everybody was sort of directing the production."

State of the Union and *Command Decision* elevated Van to a higher level of professional dignity, even though tension between Johnson and his studio continued for another full year with Metro executives uncertain about his continued popularity. The former heartthrob's draw at the box office had dropped noticeably as competition for public favor quickened after the war and new stars emerged. In 1948 Van Johnson's name was absent from every popularity poll, in part a result of bad publicity over his marriage. Fan magazines discussed Van's moods, his insecurities, his marital problems, Evie's ego, and her ambition. Some writers said that the redheaded star was through; others contended that he was rebuilding his career in a more sound and less spectacular manner. "I realized," Van said, "that success has to be won over and over again."

Through it all, Evie's belief in him, Johnson said, was overpowering. "She spoils me by matching her moods to mine," Van told an interviewer. "She has a theatrical judgment that I respect deeply. She has become my conscience and rock of faith in my career." Eve called him "Vannie" and said that she admired her husband's sensitivity and unpretentious quality but admitted that he was moody. "At least with Van there's never a dull moment," she said. "He loves his home and can't be coaxed into spending a night out 'with the boys.' Sometimes I wish he would go out." On the cook's night off, Van sometimes took over the kitchen. He often helped Eve select her clothes, and she in turn offered opinions on scripts he was offered and people he met.

The Johnsons continued a close friendship with Keenan Wynn, whom Van called "Keeno." Ned and Tracy alternated weekends with their father, and when Keenan performed in *The Skin of Our Teeth* at the Coronet Theater in Los Angeles in June 1947, Van and Evie were in the audience. For a time Eve tried to get her boys to call Van "Daddy," but no one seemed comfortable with that, so he became simply "Van" to the Wynn children.

The newlyweds gave their first party in July 1947, inviting Lana Turner, Tyrone Power, Betty Grable, Gary Cooper, Rosalind Russell, Jack Benny, and William and Edie Goetz, Mayer's daughter and son-in-law. Actress Ella Raines remembered evenings at the Johnsons' home when Evie cooked spaghetti and Judy Garland sang until eleven or eleven-thirty at night. But Van and Evie also went to dinners, parties, or premieres three or four times a week. "Every night I'd cry and beg them not to go," Ned wrote. "I'd watch, sobbing as they went down the stairs, my mother tossing running orders to the nurse and the maid as she went."

A month after their housewarming party, Van left on a personal-appearance tour to publicize *The Romance of Rosy Ridge*. He returned home in time to prepare for his first holiday season as a married man. Once his shopping was done, Van telephoned Keenan to invite him to eat Christmas dinner with the family. Wynn accepted and showed up at the Johnsons' house on Christmas day with an assortment of packages. Walking up the driveway, Keenan had second thoughts about the invitation, even though he had visited Evie and Van dozens of times since their marriage. "Minutes after Van had opened the door for me I knew I had made a mistake," Wynn wrote. "Ned and Tracy lived in this house, not with me. They were growing used to Van as a stepfather who wanted to be a good friend. Evie was brisk and hospitable as always, but now she was Van's wife, not mine. . . . I was an intruder." Within an hour after his arrival, Keenan recognized the upset he was causing in the Johnson home and left. "I hurried out and for that moment wanted never to go back," he said. "I went home to my empty house."

Yet another factor contributed to the strain Wynn felt. Eve was pregnant with Van's child. In early June she had telephoned Louella Parsons to announce the coming baby. Doctors had warned Eve not to have any more children, since this would be her third cesarean birth. But becoming a father was important to Van—both as an antidote to his own unhappy childhood and as proof to his fans that the freckled-faced boy they admired on the screen was all he appeared to be, a fact he also needed to prove to himself.

On January 6, 1948, Van's only child, a daughter, was born. Named Schuyler Van, the baby for a time was her father's pride and the object of great attention in the Johnson household. "She was plump and blond, healthy and happy," Ned Wynn recalled. "She was there to be fondled and bounced and kissed and dressed . . . and made to look like a storybook doll." But the baby also drastically changed the balance of power in the family.

Eve suffered complications after the birth and, according to reports, her life was in danger during the recovery. Evie returned home for a long convalescence amid much attention. "I saw flashbulbs popping as magazine and newspaper photographers gathered on the sidewalk in front of the house and took pictures of the pink blankets," Ned remembered. "I saw the ambulance and I saw my mother, very weak and smiling, being wheeled through the front gates on a gurney." It would be weeks before Eve was up and around again. In the interim, she had a full-time nurse to take care of her.

Van was determined that Schuyler would grow up with all the things he had missed as a child. She would be denied nothing and serve as a reminder of his success. An enormous bedroom was prepared for the infant, and she had a crib with pink ruffles and a lace canopy and drawers full of pink clothes. "I used to be afraid of having roots," Van said. "But now, a husband and father, I know the responsibility of a home and family." Yet Van could not abide vomit, and any time there was a crisis in the house, he would scream Evie's name. He proudly told fan-magazine writers, "She's quite a little personality, that daughter of mine. She has red hair, blue eyes and features that resemble her old man's."

Within less than two months after Schuyler's birth there were rumors that Van and Eve were separating. Johnson denied the reports and voiced surprise that anyone could think that there was trouble when his wife had been so ill. "Evie's getting better now," Van said in early March 1948, "but she's had an awfully tough pull, and you know how crazy we both are about the baby. Evie and I haven't even had an argument, and I say again, I've never been so happy in my whole life"

Fan magazines began to stress how brave Eve had been to give birth to another child when the hazards had been so great for her. Before long Evie claimed that she had three kids and Van, since the man she married often behaved like a child. "Van was good for a good time," Ned said, "but he was not good for a bad time. Or even for a mildly uncomfortable one. His tolerance of unpleasantness was minuscule. If it wasn't funny and rewarding instantly, it was hell on earth." Van's method of handling difficult situations was to throw a tantrum and pout, while Evie acted as if nothing had happened. But the arrival of a baby sister caused Ned to grow more troublesome. "I wandered around that year making life hell for everyone," he later admitted. "Nothing pleased me."

On the surface, life in the Johnson home was ideal—affluent, comfortable, and serene. "Van is so kind," Evie said to reporters. "He is so thoughtful and good, even about the little things." The household staff consisted of four live-in domestics—a maid, a cook, a butler, and a governess—in addition to several part-time employees, among them a laundress, a seamstress, and a full-time secretary to help Eve arrange and execute her demanding social schedule. "Making sure appearances were kept up was a full-time job," said Ned. Evie was constantly aware that people were watching her family and cautioned the children to be careful about what they said and did. "Appearances were everything," Ned emphasized. There was always the fear of an exposé in *Confidential* magazine, and fan-magazine writers still questioned the reasons behind the Johnson marriage.

As late as February 1948, gossip columnist Sheilah Graham received hundreds of letters protesting Van's sudden defection from bachelorhood. "I used to enjoy Van in pictures very much," a woman in Redding, California, wrote, "but since his type of marriage I never go to see him." Walter Strauss wrote from Baltimore, Maryland, "Home breakers are not revered. Van has played a dirty trick on Keenan Wynn. . . . He has nothing on the ball as far as acting, clothes, voice is concerned—nothing but a bunch of freckles, like an adolescent kid." An organization called the Motion Picture Research Society was formed with the sole purpose of boycotting Johnson's films: members pledged to eliminate the actor from the screen.

Yet in April 1948, Van was asked to put his signature and footprints in cement in the courtyard of Grauman's Chinese Theater in Hollywood. "It was a big day for me," Johnson said. "Evie was on the sidelines photographing the event. It gives you a wonderful feeling of security to sign your name in cement and to realize you're at last an accepted citizen of the cinema, not just a flash in the pan."

Van was the honored guest of the female workers of the local Community Chest during their annual breakfast rally in the Cocoanut Grove at the Ambassador Hotel, and in October 1948 he flew with Evie to Texas, Louisiana, and Oklahoma for a tour of veterans' hospitals. Van spent several hours on the trip visiting wards and talking to wounded servicemen. "A lot of us in Hollywood are doing this," he said. "We just want the boys to know we haven't forgotten them."

For several months Van went without making a movie. Executives at Metro-Goldwyn-Mayer were still puzzling about what to do with him. MGM finally agreed to loan him to Twentieth Century–Fox. Director Henry Hathaway had wanted to use Johnson in Fox's *Down to the Sea in Ships*, but Darryl Zanuck, the studio's production head, decided to give the role to contract player Richard Widmark instead, in an effort to change Widmark's image from the laughing gunman he had portrayed in *Kiss of Death* (1947) to something more heroic. So Twentieth Century–Fox cast Van as an English professor opposite Loretta Young in the Technicolor comedy *Mother Is a Freshman*. "I've been wanting to work at another studio," Johnson said, "just for a change of atmosphere."

Much of *Mother Is a Freshman* was filmed at the University of Nevada in Reno during the fall of 1948. "We want to be careful," Zanuck had said in a story conference, "that our campus and our school [do] not look old-fashioned. We must remember that today many of the colleges have G.I.'s on the campus, and they are not that rah-rah-rah-rah business of ten or twelve years ago." The production company was flown to Reno in the studio's private plane, and location work on the picture proved a pleasant and congenial time for the cast. "We would all have dinner together," said Betty Lynn, who played Young's daughter in the movie, and director Lloyd Bacon carried out Zanuck's instructions to keep the comedy real and not let it lapse into farce. "The idea is too good to waste on farce," Zanuck said.

Van's role in the movie almost satirized the effect he had once had on bobby-soxers, and Young seemed more thrilled with the clothes she wore in the picture than with the script. When *Mother Is a Freshman* was released in March 1949, the reviews were mixed. Some critics found the film sprightly and entertaining; others found it predictable. "Everything happens in this picture when you most expect it to," Bosley Crowther wrote in the *New York Times*. As far as humor was concerned, Crowther said, "somebody forgot to mention it."

Van spent several nights in the autumn of 1948 attending the circus when it visited Los Angeles. He was still enthralled enough with the big top to watch nearly every performance that came to town. On the circus's closing night that fall, he stayed until three o'clock in the morning to watch the crew load up. A trip to see the clowns and acrobats was Van's idea of the way to be a perfect pal to Ned and Tracy, but the problems of child rearing were beyond him. Most of the time he was content to turn Schuyler over to a governess while he withdrew into sullen privacy.

Ned and Tracy were companions for one another as youngsters and turned to each other for emotional support. Tracy said that he did not begin to understand what was going on between his parents until he was about four years old. "Dad made the best of a difficult situation and was careful to keep a very close relationship with Ned and me," Tracy said. "I never had any identity crisis as far as who my parents were. Van was Van."

In January 1949 Keenan married Betty Jane Butler, a blond Hollywood model, in a proxy ceremony in Tijuana, Mexico. During the service Wynn remembered that he had not bought a wedding ring, so he used the gold band that he still wore on his finger from the wedding with Eve. His marriage to Betty Jane lasted four years. The former model, who had once handled fan mail at Paramount, divorced Wynn in 1953, claiming that everything was a joke to Keenan and that he remained too friendly with his first wife. "She started calling only the second day after we were married," Betty Jane told the press. "She knew exactly what I had paid for my clothes and complained that I was going to spend all his money."

In the spring of 1949 rumors had it that Van Johnson was out of money and that the house he had bought was a white elephant. Reports continued to circulate that he and Evie were unhappy and ready to divorce. "The behind-the-hand stories about the Johnsons have been so bitter and black that, frankly, I have been surprised that any marriage could stand up under them," Louella Parsons wrote in her column in March. "And yet for two years this past January, the Johnsons have held up under the bitterest barrage of gossip any Hollywood couple has ever weathered."

Before the year ended Van and Eve sold their huge home in Santa Monica and began looking for a smaller one in Beverly Hills, where most of their friends lived. "Home's important to Evie and me," Van said. "The big house with its tennis courts and swimming pool was exciting. Now Evie and I are looking for a place where all the family can be closer together—where a dad can walk into the nursery and call on his daughter without formality." Such remarks sounded like dialogue from a Van Johnson–June Allyson movie.

The house Van and Evie bought in Beverly Hills had only six rooms, but they were all large and commodious. A spacious living room on the upstairs level was flanked by a master bedroom suite on one side and the two boys' room on the other. The baby's nursery was downstairs. The beige-colored, green-shuttered home, at the corner of Foothill Drive and Lomitas Avenue, had black marble in the master bathroom and vivid colors and an enormous oversized bed in Van and Evie's suite. There was no swimming pool or tennis court, but the neighborhood was impeccable by social standards. The street in front was lined with tall palm trees, and yards had trees teeming with lemons, oranges, and avocados. "We were moving to the land of milk and honey," Ned Wynn said. "Every house had a perfect lawn, a perfect wall, a perfect driveway."

Yet within the movie industry conditions were far from perfect after the war. In 1948 Metro-Goldwyn-Mayer grossed its lowest profits since the Great Depression, and a federal court had mandated that Loew's, MGM's parent company, separate its theaters from the studio. Within the organization there was constant bickering between the studio and the New York office, to such a degree that even Louis B. Mayer's position with the company was in jeopardy. Theaters were closing all over the country as the urban population moved out to the suburbs and began raising families. In

Hollywood, production budgets were slashed and the number of contracts was reduced. Although MGM's personnel still ranked among the highest paid in the business, even the industry's largest studio was in a panic.

Van's troubles with Metro over the past two years gave him real cause for alarm. He had grown accustomed to being part of America's royalty; he liked money and the things money could buy and had come to depend on Hollywood's most colossal dream factory for his identity as well as his finances. With the motion picture business running scared, Johnson knew that any more adverse publicity on his part meant the end of his career in movies. MGM celebrated its silver anniversary in 1949 in an atmosphere of tension, and Van understood that his future depended on his developing a tougher, more mature image. "Of course, I was flattered that the bobby-soxers liked me," he said. "But I couldn't go through life on their screams. All right, that's over." But the question was, did he have the wherewithal to make the transition?

Metro planned to cast Van opposite Donna Reed in *The Stratton Story* until baseball pitcher Monty Stratton voiced doubts that Johnson was the right choice to portray him in the screen biography. "Van was a star and a sweet man," said Ethel Stratton, the ballplayer's wife "but after he had worked out a little with my husband, Monty said he was gun-shy athletically and would never be convincing as a pitcher." So the studio hired James Stewart for the part and picked June Allyson to play Stratton's wife.

Van was relegated to the role of an investigator on a homicide beat in *Scene of the Crime,* a realistic detective drama filmed in a grim, documentary-like style that was uncharacteristic of Metro. *Variety* described the movie as "hard-hitting action stuff," and although Van was no Humphrey Bogart, he gave an adequate performance and looked only mildly uncomfortable packing a gun and tracking low-life characters. "Johnson was a charming man, and it was lovely to play a scene with him" said veteran character actor Norman Lloyd, who had acted with Orson Welles's Mercury Theater in New York. "He was a major star and a good actor. I always liked the fact that he carried a little lunch pail to work, much like a construction worker, and always ate in his dressing room rather than going to the commissary."

By the time *Scene of the Crime* was made, Dore Schary had been brought in from RKO to head production at MGM, while L. B. Mayer stayed on as the studio's administrative head. Schary wanted to make the kind of artistic pictures, like *Bicycle Thief* (1947), that postwar Italian realists were turning out, in sharp contrast to the glamour that Mayer favored. "Schary was the antithesis of Mayer," said Arlene Dahl, Johnson's costar in *Scene of the Crime*, "and the retrenchment at MGM during that period was quite noticeable. The limousine that used to pick me up and drive me from one stage to the other was not there; bicycles were there instead. Mayer really pampered his stars. People went to see Metro pictures because they wanted to look at beautiful faces, beautiful scenes, beautiful jewelry, beautiful clothes, and vehicles tailor-made for the studio's stars, not because of realism."

Van wondered if he could survive under the new regime. But his next picture, *In the Good Old Summertime,* was a piece of nostalgia, a musical version of Ernst Lubitsch's charming comedy *The Shop around the Corner,* and the film suited Johnson's talent well. Producer Joe Pasternak moved the setting of the story from Budapest to turn-of-the-century Chicago, and at the last minute Judy Garland stepped in for June Allyson as Van's costar. Garland and Johnson played antagonistic coworkers in a music store who unknowingly carry on a love affair by correspondence. Van was thrilled to be working with Garland, who gave the picture added value, and although *In the Good Old Summertime* was a commercial success, making the movie was not easy.

Garland was unhappy doing the film and often came to work late or did not show up at all. "Those of us who worked with her knew her magical genius and respected it," said Pasternak. Van sympathized with the torment Judy was experiencing in her life and tried to relieve the strain she brought to the set by showing her affection and making her laugh.

The two became great pals during the production, and Van found working with Garland a joy once she was there. "She needed to be patted on the head every once in a while and told she was beautiful," he said. "Judy Garland was a most natural, underrated performer and actress. I never saw her study a script." Garland had the ability to read a script, run through a scene once, and be ready for the camera. "She didn't like to rehearse too much," said Johnson. "I'm a rehearser, but I always conformed to her. I learned an awful lot from Judy Garland. She's one of the unsung ladies in my life."

The first scene in the picture that the costars have together involves an extended bit of comedy in which Johnson knocks Garland down, rips off her hat, destroys her hairdo, and ruins her umbrella. The sequence took three days to shoot, but the results are funny and masterful. Garland's young daughter, Liza Minnelli, was around the set on occasion and often went for rides on Van's back. Director Robert Leonard decided to use Liza in the movie's final scene as Van and Judy's child. "I look very uncomfortable," Minnelli said of her first appearance on film. "And no wonder. I had insisted on dressing myself and I didn't put on any panties. When Van lifted me up, his hands were very cold!"

Within a year MGM would fire Garland, and the ground around Louis B. Mayer continued to tremble. In August 1951 Mayer was forced to resign as Metro's administrative head, and the studio's remaining contract personnel sensed that their days on the lot were numbered. The golden age of Hollywood was nearing an end. Independent producers were moving in, and within a decade the big studio system would be dead. Van Johnson knew that he was a creation of that system, had been nurtured and protected by it. Could he endure in a business faced with such all-encompassing changes?

In July 1949 Van and Evie traveled to Newport, Rhode Island, for the fifteenth reunion of Van's high school graduating class. Evie gave Charlie Johnson pictures of his eighteen-month-old granddaughter, and Van visited with former neighbors and teachers. In the photograph taken at the class reunion he is in the center of the front row, decked out in a white jacket, black trousers, and a black bow tie, looking like a potentate surrounded by his minions. He was the class's sterling success, but his future in Hollywood was by no means secure.

Van Johnson and Faye Emerson in *Murder in the Big House*, the picture he made under contract with Warner Bros.

Van Johnson and Lionel Barrymore in *Dr. Gillespie's Criminal Case*, made early in his career at Metro-Goldwyn-Mayer

Robert Mitchum and Van Johnson in *Thirty Seconds Over Tokyo*,
one of Van's best-remembered pictures

Van Johnson playing tennis during his early years in Hollywood

Buddies Keenan Wynn and Van Johnson in *No Leave, No Love*

Van Johnson and character actress Geraldine Wall in *High Barbaree*

Van and Eve Johnson and their daughter Schuyler in their first family portrait

Van Johnson cooking hamburgers at the time *State of the Union* was in production

Van Johnson and Denise
Darcel in a publicity
pose for *Battleground*

June Allyson and Van
Johnson on the set for
Remains To Be Seen

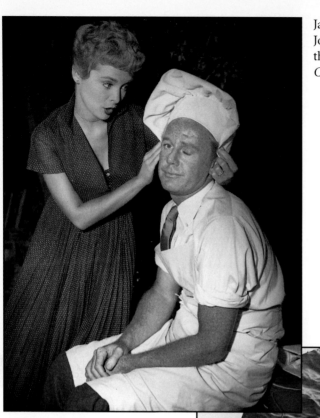

Janet Leigh and Van Johnson during the time they were making *Confidentially Connie*

Van Johnson coming out of the ocean during the making of *The Cain Mutiny*

Van Johnson in Marseilles for filming scenes in *The Last Time I Saw Paris*

On the beach at Monte Carlo during a day off from filming *The Last Time I Saw Paris*

Van Johnson in a happy publicity pose

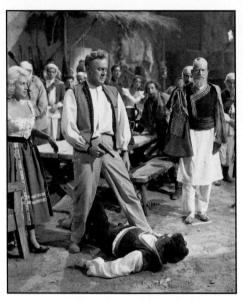

Van Johnson and Martine Carol
in *Action of the Tiger*

Van Johnson in a dramatic scene from
Action of the Tiger

Van Johnson and the press (possibly from *State of the Union*)

CHAPTER 6

Resilient MGM Star

Dore Schary began preproduction on what would be Van Johnson's finest motion picture, eventually filmed as *Battleground*, in 1947 when he was still head of production at RKO. Schary wanted to make a war movie, and writer Robert Pirosh suggested as the subject the Battle of Bastogne and the heroic stand of the U.S. 101st Airborne Division during World War II. Pirosch had fought at Bastogne and been among the troops that rescued the encircled 101st, known as the "Screaming Eagles." After the fog had lifted and American planes were able to drop food, ammunition, and supplies, Allied forces won the last major battle against the Nazis. "I was in that kind of fighting," said Pirosh. "That's where I got my material. I was writing about the foot soldier, the guy in the foxhole. Many of the things I had in the script were experiences of mine or what I had observed happening in my division. That was perhaps the easiest script I ever wrote, because it was like writing a letter home. I knew the subject."

Pirosh, Schary, and RKO's story editor, Bill Fadiman, developed the project under the name *Prelude to Love* and had Fred Zinnemann in mind for its director and Robert Mitchum pegged for the lead. But as the script neared completion, the eccentric Howard Hughes bought RKO, and Hughes and Schary clashed over control of production at the studio. When Schary resigned to become vice president and head of production at MGM, he brought Pirosh's script and the writer with him to Metro.

Louis B. Mayer, however, did not want to make the Bastogne movie. He found the story depressing and believed that the public was tired of war. Others at MGM agreed, and several producers on the lot turned the script down. Around Metro the production became known as "Schary's folly." Billy Grady, still the studio's casting director, told the new production head, "Believe me, kid, stay away from this one—it's a stinker." But Schary persisted.

Schary decided to produce the film himself and asked William Wellman, who had been a flyer in World War I and liked Pirosh's script, to direct. "Dore Schary had an awful lot at stake," the screenwriter said. "Nobody was betting on that picture except Schary and Wellman." Wellman brought a strong sense of the visual to the film. Having begun his career in silent pictures, the veteran director wanted speeches made shorter, and he worked with Pirosh to find moments where effective camera work could take the place of dialogue. "I started looking for things that could be told visually," the writer said. "Wellman gave the picture a vitality that would have been lacking without him."

Once Schary had transferred the project to MGM, he planned to use Robert Taylor in the leading role. But to make the cast look and act like soldiers, Wellman insisted on putting the actors through a modified basic training. The director hired a six-and-a-half-foot former drill sergeant and two corporals from the 101st Airborne Division, both of whom had been in the Battle of the Bulge, to teach the players how to drill, how to creep and crawl, and how to hold and fire rifles. "Taylor took a day or two of that, and it didn't fit his image of himself," said Pirosh. So Van Johnson got the part.

Van admired Schary, who was sensitive to actors' problems, and came to look on his role in *Battleground* as his best. Johnson endured the three weeks of military training that Wellman ordered and agreed that Pirosh had written a superior script. Drilling and going through army maneuvers with his fellow actors gave Van a taste of what he had missed during the war, and he weathered the hardships and thrived on the camaraderie. "When those guys trooped into the commissary, it was like a bunch of

G.I.'s coming into the mess hall," Pirosh said. "They were just half cleaned up and came in wearing their dirty fatigues. It was quite a sight for the people sitting there in their three-piece suits."

Schary would have preferred to shoot the film in and around Bastogne, but the studio hierarchy decided the expense would be too great, since weather conditions on location could not be controlled. Consequently, at least 75 percent of *Battleground* was filmed on MGM's stage 30. Snow and fog machines were installed in the ceiling, and for much of the production the stage was cooled down to below freezing. A forest of pine trees and mounds of dirt were brought in and, to keep audiences from noticing the cyclorama used as background, fog machines were kept going most of the time. "When you came into that stage, you put on a field jacket," said Pirosh. "The actors complained about the cold, but Wellman insisted on seeing real breath."

The scenes in the town of Bastogne were shot on streets in the studio's back lot, and the opening sequence at the army camp and the tanks passing marching troops at the end were filmed at Fort MacArthur. To add realism to the picture, a platoon of veterans from the 101st Airborne Division was bought in to serve as extras. The soldiers liked the idea of being in a movie and getting paid well for their work, but they rebelled when Wellman told them that they would play German infantrymen on alternate days. They finally did so, but the German-speaking parts were played by German actors.

Wellman began filming the story with the enthusiasm of a young man. Fortunately, the script had been pruned and polished so that his work was easier. After viewing the initial rushes, Schary and Wellman knew that *Battleground* rang of truth and that the project had a good possibility of success. Van quickly sensed the importance of the film and what it might do for his career. "It's just about twelve average guys," he said of the picture, "a cross-section of America."

Meanwhile, Mayer, eager to validate his supremacy with Metro's New York office, waited for Schary's pet project to fail. With his prestige at stake, Schary went through weeks of anxiety while *Battleground* was in production. Johnson understood that his own career hung in the balance. Holley, his character in the picture, was multidimensional, fun loving yet competent enough at the tactics of warfare to win him a promotion from private to sergeant during the siege of Bastogne. All in all, the part was perfect to bring out the best of Johnson's talent and promote the macho image that Van knew he needed. Pirosh's infantrymen, with one exception, were no sensitive intellectuals; they did not know why the battle they were fighting was important and wanted desperately to go home. That theme should appeal to returning veterans and could result in a movie that would catapult Van back to the top in the popularity polls.

In Wellman's expert hands, incidental characters in the picture became important, and minor moments stood out as memorable. James Whitmore was not scheduled to play the weathered sergeant that he eventually did, but the actor originally cast in the role proved unsatisfactory. When Whitmore took over he looked so much the part and spit tobacco juice so convincingly that Wellman and Pirosh began thinking up more and more for him to do. The actor improvised much of the business himself, and he received an Academy Award nomination for his earthy portrayal.

The director, known as "Wild Bill," swore a lot on the set and ranted and raved, but he had a facility for getting the best out of his actors and did not welcome suggestions. In one unforgettable sequence in *Battleground,* German planes have dropped leaflets urging the American soldiers to surrender. In the script Pirosh had infantrymen make disparaging remarks about the leaflets, then crumple them up and throw them away. As the director was getting ready to shoot the scene, actor George Murphy timorously said, "Mr. Wellman, may I make a suggestion?" When the crusty director agreed, Murphy replied that he would like to demonstrate what he had in mind to do on camera. The player started picking up leaflets and walked into the woods, obviously with the intent of using the leaflets as toilet paper. Wellman cheered and said, "I finally got a good idea from an actor!"

Another of the picture's haunting incidents has Ricardo Montalban, playing a Hispanic foot solider who has never seen snow before, become overjoyed when he awakens to find his foxhole covered with white flakes. Pirosh had in his script that the boy then gets caught in a skirmish and is wounded, with his buddies forced to leave him behind. When they come back for him, they find his body partially covered with snow and frozen to death. "I saw frozen soldiers," the writer said, "and that made an indelible impression on me." But Wellman wanted the sequence to be pictorially even more dramatic, so he arranged for a broken-down jeep to be brought to the set and had the wounded soldier crawl under it, then push snow up so the enemy could not see where he was hiding. His buddies return to find him frozen to death under the jeep. "That was much more moving than what I had written in the script," Pirosh conceded.

Van has one of the lighter, more delightful moments in the picture when he sees Denise Darcel, playing a busty Frenchwoman taking care of two orphaned children, cutting bread with the knife pointed toward her breasts. The alarmed look on Van's face as he leaps up to warn her of possible injury is funny but endearing. Darcel was the only woman in the cast with a speaking role. The actress took a great deal of ribbing from the men but proved a good sport and was well liked.

Thanks to a solid script and Wellman's expertise, filming on *Battleground* finished twenty days under schedule and almost one hundred thousand dollars under budget. Bosley Crowther of the *New York Times* judged the film "the best of the World War II pictures that has yet been made in Hollywood." Other critics found the movie powerful and well paced, its action realistic, and its despair skillfully offset with humor. *Battleground* is entertaining and immensely human and spoke to veterans who remembered similar experiences all too vividly. The public flocked to the movie, which was nominated for an Academy Award for best picture of 1949. Pirosh won the Oscar for his screenplay, and Van Johnson's career was resuscitated in precisely the way he needed to put him back on top. *Battleground* remains an exemplary war movie and one of the films for which

Johnson is best remembered. Even Louis B. Mayer had to admit that the picture was an unqualified success.

Dore Schary, a New Deal liberal, preferred to make message pictures, but a number of sleek productions were in the pipeline at MGM when he took over as the studio's production chief, movies that were more to Mayer's liking than to Schary's. Among them was *The Big Hangover*, a romantic comedy written, produced, and directed by Norman Krasna and starring Van Johnson and teenage Elizabeth Taylor. The film returned Van to the realm of trivia and had him playing an idealistic law school honor graduate who had spent hours up to his chin in hundred-year-old brandy in the cellar of a bombed monastery during the recent war. From then on, the slightest whiff of alcohol sent the young lawyer reeling. The challenge, Van said, was to make "some of that garbage" come out interesting.

Taylor was an inordinate beauty who looked far more mature than the high schooler she was. Johnson recalled passing Taylor's dressing room one day and seeing her gazing at the ceiling with a textbook in her hand and a forlorn look on her face. Van asked the girl, who seemed to have everything, what was wrong. "Oh, Van," she said, "I'm so depressed. I just feel as if I'd like to die today." Johnson chuckled to himself, remembering how often he had felt the same way as an adolescent.

Norman Krasna admitted that he was not a good director, although he claimed to know how to direct what he himself had written. Still, he proved fairly inept on the set. Character actress Rosemary DeCamp recalled filming the banquet sequence, during which the actors ate crêpes suzette. Shooting that segment of the picture went on for seven or eight days, and cast members had to eat the same dish day after day until they became nauseated. But DeCamp remembered Van Johnson as always pleasant and cooperative. "He was the one man who would stay after his work was finished to do your close-ups with you," she said, "rather than letting the script girl read his lines."

The Big Hangover opened in May 1950 at Grauman's Egyptian Theater in Hollywood and at Loew's State in New York. Reviews were mixed. Some critics objected to a film that mingled comedy with heavy doses of self-righteous sermonizing. Reviewers also did not agree on Van's work. According to the *Hollywood Reporter*, "Van Johnson has become a really fine actor and comedian, who no longer needs to depend on his boyish charm to help put over his performance." Yet a writer for the *New Yorker* said, "Miss Taylor is beautiful and cannot act. This puts her one up on Mr. Johnson."

Van was generally willing to let the studio decide what movies were best for him. The important thing to him was to keep working. Throughout his tenure at MGM he never took a suspension, and during his first nine years at the studio he averaged three pictures annually. Between 1950 and 1954 Johnson made fourteen films, for which he earned close to five hundred thousand dollars a year. He understood that he would have to take inconsequential roles along with more important ones, since that was the way the big studio system operated to meet its yearly quota of product.

In January and early February 1950, Van was busy with *Duchess of Idaho,* again playing opposite Esther Williams. Johnson is a brash bandleader in this rehash of what by then had become the formulaic Esther Williams picture. "As happy as I was to be working once more with Van," Williams wrote in her memoirs, "the recycled plots were getting to me." At one point during the filming the actress turned to her costar and said, "Didn't we do this scene before in an elevator?" But audiences had come to expect certain things from the swimmer's movies, which were consistently popular. "I was part of a group of reliable MGM box-office stars," she said, "whose films were counted on to make a certain amount of money for the studio." Pairing Esther Williams with Van Johnson assured a production of success with fans, and Johnson understood the situation as well as Williams did.

An interoffice memo described *Duchess of Idaho* as "a musical in Technicolor, based on fun, sex, and music." Shot mainly in Sun Valley, the picture was directed by Robert Leonard, a seasoned house director who was getting on in years and becoming a bit forgetful. "Esther Williams was sort of protecting Leonard," recalled actor John Lund, who also appeared in the movie, "and Van Johnson couldn't have been nicer." By that point Williams and Johnson were comfortable enough with each other to improvise parts of the script. "We knew our lives, our secrets, and our public and private personas," the actress said, "even though off camera we had little or no contact. I was aware of his marital difficulties, but none of that ever came up on the set. Nor did mine."

When *Duchess of Idaho* was released in July, *Cue* magazine found it "a big, beautiful bore." *Cue* 's reviewer liked Lena Horne's song and Eleanor Powell's tap dance but wrote, "The comedy is rapid and the pace is sleepy." Location work in Sun Valley, however, had given Van a chance to do some skiing, which he enjoyed a great deal and made the routine assignment palatable. Evie and the children had gone with him, and under Van's tutelage and that of a professional instructor, young Ned became an excellent skier.

"With Van I lived in Beverly Hills," Ned Wynn later wrote, "if not exactly in the lap, at least in the hip pocket of luxury. . . . I spent my summers at the Hotel Del Coronado, ordering hamburgers from room service, taking tennis lessons, and signing my name to the check for everything I wanted. All of these were things my father had done in his life, had found vitiating and insidious, and from which he now wished to distance both himself and me." But Van and Eve preferred an indulgent and "proper" lifestyle. They insisted on Ned attending a private school, and one or the other of them drove him to Brentwood Town and Country School each morning in a Cadillac. "Van, a WASP's WASP, dutifully trundled us off to All Saints' Church every single Sunday," Ned said. Young Wynn was baptized and confirmed in the Episcopalian Church, even though he had not set foot inside a church before moving to Beverly Hills, and Van maintained that all of the children in his household must be taught a faith by which to live.

The social ante in Beverly Hills was high, and youngsters there learned quickly that there were rules for playing life's games. "It was as if a manual had been handed them at birth," Ned wrote, "they had memorized it, and now they were operating on a plane of self-assurance and poise that I couldn't begin to match. . . . It wasn't just money. These children . . . acted as if they owned the world." Most of Ned and Tracy's friends were children of people in the film industry, such as Christina Crawford, Joan's daughter, and Bobby Walker Jr., son of Robert Walker and Jennifer Jones. "I knew I was a celebrity child," Tracy said later, "one of Hollywood's Children." Everyone of that eminence seemed to be on a predetermined level of importance, depending on their parents' rank in Tinseltown's star system.

"I was never interested in being social in the Hollywood sense during my youth," said Tracy. "I went to all the usual parties because that was expected, but I never really got off on it. For my parents it was different. . . . It was almost a requirement that one go places and be seen." As the Wynn boys grew older, Van and Evie arranged for a movie to be shown in their home on Friday nights for the children and their friends.

Eve was the disciplinarian of the family, although whenever spankings for her sons were in order she sent them to Keenan. Tracy was closer to his mother than was Ned, and both boys acknowledged later that Van tried to be a decent stepfather. "We always got along," Tracy said. "My home life was comfortable. . . . We were all pampered to an extent, of course. It was Hollywood after all. There was no harshness about my home life— none of the Joan Crawford syndrome. There were parental guidelines— just limits that we knew, understood, and respected." Tracy's main regret about his upbringing was that his family ties with the Wynns were not closer.

Ned remembered Van as "a moody, temperamental man" who often yelled and stormed out of the room in a huff. If Van was laughing, all was well. "If there was the slightest hint of trouble with one of the children, or with the house, the car, the servants, the delivery of the newspaper, the lack of ice in the silver ice bucket, the color of the candles on the dining-room table," Ned said, "Van immediately left the couch, the dinner table, the pool, the tennis court, the party, the restaurant, the vacation, and strode off to his bedroom, hands raised about his head as if he were stopping traffic, to avoid what he called a 'scene.'" On such occasions the Wynn children waited for the door to slam, while Evie pretended that nothing had happened. Sometimes the episode was chilling; other times it seemed almost laughable. Often there was pain and regret in Evie's face. But, Ned said, "denial was our stock in trade."

Some of Tracy's fondest memories of childhood were of weekends spent with his biological father. On Saturday mornings Keenan often took his son with him to the studio, where a projectionist ran the latest Tom and Jerry cartoons for the boy while his father worked. But time with Keenan also meant motorcycle rides, car races, and trips to San Francisco.

For Van, the children helped establish his image as a family man, and despite the strain in the household, the Wynn boys were fond of him. Ned frequently sought his stepfather's favor by imitating him, which amused Van. "Other than the approval of the women, I sought his approval most," Ned said, "and I figured that acting like him would gain that approval quickest. So I mimicked everything from his attitudes to his laugh." Evie maintained that she and Van wanted another baby, but the doctors had warned her that three cesarean births were the limit.

Johnson's work schedule picked up after the success of *Battleground*, and by 1951 his fan mail was back on the rise. Van was scheduled for the lead in *Pagan Love Song,* another Esther Williams film, but the script was revised and he was replaced by singer Howard Keel. Johnson then replaced Robert Walker in *Grounds for Marriage,* a light comedy featuring Kathryn Grayson in her first nonsinging role, a part originally intended for June Allyson. Grayson plays an opera singer who has lost her voice, and Van is her ex-husband, an eye, ear, nose, and throat specialist engaged to marry someone else. The part gave him another chance to demonstrate his skill as a comedian, and he proves his proficiency in a talk before a woman's club on the subject of the common cold, one of the movie's funniest scenes. In a dream sequence he imagines himself in the opera *Carmen,* singing both Don Jose and the bullfighter Escamillo, and the scene comes off quite well. When asked if he actually sang the two roles, Van replied, "That I should like to hear!"

Grounds for Marriage was escapist fare, completed two weeks after the outset of the Korean War, and was intended to help audiences forget the current domestic and international uncertainties. With television sets already in most American homes, the motion picture industry faced ruinous competition, even though advertisements ballyhooed Hollywood's latest products with the slogan, "Movies Are Better Than Ever." *Grounds for Marriage* did little to support the claim.

Three Guys Named Mike, another comedy, was initially planned as a vehicle to reunite Van Johnson and June Allyson, a formula that had worked thrice before. But when Allyson became pregnant, Metro borrowed Jane Wyman from Warner Bros. for the role of an airline stewardess, based on a real flight attendant named Pug Wells. Producer Armand Deutsch had met Wells on a flight from Los Angeles to New York and found her a unique personality. Convinced that an amusing movie could be made from Pug's life, Deutsch sent writer Ruth Brooks to live for two months with Wells and her two roommates, who were also flight attendants. Brooks created the basic story of *Three Guys Named Mike,* and future novelist Sidney Sheldon wrote the screenplay.

"I had more fun making that picture than any picture I ever produced," Deutsch said. "Most pictures are a terrible chore to produce; problems exist every day. For some reason this one was just a piece of cake." Director Charles Walters, best remembered for his MGM musicals, also found *Three Guys Named Mike* enjoyable to make. "When you've just got the flow of a straight comedy, it's easier to keep your tempo," said Walters. "It's almost twice as much work to do a musical."

Jane Wyman grew fond of Johnson during the making of *Three Guys Named Mike.* "He was marvelous," Wyman said, "funny, dedicated to his profession, and a fast study. His memory was incredible; the lines just stuck. Van loved to work and was very popular with the production company." Wyman came to know Johnson only casually on a social level, but she did have an opportunity to discover what a fabulous dancer he was. "I was flattered that Van wanted to dance with me," said the actress, who was considered a good dancer herself.

When *Three Guys Named Mike* opened in January 1951 at the Capitol Theater in New York, Bosley Crowther dismissed the movie as "an oppressively bird-brained little romance." Van plays a brilliant but boyish scientist—"just the sort of rhapsodized ideal that stalks through the pages of glamour fiction," Crowther wrote. Still, the film did terrific business.

Robert Pirosh had gained enough stature from the accolades he received for *Battleground* that Metro allowed him to direct his next picture, *Go for Broke!* Dore Schary was enthusiastic about the film and initially suggested that the writer devise a story about the Japanese detention camps created in the western United States after the bombing of Pearl Harbor. With all the tensions that surrounded the Cold War, Pirosh and Schary eventually decided to accent a positive side of a negative situation by telling the story of the 442nd Infantry Battalion, the Japanese-American combat unit that won more medals and sustained more casualties than any other during World War II. To link *Go for Broke!* with *Battleground* in moviegoers' minds, Van Johnson was chosen as the picture's star. He played a bigoted Texan assigned to train the nisei and lead their unit.

"I found that directing wasn't as easy as I had thought it would be," Pirosh said. "I was scared the first day and had a lot to learn." But Van, whom the screenwriter had come to know well during the making of *Battleground,* was his usual cooperative self and was eager to turn out the best movie possible. Most of the other actors in *Go for Broke!* were unknown players who gave the director no trouble whatever. Many of the cast members were veterans of the nisei battalion.

While *Go for Broke!* proved no *Battleground,* it did represent a somewhat clumsy attempt to right a racial wrong. Ezra Goodman in the *Los Angeles Daily News* called the movie "an honorable, authentic picture on a subject well worth filming." Other critics found the production a well-intentioned mistake. Fans were used to seeing Van in uniform and had come to identify him with military roles. His performance in *Go for Broke!* is thoroughly acceptable, and the film made modest money in its domestic run and did far better business in Japan.

By 1951 Evie Johnson had become one of the most prominent hostesses in Beverly Hills, on a par with Edie Goetz, Louis B. Mayer's daughter and the wife of studio mogul William Goetz. Some of Evie and Van's parties were informal, others were black-tie. "All of them involved having dinner at some point," said Ned Wynn. "They were big, loud, fun." The same crowd generally made the rounds of the movie colony's parties in Beverly Hills, and nearly everyone drank either scotch or vodka martinis. Keenan Wynn, who drank whiskey, was usually not invited to the big social events at the Johnsons' home.

Danny and Sylvia Kaye gave a bash for Laurence Olivier and Vivien Leigh late in 1950 at the Beverly Hills Hotel, reputedly the most lavish affair since the gala that Cary Grant had thrown for his bride-to-be, Barbara Hutton, before the war. More than 150 people attended the Kayes' soiree, during which Van danced several times with his close friend Rosalind Russell and caught the attention of the press. L. B. Mayer was said to have been on the floor that night for every dance yet left looking more fit than when he arrived. At four o'clock in the morning Danny Kaye regaled his remaining guests by playing Mary Martin to Ezio Pinza as he sang songs from the current Broadway blockbuster *South Pacific.*

Judy Garland often kicked off her shoes and entertained at Van and Evie's parties. Ned remembered Garland's drinking too much on one occasion, getting out of control, and coming into his room and sitting down on the floor while she smoked a cigarette and complained to him. Later that night Eve put Garland to bed on a sofa in the living room. Elizabeth Taylor was frequently at the Johnsons' parties, and actor Farley Granger once spent the night in their back bedroom and ended up staying with Van and Evie for two weeks.

What contact Van had with Hollywood's gay community during this time is uncertain. Henry Willson, a known homosexual who became one of the most powerful independent agents in town during the 1950s, was often a guest in Van and Evie's home. Willson represented Rock Hudson and Tab Hunter, and the gay Hudson knew Van and Eve well enough early in his career to go over and sit down with them at a Hollywood party where he knew no one else. Phyllis Gates, who worked as Willson's secretary and later married Hudson, said that she discovered that her boss was a "virtuoso" at arranging sexual affairs. "Heterosexual, homosexual, bisexual—you name it—he was a master," Gates said. The agent apparently orchestrated sexual liaisons in total secrecy and with no risk. Rock Hudson often relaxed beside Willson's swimming pool in Stone Canyon, and other gay actors doubtless did the same.

Van may have hungered for male companionship during his marriage to Eve, but how much he acted on those desires is difficult to judge. The Los Angeles police department had a close relationship with the major studios, and much pressure was exerted on the police to keep scandal involving Hollywood celebrities out of the press. Van's attitude toward his sexuality, quite rightly perhaps, was that it was nobody's business but his own. Whether or not Johnson was actively homosexual during his marriage, much of his life during the Hollywood years was a confused charade.

Van earned a princely income, had a big house and impressive cars, sported a wardrobe of loud sport coats, and exhibited an exorbitant, open-throated laugh that soared above all others at parties—all of which indicated success and happiness. Each Christmas there were piles of packages beneath an enormous tree in the Johnsons' entry hall, but no matter how profuse the gifts and the merriment might be, they were never enough to bring lasting happiness. Van usually disrupted holiday celebrations by blowing up over something that irritated him, storming out of the room, racing upstairs, and slamming doors. "From time to time Van would simply leave the house altogether and take a bungalow at the Beverly Hills Hotel," Ned said.

The Wynn boys attended all of the status-oriented birthday parties for Hollywood children—"more for the parents," Tracy said, "than the kids." They saw much money being spent, watched Van tip generously, and were assured by their mother that they would "always live in Beverly Hills." Much of Johnson's lighthearted, superficial, on-screen persona extended into his social life yet turned sour in demanding family situations. Van himself was confused about which identity was truly his. He played the effervescent role so convincingly, laughing easily on sets and chatting good-naturedly with colleagues at the studio, but such was his professional demeanor. At home, particularly under stress, he became petulant and often sulked, requiring time alone to reestablish his equilibrium. A basic loner, Van needed space; in extended periods when privacy was denied him, the pressure built into anxiety and eventually anger. With so little personal understanding, Van had no solid mooring from which to resolve the conflicts and contradictions that raged within him, and the duality in such sharp contrasts confused those nearest to him.

In 1951 Van, Evie, and the children sailed for Europe first class on the *Queen Elizabeth*. Ned remembered that they "dressed in black tie every night for dinner and ate with the captain." The Johnsons were invited to George VI's last command performance before his death, and Van wore his famous red socks to the affair. When he met the future queen, her eyes went straight to his feet to see if he was wearing his trademark. "I just like red," he told her. Tracy recalled traveling through Europe in high style, with limousines at their command, and meeting Lord and Lady "Whoozit," all of which MGM had arranged.

Van made a point of remembering people's names and of calling those he met by their first names. Virtually everyone he encountered adored the star and found him amusing. Van splashed on Tabu like water before attending parties, even though he hated most formal events and sometimes left before Evie was ready to go. An introvert trying to be an extrovert, Van experienced tremendous stage fright on the evening of his personal appearance at the London opening of *Battleground*, even though he was protected by a battalion of Metro's publicists.

Despite all of his success, Van looked into the future as he approached his thirty-fifth birthday and sensed that the pot of gold at the end of his personal rainbow might in fact be fool's gold. He no longer had the youthful appearance of the kid next door, yet he was expected to act in that manner. While he genuinely wanted to turn himself into a fine actor, Van accepted in more honest moments that he was mainly a manufactured movie personality.

He preferred to dress casually and at home spend hours by himself reading, listening to records, and painting. By the early 1950s Van had developed into a serious amateur artist. He attended Sunday-afternoon painting sessions at Claudette Colbert's house with a group of weekend daubers that included Gary Cooper, Dinah Shore, Henry Fonda, and Lilli Palmer. Fonda painted slowly, creating photographic paintings, whereas the impatient Van liked to work fast. Edward G. Robinson had told him years before, "Son, just get some paint and mess up the canvas. Then straighten it out." Johnson took the advice to heart.

He still watched at least three feature films a week and had turned home movies into a hobby, splicing them himself. He continued to like skiing and deep-sea fishing and was a fair horseman and tennis player. He exercised with barbells, even though the routine bored him and he tired easily. He never played golf, became restless at baseball games, and hated playing cards. He despised watching television, still had no interest in business matters, and was baffled by machinery. He favored dry wines, smoked four or five cigarettes a day, and considered indecision among his worst faults.

Van was really only content when he was working, and, after brief respites, he looked forward to returning to the studio, which he sometimes called the "Lion Farm." Work offered him the only sure escape from his own personal turmoil. At MGM he was bolstered by cohorts who cared for him without prying into his private world or becoming unduly intimate. Many of the actors who liked Van and enjoyed his company accepted that they would never know him beneath the surface.

In April 1951 Van began working on *Too Young to Kiss*, teamed again with June Allyson in her first movie since the birth of her child. Taking over a role originally intended for Robert Taylor, Van played a famed concert impresario who is suave and multilingual yet young and handsome enough to command a teenage following. Unable to obtain a hearing from the busy manager, Allyson's character, a pianist, connives to win his attention by crashing a children's audition as a thirteen-year-old prodigy. *Too Young to Kiss* proved a sprightly comedy but remained well within the hackneyed vein.

Johnson starred in a segment of *It's a Big Country,* one of Dore Schary's message films, which plead for tolerance and argued that America's greatness lay in its diversity. Each of the movie's eight parts had a different director, writer, and cast, and the omnibus was in production for nearly two years. Schary wrote the episode in which Van appeared, entitled "The Minister in Washington," and Wellman directed it. Johnson plays a young preacher whose congregation includes the U.S. president. The minister has a tendency to direct his sermons to the president rather than to the church membership until a gentle sexton points out his mistake. Critics found the movie as a whole fairly dull. Despite Schary's fervent belief in liberal causes, audiences showed slim interest in entertainment that contained such heavy-handed editorializing. Ignoring all of the talent involved, the *Los Angeles Daily News* dismissed *It's a Big Country* as "nothing more than an average film."

Invitation, Johnson's next film, had character actor Louis Calhern attempting to persuade Van to romance his invalid daughter, played by Dorothy McGuire. While the movie was cloaked in MGM gloss, it was a tearjerker with little to commend it except competent performances from a strong cast.

When in Rome, a better movie, was made while Van and Evie were in Europe. Johnson plays a jolly priest from a Pennsylvania mining town who journeyed to Rome for the Holy Year of 1950. On the way he meets a con man on the lam from a life sentence in Leavenworth. Paul Douglas stepped into the role of the convict after Jimmy Durante became unavailable, and Douglas and Johnson work together effectively enough to give the story warmth and plausibility. Director Clarence Brown made maximum use of the scenic and architectural wonders of Rome, and the cast and crew were delighted with an opportunity to film the story on location rather than on the studio's back lot, which would have been the case a decade earlier. When the movie was released in May 1952, the *Hollywood Reporter* called *When in Rome* "an absorbing picture filled with laughs, emotion, and beauty."

But by then the motion picture industry was in severe trouble, and mighty MGM was no exception. Executives from New York made frequent trips to Culver City to try to prevent the situation from getting worse. More than once the studio's personnel was assembled on a soundstage and told that everyone on the lot would have to tighten their belts when time came for their options to be renewed. With the advent of television and the closing of so many theaters, no one in the industry knew what the future held.

Van, at heart a sentimental idealist, was slow to despair about the impending changes because he had worked steadily since his acclaim for *Battleground*. Granted, the pictures he made in 1950 and 1951 were nothing special, but Van held his own as a box-office draw, and his salary approached six thousand dollars a week. Metro still treated its stars like royalty, and Johnson felt that studio executives were wise in balancing his roles between light, commercial entertainment and pictures of greater prestige. "I take assignments as they come," he said. "I don't claim to be an expert on scripts"

If Van had a complaint, it was that he was working too hard. "I never saw sunlight all those years at MGM," he later claimed, pointing out that he drove to work before dawn and returned home after sundown. Van had no doubt that it was a privilege to be under contract to the premier studio in Hollywood and that he was a lucky fellow. "We were innocent," he reflected in later life, remembering the "innocent movies, innocent stories, and awfully nice people" he was associated with at Metro.

At home things were less rosy. "After five years of marriage, the Johnsons have finally built exactly the sort of life they like," *Movieland* reported in 1952. "They read, they play with the kids, they've gotten the new house in order." In truth Van and Evie were having severe marital problems and had from the beginning. His dramatic exits grew more frequent, and she continued to pretend that nothing was wrong and instructed her boys to keep silent. "Guilt seeped like poison gas from person to person," Ned said of those occasions. "Somebody had made Van angry." Evie's explanation for her husband's outbursts was invariably, "He's working so hard at the studio."

Eve's family was not overly fond of Van, and he treated them as if they did not exist. Sherry, Eve's younger brother, took a wry attitude toward his sister's husband. "How's my famous brother-in-law, Van Johnson the movie star, today?" Sherry would ask with an element of sarcasm. "How *is* Laughing Boy?"

Van later maintained that he stayed in the marriage for sixteen years because of Schuyler. "Years ago I began to try to build Schuyler's defenses against a possible divorce," he said. "I taught her to paint, to ride, to read books—in general to develop her own resources to withstand the trauma of separation." Having been abandoned by his mother, Van considered divorce a tragedy for the children involved. He wanted his daughter, whom he called Sky, raised in a pristine, protected environment with all the advantages he could give her. Yet Schuyler grew up in a synthetic world full of artifice. "In Hollywood there is a tiny star who has not yet reached the cinematic heavens—although she well could," *Movieland* said of Johnson's three-year-old daughter. "With her blonde, curly hair, cornflower-blue eyes and eyelashes that form a golden fringe, she is as exquisite as anything ever painted by Renoir."

Early in 1952 Van went to the nation's capital to film *Washington Story,* in which he plays a boyish New England congressman. Written and directed by Robert Pirosh, the film takes the viewpoint that in times of crisis, America's congressmen can be counted on to forgo personal and district interests and vote for the good of the nation. "It may sound preachy," Pirosh said of the film's stand on the Cold War, "but it's really not. There are no big speeches saying we're right and Russia is wrong. But it's a picture Iron Curtain countries won't like." Much of *Washington Story* was shot on location, and MGM secured permission to shoot scenes in the Capitol building itself while Congress was in recess.

Patricia Neal played opposite Van in the movie, although the chemistry between them on the screen was not right. "It was strange casting," said Pirosh, "but that was out of my hands. Patricia Neal was wonderful, but she's a special kind of actress, so different from the usual Hollywood type." Neal was then recovering from an aborted love affair with Gary Cooper and was not eager to make the picture. "It was a piece of fluff," the actress said in her memoirs, "and I didn't know if I was up to doing it. Besides, the leading man, Van Johnson, was a close friend of Rocky's," Cooper's wife.

Dore Schary thought the theme of *Washington Story* was appropriate for the time, and once production was underway Neal found Van "a surprising delight to work with." The two enjoyed studying their lines together in the morning before each day's shooting began and became good friends. Everyone involved with the production was disappointed when the film did not do well in the theaters.

Neither did *Plymouth Adventure,* a pseudohistorical drama of the Mayflower crossing and the Pilgrims' arrival on Cape Cod. Van played John Alden in the story, which only suggested the famous romance that would develop between John and Priscilla. When Schary showed Mervyn LeRoy the script for *Plymouth Adventure,* the director was horrified. "I couldn't believe it," LeRoy said, "it was so bad. I found it dreadful." Convinced that the screenplay would make a boring picture, LeRoy turned the project down.

Clarence Brown was assigned to direct the movie, and he began filming it with high hopes. British actress Deborah Kerr had initially been slated for the role of Dorothy Bradford, but she was eventually replaced by Gene Tierney. Much research went into the project, and Schary announced that MGM's Pilgrims would wear bright and cheerful clothing, in keeping with historical truth, rather than the somber dress ascribed to them by nineteenth-century historians. Rather than being cynical and debunking, the script went in for moral and spiritual values, calculated to increase the Technicolor production's popularity.

All of *Plymouth Adventure* was shot on the Metro lot, except for one day on a beach near Oxnard, California, where the Pilgrims were shown coming ashore. Assistant director Rideway Callow later claimed that the picture suffered from having too many temperamental stars in the cast. "None of them wanted to be the first on the set," Callow said. "They'd wait and peer through the doors to see if Spencer Tracy had gone out, or Gene Tierney, or Van Johnson. I went to them and told them we were ready and nobody moved." Van finally came out, and the others followed. None of them were happy with the picture and Tracy, who played the ship's captain, complained throughout the entire ordeal.

Plymouth Adventure opened in Manhattan at Radio City Music Hall but was quickly reduced to an early run in the neighborhood theaters. Bosley Crowther said in his review that "the primary purpose of the producers is less to instruct than entertain," pointing to the romance the picture makers had invented between the Mayflower's captain and William Bradford's young wife as a primary example. Van looked as if he might be happier anywhere other than in a Pilgrim settlement, and Miklos Rozsa's score and the storm at sea, which the special effects department devised with miniatures, were about the only critical honors *Plymouth Adventure* garnered.

Steady worker though he was, Van had not been awarded a worthy dramatic part since *Battleground,* and he began to fear that his career was again on the wane. Dore Schary clearly did not know what kind of films the public wanted, and the studio's financial situation grew increasingly precarious. Schary soon called all the actors on MGM's roster to his office and asked them to take a pay cut. Van was heard to mumble, "The hell with this," as he left, and he refused to accept the reduction.

In the summer of 1952 Johnson was again cast opposite Janet Leigh, this time in a fetching comedy called *Confidentially Connie.* He plays a college professor too underpaid to afford meat for the table, even though his father is a Texas cattle baron. The Meat Institute of America protested the film's ridicule of butchers and high beef prices, but Johnson and Leigh brought freshness and charm to their amiable roles as a struggling married couple. "Van and I worked so well together," the actress said. "He was such a natural actor and never seemed to be acting, although in our conversations he played himself down. I loved working with him."

With his message pictures unpopular at the box office, Schary came to rely on proven formulas to keep Metro-Goldwyn-Mayer solvent. Van was reunited yet again with June Allyson in *Remains to Be Seen,* a rather listless mystery-comedy based on a mediocre play by Howard Lindsay and Russel Crouse. Johnson's part required him to play the drums in a nightclub orchestra; otherwise, he essentially played himself. Angela Lansbury, who plays a villain in the picture, called *Remains to Be Seen* a "dreadful movie," and the best the *Hollywood Reporter* could say for Van's performance was that he was "actually better than his poorly delineated role."

Since MGM was getting rid of many of its top stars, Van decided to seek other avenues of work. With the studio's blessing, he agreed to perform a nightclub act at the Sands Hotel in Las Vegas in the spring of 1953. He was nervous about returning to live entertainment, but Rosalind Russell more than anyone convinced Van to accept the offer. "What could I do?" he asked the actress. Russell reminded Johnson that he had begun his career as a song-and-dance man; perhaps it was time to go back to what he had once done so well. "I had twelve days to get and learn material," Van said, "work with the piano player, be fitted by the tailor, get my nerves to a white hot pitch, and start having the same old nightmares."

On the opening night of his Sands engagement, Johnson was covered with medals that Rosalind Russell and other Catholic friends had loaned him. He was so terrified that he virtually had to be pushed onto the stage. Keenan Wynn was in the audience, sitting at the same ringside table as Evie. June Allyson was also there, along with many of his professional friends. Van opened with a breezy number called "This Is Where I Belong," written by Metro's music wizard Roger Edens, who thought it would please audiences for the star to begin by lampooning his film career. Van continued with such songs as "Sing for Your Supper," "Come Rain or Come Shine," and "You're Just Too Marvelous," rendering them with enthusiasm and boyish charm. Nick Castle had staged the act, which included a soft-shoe dance by Van.

The ex–chorus boy revealed himself once again to be an exceptionally facile performer, even though he awoke every morning of the engagement worrying about that evening's show. Evie tried to bolster her husband's confidence, but Marlene Dietrich helped Van more. Dietrich walked into his suite one afternoon to hear him mutter, "This isn't for me. What am I doing here?" The German star gave Johnson a puzzled look and said, "Why do you make yourself miserable all day? Accept the fact that at a certain hour every night you will be frightened and have butterflies. But only at that hour. Everybody who is good gets butterflies." Van recognized the wisdom in what she said and began to relax.

Van's Las Vegas performances were a sellout every night. According to the *Hollywood Reporter,* his act was "good, clean fun, high-pitched entertainment," and by all accounts Johnson's debut as a nightclub headliner was a howling success. "I wasn't sure how my act would go," Van said, but "I made up my mind that I'd give it one big blast." He put all the vigor he had into the show and thrived on the rapport he established with audiences. On the last night of his engagement at the Sands, all the waiters and musicians wore red socks as a token of their affection for him.

The Las Vegas casinos had no allure for Johnson, for which he thanked his New England upbringing. Van claimed that he was the only performer who ever played the Strip and walked away with his salary. "I've never gambled," he said. "I don't know where to put the chips. I'd stand there after the show and watch some of those poor strained faces. You know they're going to wind up without carfare home."

Van repeated the act in Toronto, Montreal, and Chicago and was soon flooded with offers for live performances. Rosalind Russell's husband, producer Frederick Brisson, proposed starring him in the original production of *The Pajama Game,* and Johnson later considered accepting the lead in the Broadway musical *Li'l Abner.* Since his present contract with MGM was expiring in December 1953, Van weighed the stage bids seriously. "From now on, as film assignments permit," he said, "I'd like to alternate between screen and stage. There is nothing more gratifying than that instantaneous audience reaction. It's inspiring and stimulating, something we in Hollywood often forget."

Van worried that his movie audience had outgrown him, a possibility that depressed him. The discipline he had learned at MGM prepared him well for other venues in the entertainment business, and the image he had created on the screen was so indelible that he would command public attention for many years to come. But Van was a product of the big-studio era, and he had enjoyed and been spoiled by all the perks and comforts that Metro lavished on its stars. To be cast adrift by the studio at age thirty-seven was a frightening prospect, and Van talked braver than he felt.

Always moody, Johnson's demeanor assumed darker hues as his MGM days neared an end. He bickered more with Eve, and one night he walked out of a party and left his wife there to find her own way home. As the Wynn boys grew older they became more difficult, especially Ned. "Smart-aleckism was my forte," said an adult Ned, who often was in trouble during the years he attended the Harvard School in the San Fernando Valley. "Each time I got into trouble my father was sent for," Ned recalled. "In this way I saw a lot of him. There was a watchful truce between my mother and Van and my father."

Tracy was better behaved, but on one occasion he burned down part of the guest house after playing with matches. Keenan worried that his sons were growing up sissies and too much the mama's boys. Evie made sure that Ned and Tracy went to boys' clubs and summer camps on Catalina Island, where she hoped they would learn to be like other children, but their privileged status ruled out their being normal.

Things were different when the boys were with Keenan. Ned remembered weekends when he "got to eat richly poisonous hot dogs, pee in filthy men's rooms, and sit in the local dives with my father while he stood rounds of drinks and accepted the glad-handers, stuffing ten-dollar bills into the pockets of old punch-drunk fighters and broken-down race car drivers." Ned claimed he loved every minute of those times. "I was great around adults," he said, "and I much preferred them to children."

On reflection, Tracy felt that his parents had done a good job of raising him and his brother under the circumstances. "They were wise in not being too structured with us because kids react against too much structure," Tracy said. "We were given choices." The younger Wynn's biggest resentment came from being sent to military school, which he hated. "In third grade I went to school from seven-thirty in the morning until five-thirty in the afternoon," Tracy said. "They made us march." The boy also had to take piano lessons for seven years, although he could not play a note as an adult. "I was in my teens before I realized that all of those things were status symbols," Tracy said.

Soon after Van's successful 1953 nightclub appearances, he went to Florida to film *Easy to Love*, his fifth and final movie with Esther Williams. Part of the picture was shot in Cypress Gardens on Florida's Lake Eloise, and the company lived two or three miles from the location and had cars and drivers available to take them back and forth. Van liked working away from the studio with Williams because the swimmer made good lunches for her costars, who included singer Tony Martin and actor John Bromfield. But *Easy to Love* was a routine assignment, and everyone connected with the production found it a drag. "It got so that I'd go down to the studio and see June Allyson or Esther Williams, and so help me," Van said, "I could write the story before the author could even get the paper into his typewriter."

Charles Walters directed *Easy to Love*, and Busby Berkeley choreographed the picture's big swimming numbers. "It was corny and we knew it," said Walters. "It was a matter of make this one as much fun and believable as possible." Berkeley was a heavy drinker, although his nightly bouts seldom interfered with his work. The aquatics he arranged for Williams, which included a lengthy waterskiing ballet filmed from a helicopter, proved the picture's only memorable parts.

When *Easy to Love* was released in November 1953, the reviewer for the *Los Angeles Daily News* found the movie "light, carefree, and eye-filling." Van handled his familiar role in his usual smooth manner, and the combination of swimming, comedy, romance, and music assured the Technicolor production reasonable traffic at the box office.

Van next was loaned to Twentieth Century–Fox for *The Siege at Red River,* a Western set in the Civil War period. In the picture Johnson poses as a patent medicine salesman but is actually on a secret mission for the Confederacy to capture a Gatling gun from the Yankees and smuggle it to Southern sympathizers in the West. The movie was called *Gatling Gun* in an initial script, and the story's tension stems from a danger that the weapon might fall into the hands of renegade Indians. Director Rudolph Maté argued that the film must unfold like a modern-day spy hunt, with plenty of action, but it also offers moments of humor.

Filming outdoors in the desert necessitated the company's working in temperatures of 115 degrees with no protection from the sun, which Van particularly found uncomfortable. "I've got this plate in my head," he said. "Extreme heat and extreme cold always affect it." But Johnson liked his leading lady, Joanne Dru, found her good-humored, and thought she was "the greatest trouper in the world."

The Siege at Red River wrapped on October 5, 1953, and opened six months later to assorted notices. "Van Johnson not only turns out to be an excellent horseman and singer," the *Los Angeles Examiner* reported in an overzealous review, "but also looks and acts better than ever. Right now it's kind of hard to remember him as the raw young actor of a few years ago, he's getting that smooth and versatile." Van was better as a medicine show performer in the picture than he was as an Indian fighter and brawler, where an obvious double was used.

Van's last picture as an exclusive Metro player was *Men of the Fighting Lady*, a realistic look at the war in Korea, including some footage of actual bombing raids. Keenan Wynn also appeared in the movie, which was photographed in the inferior Ansco Color. The film's climax has Van guiding a blinded squadron member by radio to a successful crash landing on the flight deck of an aircraft carrier. Since the rescue was based on official files, including actual dialogue, the sequence comes across as moving and plausible. Critics rated *Men of the Fighting Lady* above average, although the picture adds up to less than gripping entertainment. Van neared the end of his MGM tenure back in military uniform, this time flying jets, but the effort involved in keeping his portrayal fresh shows on the screen. "I was in all branches of the service," Johnson said of his Metro years. "Finally I had enough points to get out."

Keenan Wynn also left MGM soon after finishing *Men of the Fighting Lady* and in the months ahead launched a successful career in live television. "It saved my life," Wynn said, "because I was rediscovered as an actor in live television." Never hung up on being a celebrity, as Van was, Keenan looked back on his period at Metro with disgust. "I was at MGM for twelve years," Wynn said, "and played the same faithful buddy–type role in sixty-eight pictures." The actor deprecated the films he made there and liked to rename them to fit the attitude he had toward them. *Kiss Me, Kate* became "Kiss My Kootch" and *Desperate Search* he called "Desperate Crotch." Wynn said he could have phoned in what he did in *Annie Get Your Gun* but later claimed to be one of the last Hollywood character actors to become famous.

By 1954 most of Metro's big stars were leaving the studio either of their own volition or because their options were permitted to lapse. That year the studio dropped Clark Gable and Greer Garson, once king and queen of the lot. "I can't believe I won't see your lovely red head around the pickle factory any more," Van Johnson wrote to Garson in March. "I know you'll be much happier wherever you go." Sandy Descher, a child actress who would work with Van on *The Last Time I Saw Paris* in 1954, happened to be in the office of the studio's drama coach, Lillian Burns, when Gable left the lot. Burns called the girl to the window and told her to watch history being made. "Clark Gable was standing outside the Thalberg Building," Descher recalled, "ready to leave MGM forever. Gable saluted the studio's administration building and drove away."

Van would stay at Metro to fulfill two more commitments, but by the summer of 1954 he would be a freelance actor. Louis B. Mayer had already departed, as had Esther Williams, Spencer Tracy, Deborah Kerr, Kathryn Grayson, and many more. Lana Turner stayed until 1956, but her final days at the studio, the actress said, "were like working amid the ruins." The wardrobe and prop departments had been decimated, and most of the publicity people Turner had known for years had been discharged. "It was all doom and gloom," she said.

Van viewed the termination of his contract with the Lion Farm as a mixed blessing. Although he would be free to develop as an actor, Metro had made him a star and been his professional home. For twelve years MGM had promoted Van, protected him, and awarded him preferential treatment. In return he had been a faithful employee, made millions for the company's stockholders, never turned down a role, and only once had asked for a raise. But times were changing. Dore Schary's days at Metro were also numbered, and a new regime already was attempting to seize control of the studio. "They were great years," Van said of his time at Metro, "but the studio didn't equip me for facing the outer world." Almost thirty-eight years old, Van Johnson, the eternal boy next door, at last faced the terrifying prospect of growing up—and without Louis B. Mayer's guidance and MGM's minions to coddle and support him.

CHAPTER 7

Freelance Actor

Johnson was playing at the Sands casino in Las Vegas when producer Stanley Kramer offered him a role in *The Caine Mutiny,* the film version of Herman Wouk's Pulitzer Prize–winning novel. Van had read the book and was excited by the possibility of appearing in the picture, although he assumed that he would be playing the fresh-faced ensign, Willie Keith. Much to his surprise, Kramer wanted him for Steve Maryk, the USS *Caine*'s idealistic executive officer, who takes command of the beat-up minesweeper during a typhoon and is later charged with mutiny. Maryk is a dramatic part, and *The Caine Mutiny* would be an important movie, both an Oscar nominee and a box-office winner. Van was ecstatic at the chance to break out of his mold and play a complex, forceful character. "A role like Maryk after all these years!" he said. "Believe me, I'm grateful. Nobody can say it wasn't time for a change."

Van knew that the parts he had been handed in recent years at Metro were flimsy and one-dimensional. He had been typecast for so long that he feared he might have lost the ability to stretch as an actor. Yet Kramer seemed confident that Johnson could play a demanding, introspective part. "I was in a rut," Van said; "Stanley Kramer saved my life."

MGM agreed to loan Johnson to Columbia for *The Caine Mutiny,* and Kramer secured a two-million-dollar budget for the picture from studio head Harry Cohn. Humphrey Bogart, Fred MacMurray, and José Ferrer were also cast in the film, and Edward Dmytryk was set to direct. Cohn mandated that the shooting schedule could not extend beyond fifty-four days and that the completed movie must not run longer than two hours, which necessitated cuts in the script.

Much of *The Caine Mutiny* was photographed in Hawaii, and Van and Evie sailed to Honolulu aboard the *Lurline,* a Princess Line ship. Also on the cruise were Janet Leigh and her second husband, Tony Curtis, and the two Hollywood couples spent most of their time together and enjoyed the voyage immensely. They sunned, dined at the captain's table, danced, and even took hula lessons. When the ship docked in Honolulu, kayaks and catamarans came out to meet the passengers, and divers bobbed around the boat while the press vied for photographs and statements from the Johnsons and the Curtises that could be embellished into something newsworthy.

The first few days on the set of *The Caine Mutiny,* Van seemed nervous and unsure of himself. "He was trying too hard to be tough," Dmytryk recalled. "Although he was marvelous in the part, it was difficult for him to do, because Maryk was not the boyish-type role that he was used to playing." The film crew helped bolster Van's confidence by being a responsive audience. "Actors are very sensitive," Johnson said, "and need to be built up. Everyday I have to be told that I'm good. I really do." But Van proved a hardworking professional and won the company's respect, with the possible exception of Bogart, who expressed reservations about Johnson's ability to delineate character. "Van wasn't a great actor," Dmytryk said, "but he gave the performance, and that's what counts. He was the most cooperative actor I've ever worked with."

Part of the filming of *The Caine Mutiny* took place in the navy yard at Pearl Harbor, and before shooting started, there had been some protests against the picture on the grounds that it would depict the U.S. Navy in an unflattering way. For three years, amid the ugly backwash of the McCarthy era, Hollywood had been afraid to touch Wouk's novel. But Stanley Kramer had a reputation for daring, and he mollified the navy by softening the author's characterization of Captain Queeg, making him less a madman and more a veteran skipper suffering from battle fatigue.

In Hawaii the navy gave Kramer's production company full cooperation. An alert young gunner's mate saved Van from possible injury by shooting a shark in the water just ten yards away from where the actor was swimming. The incident occurred about twelve miles south of Pearl Harbor. Johnson had dived into the ocean, fully clothed, to retrieve a line, as the script required. The navy rifleman was standing on a camera tugboat, and he stopped the shark with a single bullet.

Dmytryk managed to blend the diverse acting styles of his high-powered cast and evoked a superb performance from Van. Gone was the lightweight geniality that had won Johnson fame. Riddled with conflict, Maryk was a far darker character than Johnson had previously played. With his self-assurance restored after the first few days of shooting, Van felt like an actor again. "That's what I'm after now," he said, "after years of being just a star."

The Caine Mutiny was unquestionably Van's best opportunity to prove his dramatic skill since *Battleground*. "Thanks to that picture," he said, "I won't have to worry about my career not lasting. It proved to me . . . that I hadn't gone as far as I could." Johnson later met Herman Wouk and claimed to have gotten down on his knees to thank the writer. "If it hadn't been for his *Caine Mutiny*," Van said, "I'd still be at Metro. That movie was a great break for me."

With his success in Las Vegas and his acclaim as a serious actor in *The Caine Mutiny*, Van Johnson once again became a hot property. Even MGM's interest in the former teenage idol was restored, and he demanded that the studio's executives treat him with respect. At the beginning of 1954, Van wanted a contract that gave him a percentage of his films' profits. "I can't work for salary," he said. "After twelve years all I've got to show for my work are a bunch of leather-bound scripts and photographs." He pointed out that he had relatives to support and a large staff to pay. Metro offered him a new contract, but Van did not want to be tied exclusively to any one studio. As many other stars were doing at the time, he decided to freelance. He agreed to do two more pictures for MGM but also signed a five-year contract with Columbia to make one picture a year for the smaller company.

Having put a stamp of maturity on his work, Van was eager to demonstrate his newfound versatility. He felt buoyant, even cocky, as he entered his final months under contract to MGM. "All of a sudden, I'm not scared anymore," Johnson said. "It took twelve years, but it finally happened. I've grown up at last. I know I can stand on my own two feet."

In late 1953 Van began work on *Brigadoon,* Metro's rendition of Alan Jay Lerner and Frederick Loewe's successful Broadway musical. Since the story told of a Scottish village that comes to life one day every hundred years, producer Arthur Freed, director Vincente Minnelli, and dancer-choreographer Gene Kelly initially planned to shoot the fantasy on location. "We thought *Brigadoon* was going to be one of the great revolutionary breakthroughs in screen history," Kelly said, "because CinemaScope had come in and widened the screen. Our hope was that we would do *Brigadoon* as an outdoor picture the way John Ford would do a Western." But when Kelly and Freed went to Scotland to scout locations, they saw nothing but gray skies and decided that weather conditions there were too drab to photograph well.

The studio next decided to film *Brigadoon* in the mountains in back of Carmel, California. "We wanted all the clans to gather out-of-doors," Kelly said, "with the bagpipes skirling and the drums banging away." But the financial situation became so grave at MGM before production started that the movie's budget was cut, which meant that *Brigadoon* had to be shot on a studio soundstage with synthetic backdrops. "The art directors had a hell of a job on that picture," cameraman Joseph Ruttenberg recalled. "George Gibson, the scenic artist, painted a background that looked amazingly realistic, and they built mounds and elevations on the stage. Then they had to blend the grass and vegetation to match the colors of Gibson's painting."

Since *Brigadoon* was ultimately shot on a soundstage, it should have been a singer's picture, but dancers had been cast in the leading roles when the intention was to film the story outdoors. Kelly particularly wanted to give the movie great movement and the look and feel of the fresh air, which was difficult to achieve on a soundstage. "We lost a lot of our enthusiasm for making the picture," the dancer said, "and none of us were very happy with *Brigadoon*. Alan Lerner wasn't happy with it at all. But we were professionals, and we did the best we could. Vincente Minnelli and I never felt that it was our picture."

The director, an unabashed sensualist with decor, which he had demonstrated in such musicals as *Meet Me in St. Louis* and *An American in Paris,* had no worry that *Brigadoon* would be visually arresting, but he had misgivings about its slender story. Lerner and Loewe's score was melodic and haunting, and interior scenes were lighted to look like Flemish paintings. Low-lying Scottish mists were created with dry ice on the set, whereas denser fog was made from vaporized oil. Clusters of plastic trees were rigged with live foliage, and a seventy-five-foot stream was devised to ripple through an artificial glen.

Gene Kelly seemed remote and emotionally down during the production, aware that by the mid-1950s, film musicals were on the decline. Minnelli disliked the shape of the CinemaScope screen, considering it a distortion, and since *Brigadoon* was shot in both a wide-screen process and a regular version, Van complained that he should receive two salaries. Minnelli later said that Johnson gave him an abundance of riches as a performer, although Van had a tendency to overdo. "His portrayal of Gene's sidekick was magnified, if not magnetic," Minnelli said. "Van was cursed with the mugger's face, and every director had to watch him to make sure he wasn't too expressive." Johnson claimed that he sang "about four notes" in the picture and admitted that Fred Astaire need not worry about having any competition from Van as a dancer.

Before the musical opened in September 1954, Metro's New York publicist, Howard Dietz, said, "We just saw *Brigadoon*. For me it was the most beautiful picture I've ever seen." Critics disagreed, for the most part. Bosley Crowther of the *New York Times* found the movie "curiously flat and out-of-joint, rambling all over creation and seldom generating warmth or charm . . . pretty weak synthetic Scotch." And a reviewer for *Newsweek* wrote, "Despite the resurgence of good films, Hollywood can still put its worst foot forward in the classic manner."

Van fared better with *The Last Time I Saw Paris,* the last MGM movie he made under contract. Based partly on F. Scott Fitzgerald's short story "Babylon Revisited," Johnson plays an alcoholic writer who in recovery tries to reclaim his daughter from the custody of his embittered sister-in-law. Writer-director Richard Brooks moved the time of the story from the roaring 1920s to the post–World War II period, and lovely Elizabeth Taylor was cast as Van's wife, who dies as a result of her husband's drunkenness.

Van had never played a true alcoholic before, and he was worried about how to handle the assignment. Casting director Billy Grady claimed that Johnson had also become temperamental. The first day's shooting on *The Last Time I Saw Paris* called for a street scene that involved five hundred extras. The sequence was to be filmed in downtown Los Angeles, and Van's presence there was needed. Since the star was vacationing in Palm Springs at the time, producer Jack Cummings wanted confirmation that the actor would report for work at the appointed time. Although Van had requested that he receive no phone calls during his three-week holiday, Cummings became concerned enough as production time grew near to phone the vacationing actor at the Palm Springs Racquet Club. When Van refused the call, the producer was incensed.

Grady had had other occasions to observe Johnson's displays of temperament, so he waited until the last minute to call again. With the shooting of the crowd scene scheduled for Monday, the studio's head of casting finally asked Van's agent to give the obstinate star a call to corroborate the coming week's schedule. When the agency refused, Grady grew furious and rang the Racquet Club himself. Van came to the phone but barked,

"How dare you call me when I'm on my vacation," and slammed down the receiver.

Grady and Cummings spent a miserable Saturday and Sunday, wondering whether their male lead would show up for work the next week. "All I could see were 500 extras on Los Angeles' Main Street ready to work on Monday morning," Grady wrote in his memoirs, "and no word from Johnson that he would be there." As it turned out, Van arrived on the set early that Monday and delivered one of the best scenes in the picture. Still, Grady remembered the days when "Van wouldn't go to the bathroom without a long-cord telephone." The casting head assumed that the star's recent success in *The Caine Mutiny* had convinced him that he could get away with inconsiderate behavior.

Although Van gave one of his finest performances in *The Last Time I Saw Paris,* screenwriter Julius Epstein, who with his twin brother, Phillip, had drafted the original script several years before the picture was made, thought that the revised version was terrible. MGM had bought the Epsteins' script from Paramount, and Richard Brooks had rewritten it and pushed the time of the action forward. "The story lost all meaning," Julius Epstein said. "It was one of the best scripts my brother and I ever did, but it turned out one of my greatest disappointments. I'm still very bitter about that."

Although a second unit went to Paris to shoot backgrounds for the film, most of *The Last Time I Saw Paris* was made in the studio. One of the movie's particularly touching moments is a scene on a park bench between Van and nine-year-old Sandy Descher, who plays his daughter in the picture. "We had to keep taking that scene over and over," Descher said, "because one or the other of us would break down and cry. Richard Brooks said that he wanted the audience to cry, and that if we did, they wouldn't. Van was a delight to work with, but he was never fully appreciated as an actor."

Johnson's love scenes with Elizabeth Taylor are less convincing than his tender exchange with the child actress. Although Taylor looked her most desirable in *The Last Time I Saw Paris*, Van comes across as fairly asexual, as he does in the pictures with June Allyson and Esther Williams. He lacked the animal magnetism of Hollywood's more notable screen lovers, had none of the danger of Errol Flynn or the hirsute quality of Tyrone Power or Peter Lawford, and emitted no erotic sparks on an adult level. Going into a clinch, he seemed ill at ease, strangely distant, and fundamentally sexless.

Yet *The Last Time I Saw Paris* is one of the few movies of which Van would be proud, for his performance is at times sensitive and moving. "Some of his scenes in that picture reached out and tore the heart of everyone who saw it," Evie said. Many thought that Johnson should have been nominated for an Academy Award for the film and were surprised when he was overlooked. When Van and Eve returned home the night of the Academy nominations, their phone started ringing with people calling to offer condolences, and telegrams and letters of protest poured into the studio the next day. But critics were not as impressed with the picture as the public seemed to be. Bosley Crowther called the film "a nigh two-hour assembly of bistro balderdash and lush, romantic scenes," and the *New York Times* critic found Van Johnson "too bumptious when happy and too dreary when drunk."

With his MGM contract behind him, Van claimed to feel freer and happier than he had ever been in his life. "I shall make fewer pictures from now on," he said, "but they'll be good ones." He acknowledged gratitude to Metro but complained that he had sometimes canceled trips and sat around for weeks waiting for a call from the studio, only to be told at the last minute that he would not be needed. "Now that I'm not tied down to a studio contract," he said, "the Johnson family is going to get around and see the world."

The golden years of Hollywood were coming to an end, and even Van recognized that the glory days of the big studios were winding down. The future of the industry was uncertain. "Where are we going?" Johnson asked of the motion picture business in 1954. "Whatever happened to the little old black and white [movies], with the close-ups like Garbo used to have?" Although Van had enjoyed a phenomenal year, he was not as sure of what lay ahead for him as he liked to appear. No longer would he have Metro-Goldwyn-Mayer to lean on, and he lacked the resources to stand confidently on his own. So he depended more on Eve, which added confusion and further resentment to their already complicated marriage. Van continued to exude a movie-star radiance, yet he faced each new assignment with trepidation.

By 1954 the Johnsons' marriage had assumed an edge even in public. Singer Rosemary Clooney and her husband, José Ferrer, who had known Keenan and Eve in New York, invited the Johnsons to a small dinner party shortly after Johnson worked with Ferrer on *The Caine Mutiny*. "Van had a tendency if the dinner conversation moved too much toward Keenan to get upset and start needling Evie," Clooney recalled. "I thought it was rude, and I told him so. Van was annoyed with me for a long time after that. But he was really not nice to Evie that evening."

Other acquaintances claimed that Eve was frantically jealous of her husband and accused him of having all manner of romantic attachments. Whatever alliances Johnson may have had during his marriage were carried out discreetly, although there was always fear of exposure in the tabloids. A New York newspaper reported in June 1955 that the vice squad was watching Johnson's activities, but the article did not disclose the reasons for the surveillance. Van admitted that he and Evie had their ups and downs, yet he staunchly repeated that she provided him with the only home and stability he had known. "The faith and belief that Evie has in me [are] way beyond what any man should expect," he told fan-magazine reporters. "Her belief in me . . . has bridged many a possible disaster or crisis."

Evie occasionally returned to acting and in 1952 played a part in Rosalind Russell's movie, *Never Wave at a WAC*, but she devoted herself primarily to designing handmade furnishings for their house, being one of Hollywood's foremost hostesses, looking after details of Van's career, and traveling with her husband to the various locations where his films were made. But friends viewed the marriage as more of a business than a union of mutual affection.

Van wanted Schuyler to grow up a proper lady, although his daughter's governess saw more of the child than he did. Janet Leigh once met Schuyler with Evie on a shopping trip in Los Angeles. "She was just a little girl then," Leigh said of Schuyler, "and looked a lot like Van, with her red hair and freckled skin." Sky would soon be enrolled in the fashionable Marymount School in Bel-Air, also attended by a number of other Hollywood children.

Ned Wynn maintained that his goal as a youngster was never to grow up. "I was actually physically frightened of becoming an adult," he said. Van seemed more at ease with his stepson when the boy acted mature and did not put too many demands on him requiring parental support. "Money he could provide and was always quite generous in doing so," Ned said. "But in exchange he wanted an intelligent, funny, urbane companion in a son, so I learned to be an intelligent, funny, urbane companion."

Van's mother, Loretta Neumann, reappeared in her son's life in November 1954, when she sued him for nine hundred dollars monthly support. Johnson refused to pay, pointing out that his father had raised him with no help from Loretta. By 1954 Van's mother was sixty-one years old and twice divorced, and until recently she had been a dietitian at Metro-Goldwyn-Mayer. Van told reporters that he was "terribly shocked and hurt at the proposed court action" and claimed that he had always been willing to support his mother in a reasonable fashion, which indeed he had. Loretta insisted that she could no longer work because of extreme nervousness, hypertension, arthritis, and a stomach disorder. The suit ultimately was settled out of court. Van agreed to provide his mother with four hundred dollars a month and to assume responsibility for some back taxes and other bills she owed.

Thirty-seven-year-old Keenan Wynn married twenty-one-year-old Sharley Hudson in San Juan, Puerto Rico, in January 1954, although the actor's previous wife claimed that the divorce from her was not yet final.

Wynn told the press in July that the Puerto Rican rites had been exchanged at the end of a hectic tour of Africa, Iceland, and Greenland, where he had entertained troops, and that he and Sharley planned to have a more leisurely wedding ceremony performed in Los Angeles the following summer. The couple bought a two-story colonial home on Fontennelle Way in Bel-Air and eventually had three daughters. Tracy Wynn later referred to Sharley as a "great lady," and Keenan's marriage to his third wife, despite stormy times and periodic separations, lasted until the actor's death.

In June 1954 Van sailed for England, where he was slated to make *The End of the Affair* with Deborah Kerr, a friend from Metro days. For a time, Evie stayed behind in Beverly Hills to supervise the construction of a swimming pool in their yard. Keenan and Sharley lived in the Johnsons' house once Evie had joined Van in London, and the newlyweds looked after Ned, Tracy, and Schuyler.

The End of the Affair would be Johnson's second picture for Columbia, and Edward Dmytryk again directed. Based on a novel by Graham Greene, the film's initial script was written by Lenore Coffee, but in England the script was revised, although Coffee claimed it showed no improvement. Censorship problems necessitated the changes, since the story, set during World War II, deals with an adulterous love affair between the wife of a stiff-necked British government employee and a moody American author. The woman faces the personal crisis of deciding whether sex or religion will be the stronger force in her life. In the revised version the moral aspects of her dilemma are emphasized more than the romantic. Van's character, a somewhat embittered novelist with few scruples, dies in the end, giving the actor a chance to look sick and unhappy after all of his happy-go-lucky roles at Metro. "What a dream part," Johnson said. "It was probably the happiest picture experience of my entire career."

Van found working with Deborah Kerr a joy, and in his autobiography, Dmytryk remembered both actors with great affection. "Rarely have I seen two people of comparable skill and talent work together so effortlessly and with so little self-indulgence," he wrote. The director observed no trace of temperament from either star. They were always on the set by 8:30 in the morning, drinking tea and chatting with the crew, ready to go to work.

But the perceptive Dmytryk, who had endured his share of agony during the House Un-American Activities Committee's investigations of Hollywood and eventually was sent to prison for contempt of Congress, detected the tumult in Johnson's personal life. "At that time Van was one of the most admired and least understood stars in the world," the director said. "He loved films, and when he wasn't working in one he was usually watching one. When there was trouble at home—and often when there wasn't—he'd head for a theater as soon as the doors opened and stay until they turned him out at closing time. This activity undoubtedly served to take his mind off the constant battle being waged within him." Dmytryk noted that Johnson was painfully shy but understood that he had to mix with people for professional reasons. "So he allowed his wife or his agent to drag him to parties where he would spend a miserable evening hiding out in some secluded room," the director said. "Yet in the hustle-bustle of a movie set, he felt completely at home."

Van did experience some trouble adjusting to the relaxed atmosphere of a British movie company, and while Kerr was surrounded by old friends from her British film days, Johnson felt out of his element. Kerr's aunt visited the set one day and brought along her ten-year-old daughter, Harriet. The child watched as Dmytryk completed a sequence in which Van was severely injured during an air raid, and the girl became convinced that real blood was spurting from his head wound. She grew so distraught that she had to be taken from the set. Johnson followed her out and finally convinced the child that what looked like blood was only makeup.

Like Van, Kerr had recently gotten free of her MGM contract and looked forward to playing more demanding roles than the historical epics in which she had been cast after being brought to America. The actress thought *The End of the Affair* would be an interesting challenge since it gave her an opportunity to play a complex, flawed woman, a change from the noble ladies she had played at Metro. But critics found Johnson and Kerr mismatched in the film, and several reviewers complained that Van did not appear much like a passionate lover. "What's really bad is Johnson's tendency to look like a St. Bernard when he becomes thoughtful," a writer for the *New York Post* remarked. Other critics objected to Dmytryk's over-playing the mysticism in the story, which called for Kerr's character to promise God that she would give up her lover if the American survived. Even with the religious element stressed in the revised screenplay, puri-tanical audiences in the United States were shocked by the implication of adultery in the movie, particularly when it involved Van Johnson.

Actor David Niven invited Van and Evie to spend a weekend at his country estate while they were in England, and in London the Johnsons ran into Louella Parsons. "Van," the gossip columnist exclaimed, "you've grown up at last." Johnson gave Parsons a wry smile. "Don't you think it's about time?" he replied.

Once *The End of the Affair* was finished, Van and Evie boarded a plane for the Riviera, where they enjoyed a brief vacation. They arrived in New York on the *Queen Elizabeth* in September 1954 and returned to Beverly Hills soon thereafter. Johnson would not start his next movie until late spring. During the hiatus he spent a great deal of time painting, which he claimed brought him more pleasure than did acting. He particularly liked rendering scenes from his New England boyhood—farmhouses he remem-bered, elm trees bright with autumn foliage, and views of the sea and shore around Newport. He shopped, watched movies, and developed more of an interest in television programs. "Sometimes I think I could be a bum," Johnson said, "just painting or making straw hats on the beach at Aca-pulco. . . . A lot of people are hard workers because they know they are ba-sically lazy. I'm one. I've never really had a chance to be lazy, but some-times I daydream about being a terrific beachcomber."

Van received offers for movies and stage work, but he seemed in no hurry to make decisions. Frederick Brisson was still trying to interest him in signing for a company of *The Pajama Game*, and Van conferred several times on the telephone with the producer and George Abbott, the show's director, and even traveled to New York to discuss the possibility of appearing in the musical, which he thought offered him a good role. "I walked out on the stage of the Winter Garden Theater and looked out at those seats and got sick to my stomach," Johnson said. "With three kids and a big house to run in Beverly Hills, I didn't want to risk it." He later regretted turning down Brisson's offer.

In November 1954 Van joined Elizabeth Taylor in Manhattan for the opening of *The Last Time I Saw Paris*. "In New York I'm King of the Asphalt," Johnson said. "Along about twilight I get out of that hovel at the Plaza and walk from river to river." He saw a number of Broadway shows while he was there, wrote fan letters to performers whose work he particularly admired, and toyed with the idea of finding a suitable play for himself. "I am not sure I want to go on the stage," Van said. "I get such butterflies every time I walk before the footlights."

Johnson already was feeling lost without MGM to guide him. He remained unable to shake off his boyish image, yet as he neared forty, trying to be the bouncy youth was not fashionable any more. "I'm glad the bobby-soxers no longer bother me," Van said in 1954. "They're all grown up and married now, and I appeal to sweet old ladies. It's a nice, substantial, relaxed career." Yet he missed the limelight and the security he had enjoyed when Louis B. Mayer was in charge of his career.

Van would liked to have played Texas rancher Bick Benedick in the movie version of *Giant*, opposite Elizabeth Taylor, but Warner Bros., where the picture was made, instead offered him *Miracle in the Rain*. Production began in New York City early in May 1955, with a budget of $1.1 million and a forty-eight-day shooting schedule. Van was paid $150,000 for the film, whereas his costar, Jane Wyman, earned $120,000. Rudolph Maté directed the romantic story, which a Warner Bros. publicist hailed as a "dramatic presentation that should win Academy Awards in many departments."

Set in 1942 and written by Ben Hecht, *Miracle in the Rain* appeared first as a magazine story in the *Saturday Evening Post,* then was turned into a television drama starring Phyllis Thaxter and William Prince. The plot involves a young woman who falls in love with a happy-hearted soldier on leave during World War II. Their romance ends tragically when the soldier goes back overseas and is killed. The girl's spirit is broken by the loss of her loved one, and she becomes seriously ill. In delirium she leaves her sickbed and makes her way through a downpour to pray for him in St. Patrick's Cathedral. Outside, she again sees her lover. Right before she dies, the girl tells a priest of the miracle. He thinks that she has been hallucinating until he sees a coin clutched in her hand that the soldier had taken with him overseas.

Warner Bros. hoped that *Miracle in the Rain* would appeal to audiences eager to believe that love never dies. Van's character is amusing, tender, full of dreams. Aware of his long-standing success in wide-eyed juvenile parts, Warner executives counted on a combination of Johnson's wartime image and his recently demonstrated ability in more mature roles to make the mawkish *Miracle in the Rain* appealing and convincing. Jane Wyman had enjoyed enormous success the year before in the highly sentimental *Magnificent Obsession,* and Universal had already cast her in the equally maudlin *All That Heaven Allows.* Stories with a religious theme were popular during the 1950s, and the thinking was that if *Miracle in the Rain* were released at the right time, Warner Bros. might have a major success on its hands. "I've always felt that the faith theme of *Miracle in the Rain* might mean extra dollars to the company if the picture were released, at least in some key situations, between Thanksgiving and the first of the year," producer Frank Rosenberg wrote in a memo to Jack Warner. "Frequently, as you know, the very atmosphere of the moment makes the public more receptive to a particular type of story."

Van and Evie were put up in a suite in the Hotel Pierre, overlooking Central Park, while *Miracle in the Rain* was being made, and they had a car and chauffeur at their disposal. Johnson and Wyman rehearsed with Maté for a week before shooting on the picture began. During that time Wyman was surprised to learn that her costar could handle drama as adeptly as he did comedy. "Van could play both ends of the piano," the actress said. "He was a fun person, but there were all kinds of wonderful facets to his personality."

When Johnson had read Hecht's story in the *Saturday Evening Post* years before, he told his friend Robert Walker that he should play the soldier in *Miracle in the Rain,* since it was the kind of role that Walker did so well. By the time the film was made, Walker was dead after having developed a chronic drinking problem and suffering severe bouts of depression. "I thought of him every day when I was working on that set," Van said.

Several scenes in *Miracle in the Rain* were shot in Central Park, while the New York police department kept a curious gallery of fans from interrupting the crew as they worked. Warner Bros. made a donation to St. Patrick's Cathedral and in return secured permission to use the sanctuary of the church for filming after ten o'clock at night. For a full week the company worked in the cathedral between midnight and dawn, mostly in front of St. Andrew's altar, using added lighting to brighten the interior. To create convincing rain for the movie, sidewalk hydrants were tapped and a steady shower was aimed at the great cathedral doors while scenes were played.

The cathedral's organ was heard in the film, and the St. Patrick's Boys Choir supplied the choral work for the last part of the picture. Since Hollywood studios discovered in the 1950s that a title song was a good way to publicize movies, Johnson and Wyman recorded "I'll Always Believe in You" for the soundtrack, and the record was released under the name "Miracle in the Rain."

Shooting on the picture proceeded with remarkable speed and was completed on July 7, 1955, six days ahead of schedule. Van had managed to take a few days off from location work to visit his father in Rhode Island, and once *Miracle in the Rain* wrapped, he and Evie left from New York to spend the summer in Europe. They attended the film festival at Cannes, visited Paris, and did not return to Beverly Hills until early fall.

Meanwhile, Warner Bros. prepared a publicity campaign to launch *Miracle in the Rain,* taking out advertisements in such women's magazines as *McCall's, Redbook,* and *Ladies' Home Journal* and holding a national "A Miracle Can Happen to You" contest. Since Jane Wyman played a lonely stenographer in the picture, thirty-two secretaries, winners of the "Miracle Can Happen" contest in various cities, were brought to Hollywood for a three-day, all-expense-paid tour, during which they met movie stars and were feted in a royal manner. Producer Frank Rosenberg thought *Miracle in the Rain* merited special attention from the studio. "For all I know," Rosenberg said, "the picture may turn out to be a resounding bust, but at least we ought to give it a chance to catch on instead of releasing it in a routine way."

When the movie reached the theaters in April 1956, it received lukewarm notices and played to generally small audiences. The *St. Louis Post-Dispatch* dismissed the film as a "tearjerker that is as unabashed as any we've encountered." Most critics conceded that Johnson and Wyman gave strong performances and were ideally matched. "Together they are in true emotional balance," the *Los Angeles Examiner* reported. "No one can give more of himself than Van." Both stars were disappointed in the film's poor box-office showing, but Johnson still commanded some of his old following. After members of the Los Angeles chapter of the National Secretaries' Association saw the picture, they voted that Van would make the perfect boss. "He's genial and full of spirit and has a soothing voice," the organization's president said, "and he's cute, too."

While vacationing in Palm Springs after the completion of *Miracle in the Rain,* Johnson announced that he was again considering a nightclub act. This time he would perform at the Hotel Fontainebleau in Miami Beach and possibly the National Hotel in Havana. Neither Van nor Evie precisely understood their family's overall economic situation, since a business manager took care of their monetary affairs. "There is a certain arrogance about having a lack of knowledge where financial matters are concerned," Ned Wynn later wrote. Van contended that he had always been conservative with money, and to a great degree that statement was true. "I'm really a hamburger and a glass of beer type guy," he said. Yet he was always quick to pick up checks when dining out with friends, much to Eve's disgust. Far worse, he had been talked into investing in some oil leases and tax shelters that eventually proved unprofitable.

In the fall of 1955 Van spent two weeks in Tucson and Nogales, Arizona, working on *The Bottom of the Bottle,* a grim story in which Johnson plays an alcoholic who has broken out of prison and is trying to reach his wife and children. "I'll do anything to go in a different direction every time," Van said of his realistic role. "It's very important to keep audiences surprised." *The Bottom of the Bottle* was a Twentieth Century–Fox film, made as Darryl Zanuck was preparing to leave the studio as production head. Johnson found working for Fox pleasant and admired Henry Hathaway, who directed the picture. "Hathaway doesn't miss a trick," Van said. "He's a rock of Gibraltar." But the veteran director disliked *The Bottom of the Bottle* and complained later that the studio's main purpose in making it was to get rid of some old commitments. "Joseph Cotton and Van Johnson as brothers didn't go very well," Hathaway said. "Neither did Van's playing that kind of hard-bitten guy, who should have been acted by a John Garfield or a Humphrey Bogart. It was a good story and could have been a lot better, but you just didn't believe the people in the film."

Audiences were not used to seeing Van Johnson as a man driven to such desperation, although he seemed highly effective in a scene where he spoke tearfully to his destitute family. *Variety* said that Johnson turned in "an earnest, sincere performance," but *The Bottom of the Bottle* was released with no major buildup and did not do well in the theaters. "Consequently most people were unaware that Van did a magnificent job of acting in it," Evie said.

Twentieth Century–Fox then considered Johnson for the lead in *Boy on a Dolphin,* but Alan Ladd ultimately got the role. Van was interested in the picture primarily because it was to be shot in the Greek Islands. "I'm a gypsy," he said. "After I'm home two days, I'm wild to go somewhere." Without MGM as an anchor, Van seemed to be growing more restive. "I am location mad," he said. "What other way can you see the world so well?" It got to the point that he would not even read a script unless the picture was scheduled to be made at a foreign location.

Johnson hoped that he would be sent to London when he agreed to make *23 Paces to Baker Street* for Twentieth Century–Fox, but only a camera crew went to England. "I've gotten myself into more pictures because they were going on location," Van said, "then found that only the second unit goes out, and I get stuck at the studio." In *23 Paces to Baker Street,* he plays a blind playwright who stumbles onto a kidnap scheme, and again Henry Hathaway was the director. The picture's plot was exciting, particularly after the playwright that Van plays goes sleuthing and puts his own life in jeopardy. Johnson turned in a mature portrayal as a man who chafes under his blindness, feels useless despite his professional success, and is peevish and resentful. "Johnson gives a high-strung, perceptive performance," the *Mirror-News* reported. Yet the thriller's box-office returns were slight.

In public Eve remained her husband's strongest booster. "Without a doubt," she said, "Van's performance in *23 Paces to Baker Street* is one of his greatest." As for herself, Evie claimed to be thoroughly absorbed in her home and family. "Van is king of his castle and his castle is home," she told *Photoplay.* "He is the foremost ruler of all time. He is so much stronger than I. . . . I couldn't stand a weakling, so I secretly delight in his aggressive, no-nonsense approach." Yet there were times, she said, when she felt like shaking her husband for his lack of aggressiveness in making demands that would increase his power within the industry. "Van has achieved stature with everyone except himself," Eve told reporters. "It's as if the actor, Van Johnson, were a separate entity—a symbol, totally unrelated to him."

From the outside the Johnson marriage appeared to have settled into an agreeable relationship, and both partners strove to keep up the image. "When we're alone," Evie told fan-magazine writers, "we never stop talking. We don't need people. After a good dinner, we can sit in front of the fire and talk, become stimulated, interrupt each other with thoughts, opinions, and new ideas until the late hour precipitates contented yawns and we trundle off to bed, full of the richness of togetherness." Van continued to take the children to church every Sunday when he was in Los Angeles and seemed to have found a stable home life. His fame had endured despite the collapse of the big studio system and the loss of the country-club atmosphere that had enveloped Tinseltown a decade earlier.

"Van is completely honest," said Evie; "he can't say anything he doesn't mean. He only acts when he has to. He's for real—a human being without a facade." Yet so much of the Johnsons' life was a facade, built on dishonesty and subterfuge. Within a year stories would appear in the tabloids that smeared Van's reputation. His confidence, never strong, was shattered by the shabby treatment he received in scandal sheets that attacked Hollywood stars with as much innuendo as fact. Furthermore, his popularity began declining, which hurt Van more than he was willing to admit. The bobby-soxers who used to squeal his name had become matrons with children of their own and viewed him as a reminder of their youth. Van feared that more bad publicity could cause him to lose his following and all he had worked for, yet he tried to maintain a brave front and contrive an air of self-assurance. "Since playing this part of a blind man," Johnson said after *23 Paces to Baker Street* was finished, "I often think how we take for granted the sunset and sunrise. We are so lucky." Privately, he feared that his luck had run out, and the disconnect between his moody temperament and his sunny public image widened.

Van courted his public and needed its affection. He knew that he must let go of his old image yet was uncertain about what direction he should take to make himself viable to a new generation. He hated to make decisions and missed more than ever having paternalistic studio executives to do his thinking for him. "I procrastinate and vacillate," Johnson said. He had signed the five-year deal with Columbia for a hefty fee per picture but balked at the first script the company offered him, and the studio terminated the agreement. "I think it's the exciting part of this business," Van told reporters, "this blowing hot and cold, the dark and the light, the ups and downs." But the insecurities of freelance acting frightened him. Although not yet desperate, by early 1956 Johnson was willing to do almost anything to resuscitate his sagging career.

That January he reported to Universal-International for *Kelly and Me,* a throwback to the musicals of the 1930s, with Van playing a second-rate vaudevillian. Kelly was the dog his character used in his act, and the picture was directed by MGM veteran Robert Z. Leonard, whom Van and other Metro employees called "Pop." "Johnson is quite good as the corn-ball entertainer and performs a few song-and-dance numbers with ease and charm," the *Motion Picture Herald* said of Van's performance in *Kelly and Me.* The star earned a percentage of the profits, but the film was judged old-fashioned and mediocre and did not make big money.

Later in 1956 Johnson returned to Metro for *Slander* on a one-picture arrangement, but even producer Armand Deutsch later admitted that the movie was labored and flat. Van could relate to the film's theme, since *Slander* deals with the effects of a *Confidential*-type magazine story on a rising television personality's private life and career. In the movie Johnson plays a young puppeteer who is chosen to star on a network children's program. Just as the performer begins to achieve success, the editor of a slanderous magazine discovers that the puppeteer had served a prison term for armed assault in his youth. The editor threatens to print the story unless Van's character informs on a bigger celebrity whom the puppeteer had known as a boy. When he refuses, the budding television star is exposed and his career is ruined.

During the time Van was at Metro making *Slander,* Elvis Presley was shooting *Jailhouse Rock* on the next soundstage. For the studio's former heartthrob, Elvis's presence seemed to symbolize the changes that had taken place in Hollywood as well as the shift in public taste. *Slander* would be Van's last feature film made in California for the next four years.

Evie had purchased a home in Palm Springs while her husband was away on an assignment, and with film offers slowing down, the two of them spent much of their free time replacing furniture in the new house and painting the interior. Johnson continued to enjoy his artwork and passed on some of his knowledge to Tracy and Schuyler. But money became more of a concern when the government demanded $117,000 from the Johnsons for additional income tax. Van and Evie were both big spenders: they were fond of antiques, drove Cadillacs, and by the mid-1950s had two homes to maintain and three children in private schools. To maintain the lifestyle to which they were accustomed, Van needed to keep working.

Anxious about money and his draw as a performer, Van began watching his diet and more seriously considering offers from television producers. He had already made guest appearances on Lucille Ball's and Loretta Young's weekly shows, and in late 1957 he starred in *The Pied Piper of Hamelin,* an NBC special that was later shown in a few movie theaters. In 1959 he would appear in "Deadfall" on *Dick Powell's Zane Grey Theater,* but he lost the part of Eliot Ness on *The Untouchables* when Evie insisted that he hold out for more money. Desi Arnaz, the show's executive producer, replaced Van with Robert Stack. "I went to costuming," said Stack, and "found a tailor greeting me with the 1930 suits already cut for Van Johnson." When the series soared to popularity, Van realized the mistake he had made.

With Europe becoming more and more active in moviemaking, the Johnsons decided to take advantage of a current tax break and move to England for a time. They sailed for Europe on the *Queen Elizabeth* in the summer of 1957 and settled in London in a flat at 44 Mount Street in the heart of the Mayfair district. The children were enrolled in a tutorial school, and Van began making *Action of the Tiger* with a British film crew. Ned later said that it had not occurred to him that Van's career was faltering. "We still had plenty of money," the older Wynn boy recalled, "and no one seemed to be worried." But Ned was growing up personally alienated and unstrung, not really comfortable with either Van or Eve. "Sometimes I'd actually go to class," he said of his months in England, "but most times I'd only go for an hour and spend the rest of the time riding around London on the buses or the Underground."

Action of the Tiger was a poor melodrama, directed by Terrence Young and costarring Martine Carol. Van was miscast as a tough soldier of fortune, and the poor casting combined with a fuzzy plot to give the movie comic overtones. *Variety* was kind when it noted, "Johnson never entirely convinces as the adventurous American who fights his way out of trouble with brawny fists." And the picture died in the theaters.

The Last Blitzkrieg was filmed in 1958 entirely in Holland, mostly at Cinetone Studios in Amsterdam, with Arthur Dreifuss directing. Sam Katzman produced the picture on a modest budget for release in the United States through Columbia. Van plays the son of one of Hitler's top generals, even more of a miscasting than his role in *Action of the Tiger.* His character is a Nazi spy, well schooled in English and American customs, who is disguised as an American and sent behind Allied lines to commit acts of sabotage. "Johnson," according to *Motion Picture Herald,* "is a bit hard to take as a confirmed Nazi."

Van and Evie considered putting their home in Beverly Hills up for sale and buying a place in Connecticut, essentially midway between Hollywood and Europe. They decided instead to spend a year in Switzerland. "We talked about it for some time before we actually moved there with Schuyler," Van said. "I suppose we both thought it would be a good time for regrouping ourselves and maybe even save our floundering lives together." Johnson claimed that he was "fed up with Hollywood," tired of being typecast, and wanted out of the routine he was in. But his attempts at finding different movie roles were not succeeding at the box office.

Ten-year-old Schuyler was becoming confused by their unsettled life, and the Wynn boys, in varying degrees, were growing up anxious and resentful. Aware that his career and marriage were crumbling, Van himself seemed on the edge of a nervous breakdown. Yet he tried to project the role he played best—the easygoing, lighthearted Van Johnson. "At first it seemed wonderful," he said of living in Switzerland. "The scenery was fabulous. We'd have dinner one night with Deborah Kerr and Peter Viertel, then with Audrey Hepburn and Mel Ferrer. I played tennis every day with Charlie Chaplin. I sent smoke signals from Alp to Alp to Paulette Goddard." But Van later admitted that the scenery soon started to close in on him. "One morning I woke up and the mountains were at the foot of my bed," he said.

Schuyler lived with her parents on the shores of Lake Lemans, near Geneva, while Ned was sent to a boys' school in Zermatt. The students at his school mainly were children of European and Asian millionaires, and many of them were misfits. Ned maintained that the place was "really just a skiing club for spoiled brats." Tracy went to school in Gstaad. "It was great speaking French and meeting all those incredible jet-setters," the younger Wynn recalled. "Meeting them, but not necessarily liking them." Meanwhile, Eve talked about suing Keenan to set up trust funds for their two sons.

Van had learned a smattering of French, but he never fit comfortably into the European lifestyle. He was invited aboard Aristotle Onassis's yacht, the *Christina*, where he met Winston Churchill and visited with Greta Garbo, and saw old friends and made new ones in Switzerland. He dodged autograph seekers, whom he seemed to detect before they even appeared. Sometimes he was nice when fans invaded his privacy, but sometimes he exploded. "Or he could do his middle-ground, controlled-furious sarcastic attitude," Ned said.

What troubled Van most and caused him to become irritable was that there was so little going on in his life. "I was simply bored to death most of the time," he later admitted. He soon grew desperate for something to do. "I was terribly unhappy," Van said, and "was running away from everything. The marriage was bad and so was my outlook." The cost of living in Switzerland was expensive, and he was not working. He quickly realized that he had made an almost fatal mistake as far as his career was concerned by moving to Europe. "I found out the hard way," Johnson said, "out of sight, out of mind. You have to be where the action is. The phone didn't ring for me."

A whole new generation had come along since Van's heyday at MGM. Many young people knew him only from television late, late shows. When Edward Dmytryk requested Johnson for a role in a film at Twentieth Century–Fox in 1959, the director was told by studio executives that Van Johnson was box-office poison. Van heard about the remark and agonized over the slight but had no notion of how to reverse the tide.

Depressed, he accepted whatever offers came his way. *Subway in the Sky* (1959), for example, was a suspense drama set in postwar Germany. The black-and-white film was made in England, with Hildegarde Neff as Van's costar, and contained a passable number of stock thrills for audiences. "Johnson goes through his beset role with standard competence," *Film Daily* remarked. *Web of Evidence* (also 1959), based on A. J. Cronin's novel *Beyond This Place,* was filmed in Liverpool and New Brighton and costarred Vera Miles. Directed by Jack Cardiff, the melodrama has Van as the American son of a man sent to prison in Great Britain for a crime he did not commit. Johnson delivered an honest performance, but the plot is confusing.

The Enemy General was another Sam Katzman production, made in France and Italy for release through Columbia. George Sherman, a Hollywood old-timer who specialized in action movies, directed the suspense drama, Jean-Pierre Aumont costarred, and Van played an American OSS officer during World War II. In the film Johnson joins Aumont, playing a French resistance leader, to rescue a Nazi general who is ready to defect to the Allies. Van's performance is compelling, yet *The Enemy General* did slim business when it was released in October 1960 and quickly vanished from the theaters.

Disappointed with the results of his recent professional efforts, Van grew distant and withdrawn in his private life. The strain affected his relationship with Evie, and he turned violent. Ned recalled hearing muffled shouts and a scream one night. "I lie in bed remembering similar sounds from years before," Ned said. "But I'm older now, and I know what it is. This time it's stepfathers and mothers." Wynn heard a second shout that night, this time from Van. There was a crash, and the boy sat up in bed. "Later I learn that he has thrown my mother over a table and onto the floor," Ned wrote. "Then he has thrown a chair at her."

Ned Wynn remembered several big rows between Van and his mother over the years, but some of the biggest apparently took place in Europe. "I had never been present," Ned said, "and only knew about them later when Schuyler told me." Once Van hit Schuyler so hard that the girl slammed into a wall. "No one talked about these things," Ned said. "They were never discussed. Van was very big and very frightening, and he was the star, the guy making the bucks, the guy with the career that we had to protect."

Tired of Europe and exasperated with Van, Evie returned to the United States with Schuyler. "I wanted to get back to California and my home and my friends," Eve said. She soon announced an official separation from her husband. Van stayed in Europe, hoping for work. He later told Hedda Hopper that it broke his heart when Evie pulled Schuyler out of school in Switzerland without his knowledge. "She was doing so well with French," he said, "was riding horses and skiing."

Ned remembered his stepfather coming to Zermatt to fetch him after Evie went to California. When Van arrived in the Swiss village, Ned was surprised that he was alone. "I found that in the mountains Van was different from the way he was at home or even in London," Ned recalled in his book. "He was entirely relaxed. He seemed happiest now when he was away from the family; for one thing the duties of husband and father, something he had prized so much a few years earlier, had become onerous to him." Johnson had had the wife, the family, and the big house, but none of those things seemed to possess the allure they once had. "It was no longer what Van wanted or needed in his life," Ned said. "Being away from it he could ease up. And I think that while he truly loved us, he could only take us in short bursts and then only one at a time."

In Zermatt, Ned skied with Van, proudly ordered dinners in German, and for a brief time felt like his stepfather's friend. "Van was always a tremendous faker," Ned said, "pretending he was glad to see you when he wasn't. But here he was genuine, unguarded, at ease." The two of them remained in Zermatt for two weeks, then went to Geneva and boarded a plane for the United States, where Van was to make some television appearances. The aircraft stopped in Copenhagen, and Ned decided that he would like to stay in Denmark for a while and look around. Van gave his stepson some additional money and left the boy behind. "I never saw him that happy again," Ned said.

Wynn had no concept of the pressure Van faced or how the rapid decline in professional stature devastated him. The mask of Van Johnson, movie star, concealed most of the insecurities and apprehensions that lay inside the frightened star. "He was an actor," Ned said. "Appearing to be what he was not was his job, after all." Van played the part well, but through the years the burden had grown heavy. He had become more short-tempered, curt, and sarcastic when not on public display, with a growing need to put Evie down. He referred to her as the "mother of all living things," and while his rancor was often cloaked in humor, the intensity of his anger was becoming too much for Eve to tolerate.

Shortly after returning to their home in Beverly Hills, she filed for divorce in the superior court in Santa Monica, charging her husband with unspecified acts of extreme cruelty and causing her "grievous mental suffering." Six weeks later Eve filed suit against Keenan Wynn for more than thirty thousand dollars, accusing him of "fraud and breach of contract" in their property settlement and of failing to pay the designated child support. Evie claimed that she was too upset to talk about her split from Van but told reporters that he had rented a flat with one bedroom in Switzerland and did not expect her to return.

Van lived alone in Europe for six months. He gave up drinking and went on a junket with a number of other celebrities to open Hilton Hotels in Cairo and Athens. Yet offers for work were few, and those he received were disappointing. "When you hide out like I did," Johnson later said, "the telephone stops ringing because no one knows you're around." He told Hedda Hopper that he and Evie had had only three happy years together, yet the solitude of life in a foreign country without her and the children soon caused him to ache with loneliness and depression. "What's the good of having a million dollars in a drawer in Switzerland," he said, "if you can't be with your family and eat an American hot dog once in a while?"

With nothing more pressing to occupy his time, Van attended the Cannes film festival, where he saw eighteen movies in fourteen days. "It made me feel a part of things again," Johnson said, "however vicariously." One night he spotted Shelley Winters and Rita Gam in a restaurant. Winters waved to him and shouted over the crowd, "What's with the Swiss bit?" Van joined the two actresses and explained his situation to them. "Why don't you do a Broadway play?" Winters asked. The thought registered with Van and had some appeal.

He walked back to his hotel a few nights later, and on the desk in his room was a letter from Ben Segal, an American producer, who wanted Johnson for a production of *Damn Yankees* in a summer theater in Wallingford, Connecticut. Johnson decided to accept the offer. "My hand shook as I wrote Segal," he said. Van remembered the torment of facing a live audience, and this would be theater-in-the-round, an even more terrifying experience. Yet he took comfort in the knowledge that Wallingford is a long way from Hollywood and outside the spectrum of major critics. "I knew I had to start my life again somewhere," he said, "and this was the only offer I had."

Van flew to New York in June 1960 and called Evie. She agreed to meet with him in Manhattan to talk things over. "New York never looked so beautiful," Van said later. "Even the taxi drivers were friendly." He and Eve made an attempt to patch up their differences, and she agreed to withdraw the divorce action and began helping him learn his lines for *Damn Yankees.*

When Johnson met with reporters in their hotel suite, he seemed almost as eager and youthful as when he was the freckled-faced heartthrob of the early 1940s. "I'm too American to stay in Europe," he told the assembled press. "I expect to live here and do a Broadway show." With Eve back at his side, some of the Van Johnson bravado of Metro days appeared to return. "Today I think you have to go where the work is," he said. "I'm going to play it by ear now." But he also knew deep inside that his personal life was wrong. His marriage was a charade. The tension and bitterness he and Evie had each harbored for years was ready to ignite. All that was needed was an external force, little more than a seductive gleam, and their imitation marriage would be finished.

CHAPTER 8

Holding Together

Van's performances in *Damn Yankees* in Wallingford proceeded shakily but adequately for three weeks. His fee was $7,500 a week, almost a match for the $8,000 a week he had been making during his final Metro years. After Wallingford he waited for movie offers, but none came. Van and Evie spent a great deal of time at their place in Palm Springs, but their relationship remained uneasy. Lying out by the pool one day, Johnson realized that he would be forty-five years old in August. "If you don't start doing something now," he told himself, "you never will."

His experience with *Damn Yankees,* while not altogether satisfactory, gave him courage. When Van learned that a cast was being assembled for a production of *The Music Man* in London, he asked to audition. "I hadn't had to beg for a chance like this since I understudied Gene Kelly in *Pal Joey* twenty-odd years ago," Johnson said. He had seen the Meredith Willson musical on Broadway with Robert Preston in the lead and knew that the role of Professor Harold Hill, a traveling salesman working the territory around River City, Iowa, was ideal for him.

The Music Man was in its fourth year at the Majestic Theater in New York, the biggest hit on Broadway since *My Fair Lady* opened in 1956. British impresario Max Bygraves flew to America three times to see the show and hoped to produce the musical in England, changing a couple of lines to make the Midwestern con man in the title come from London rather than New York. But Meredith Willson objected to having his show tampered with, and Bygraves was eventually outbid for the British rights by his friend Harold Fielding, who eventually presented *The Music Man* in London in association with Kermit Bloomgarden, the show's original producer. Willson, Fielding, and Bloomgarden agreed to cast Van Johnson in the name part, even though it would be the star's first appearance on the British stage.

The London production of *The Music Man* would be a close copy of what audiences had enjoyed in New York, although English audiences were not expected to respond to the musical's nostalgia with the same intensity that Americans did. After a short provincial run that began in Bristol, the production opened before an enthusiastic audience at the Adelphi Theatre in London's West End on March 16, 1961. British critics welcomed the old-fashioned show with reservations but predicted that the musical would be a popular success and that the Adelphi Theatre would be filled for a long time with people eager to buy tickets.

"Not since Danny Kaye last visited the Palladium or the Pied Piper made his deal in Hamelin," the *London Daily Telegraph* reported, "has music worked more potent magic." The critical consensus was that Van Johnson brought enormous vigor to the title role, but several reviewers objected to the show's false innocence. *The Daily Mirror* said that Van played Harold Hill "with the absorbed air of a man trying on a new suit," yet the reviewer maintained that "the result is still a tormenting evening in the theatre" and said that he hated the music. "Van Johnson sings the hero as becomes a man who hardly knows one note of music from another," the *London Times* recorded, "but has the salesmanship to start a tune which more natural singers take up with a will." Although English audiences seemed enchanted with Willson's sentimental portrait of the simple life of yesteryear in the American heartland, the critic for *Queen* found *The Music Man* a "really far-out example of the conspicuous waste upon which the form, like many other aspects of the American economy, now depends. The musical long ago reached the limit of necessary noise, energy, optimism, and naïveté, the four cardinals of the genre, but more and more is still being added, like fins to American cars."

Van's notices were mostly positive, even though *The Tatler* noted that he seemed to be scant of breath in the dances, which were performed at breakneck speed, and the *London Sunday Telegraph* remarked that he could "hardly have been chosen for his voice." By general agreement the "Shipoopi" number was the production's brightest spot, and Van was not part of it. Reviewers generally judged Johnson's performance to be perky, attractive, and good enough but lightweight rather than spellbinding. Audiences, conversely, loved him. "With the British it's once a star, always a star," Van said. "I never felt so popular."

In the United States, Johnson's London performances were hailed as an unqualified personal triumph. Van later claimed that his success in *The Music Man* helped him to overcome his fear of live audiences and changed his life as a performer. "The stage is a lot harder than motion pictures," he said. "You've got to go on every day. But it's more stimulating and rewarding, especially when the audience smashes you with applause." He found satisfaction in contact with live audiences and learned to relate to them in an intimate way. "You can't entertain from atop an ivory tower," he said.

Although appearing in *The Music Man* for a year in London was stimulating, it also was exhausting. Van thought that Meredith Willson must have wondered, "Now how can I write a part that will tax a leading man to the extreme." Johnson got his timing back for stage performances, and the musical did much to restore his professional confidence. As an English schoolgirl, his leading lady, twenty-six-year-old Pat Lambert, had idolized Van, and he came to admire her and the British lifestyle. "It's such a gentle existence," Johnson said. "They take time to live."

Evie, Schuyler, and Tracy were in London with Van, and in April the Johnsons moved out of the Claridge Hotel and rented a three-bedroom flat in Bayswater from local television personality Edana Romney. They left the flat after a week and moved into smaller quarters in Kensington. In September, Romney sued the Johnsons for unpaid rent. "My husband

and I are prepared to go to court if necessary over this dispute," Evie told a reporter for the *Daily Mail*.

But a far bigger altercation took place in mid-September 1961, when Van removed his clothes from the apartment in which they were living and left Eve, determined to seek a divorce. This time their parting was permanent. "Van picked the fight that led to our separation," said Evie, and "he gave the first statement to the press." She went to Rome, where Van sent a lawyer to talk to her. "He wanted to know how much I would need to live on," Eve said. "Van can have a divorce if he wants one."

She returned to Beverly Hills in January 1962 and told her son, Ned, then a student at the University of California in Berkeley, that Van no longer wanted to be married. "I finally gave my mother some attention," Ned later wrote, "and realized that for one of the few times in her life, she was showing me the face of her own pain. She was telling me something vital." Van had left her for the lead dancer in *The Music Man*. "A man," Evie told her son. "A boy really. He's the lead boy dancer." Ned's emotions were so confused by the report that he almost missed the point. "I saw [Van] once," Eve said to Ned. "Through a window in the theater. He was with another man, his dresser, that time. But he left with this dancer—this young boy." Ned did not know how to respond to the news. "I never listened," Evie continued. "Laird Cregar told me. Laird told me years ago. And Henry Hathaway told me. I didn't listen. I thought it was just rumors."

Ned realized that he really did not want to know the details of his stepfather's sex life or of Van's rejection of his mother. "My curiosity just evaporated," Wynn said. "I felt as though it were inevitable that Van should leave her." So the marriage had ended—what of it? "Screw him," said Ned, still in his smart-aleck phase. "He's an asshole." Evie explained that she had thought she could change Van, make him what she wanted him to be, cause him to be completely straight. But Ned felt distant from the whole situation. "It was beginning to dawn on me," Wynn wrote, "that I was a guest and had always been a guest, wherever I had lived."

Van moved into the Connaught Hotel in London, a glorified theatrical boardinghouse that served good food. He ran into Rex Harrison in the lobby there one day, visited David Niven, and spent time with Binnie Barnes and her husband, Mike Frankovich. On weekends the Gilbert Millers invited Johnson to their home. "No more marriage for me," Van said. "Once was enough. I just figure it wasn't in the cards for me." He did not mind the English climate and spent Christmas that year with Ivan and Lady Foxwell, a British producer and his wife, at their farmhouse outside Bristol. Cary Grant came to see *The Music Man* while he was in London, and Van visited Beatrice Lillie at her home on the Thames. He seemed happy, free of the old burdens and without some of the old insecurities, yet he remained thankful for the stature and fame that motion pictures had given him. Hollywood had been good to Van, and he had few regrets about the movies he had made or the pretense with which he had lived. Now he was ready for a different lifestyle and ready to explore new professional challenges. "I take care of myself," he said. "I don't stay up late. I eat the right food and think good thoughts."

How long Van's relationship with the boy dancer lasted is not recorded. Although Johnson's orientation was probably more homosexual than heterosexual, Van most likely was one of those people that Eros did not arouse deeply. He certainly came from a generation that did not see sexual preference as the most essential part of its being. Van was not immune to the charms of women and would have resented being labeled in facile ways that might diminish or limit him. Yet with advancing age, his sexual ambiguity shifted markedly toward an attraction for young men, who reminded him of his youth and reinforced his boyish appetites and demeanor.

During one performance of *The Music Man* in London, Van raised his left hand in the opening scene to wave good-bye to the fellow actors on stage and caught his finger in the door of a prop train, severing the tip of his middle finger. He staggered off the stage and collapsed in the wings as the curtain came down five minutes after the show began. Van was taken to his dressing room, where a tourniquet was applied, then driven to Charing Cross Hospital. While the performance continued with his understudy, Johnson lay in the hospital in stage makeup. Finally he asked, "What are we waiting for?" A doctor replied, "We're waiting for your finger to come over from the Adelphi Theatre." Sure enough, a stagehand had been sent to retrieve the end of his finger and bring it to the hospital, where doctors grafted it back on.

"I have been shutting this door every night for 219 performances," Van told the press. "Tonight on the 220th, I had to catch my finger. When I got off the stage I just blacked out." The next night he was in too much pain to go on stage. "I gather the graft has not taken as well as they expected," Johnson told reporters. He did not return to the show for two weeks, during which time producer Harold Fielding grew uneasy about the length of Johnson's recovery and Van received no salary. "Since I've been off I haven't had a phone call from Mr. Fielding or his office," Johnson told the *Daily Mirror*. "If the producers want me out, I wish they would say so. . . . All I want to do is get back, finish my contract, and get out of here." When the star finally did return to *The Music Man*, a big welcome awaited him at the theater. Van finished his contract in March 1962, but he brought legal proceedings against Fielding, alleging negligence at the time of his accident. "It seems a miracle that the finger has healed," Johnson said.

Meanwhile Evie, full of bitterness, complained in Beverly Hills that she was without funds to meet living expenses for herself and Schuyler. She said that she owed $1,100 in grocery bills and prepared to sue her husband for separate maintenance. Eve asked for alimony and child support of $5,000 a month and stated that Van had grossed approximately $250,000 in 1961. She knew the amount because she served as her husband's business adviser. Johnson maintained that he knew nothing of his business affairs because everything he made went to a manager for distribution. "I'm not very bright about business," Van said, "and I make no bones about it. I'm an actor."

Johnson returned to the United States on the *Queen Elizabeth* after completing his contract with Fielding. Van stayed in New York for a few days to make some television appearances and returned to Los Angeles in April 1962 for a four-week run in *The Music Man* at the Cocoanut Grove in the Ambassador Hotel. Janet Leigh and a party of forty people were in the audience for opening night, as were June Allyson, Keenan Wynn, Rosalind Russell, Jack Benny, Peter Lawford, and directors Mervyn LeRoy and George Sidney. Sandy Descher, the former child star who had worked with Johnson in *The Last Time I Saw Paris,* saw Van on stage at one of the Los Angeles performances and started to cry. "We always cry when we get together," Descher said.

When Ned Wynn came to see the show, Van reserved a ringside table for his stepson. "He was great as always," Ned said. "To me he was the quintessential Professor Harold Hill, larger than life, an amiable, ambling giant, the man who could span the universe in three strides and sweep me up in his arms those eons ago." Van and Ned ate supper together after the performance and talked about everything except Evie and Schuyler. "Why he left, the breakup of our home, all that was not mentioned," Ned said. "It was as if he were on the road, and we just met up and chatted."

Rehearsal time for the Cocoanut Grove's production of *The Music Man* had been limited, and Van was clearly nervous about his homecoming. He perspired a great deal at the opening performance and was pleased but shaken by the gala audience that turned out to greet him. Critics said that Johnson's portrayal of Harold Hill was more subdued than that of either Robert Preston or Forrest Tucker, who played the role in the national company, but that the contrast was interesting and that Van sang and danced well. Johnson gained assurance as the engagement at the Ambassador Hotel progressed, and he finished the run there quite successfully.

Van spent time with Schuyler while he was in California. He took her to church and ate pancakes and drove along the beach with her afterward. He waited in a courtroom with Evie while their attorneys conferred with a judge, but neither of them spoke or looked at the other. Van sold four thousand dollars worth of stock to apply to Eve's separate maintenance expenses and was informed by the court that it was his responsibility to keep up mortgage payments on the home in Beverly Hills and the place Eve had bought in Palm Springs.

Johnson devoted the summer of 1962 to touring with *The Music Man* on the straw hat circuit, starting in Warren, Ohio. The performances were standing room only every night and broke house records everywhere the company played. "I only wish I'd done this five years ago," Van said. "They just keep applauding and applauding. I come off the stage with tears in my eyes every night." He lost twenty pounds during the summer, lived mainly on steak and milk, and played such places as Tonowanda, New York, and Framingham, Massachusetts. "Life is just one motel and laundry bag after another," he said. "Every time I check into a new motel in the middle of the night, I think of Janet Leigh in *Psycho*."

Meanwhile, Evie stormed angrily about Van and spent a good part of her time at home bustling. She bustled in the kitchen, in the garage, in one room after another, creating jobs for herself. "While she bustled," Ned said, "Schuyler and I would sit around the house and smoke weed and laugh till the tears came. The sixties were upon us. . . . My mother dealt with the drug era as if it had never happened." Eve was still Mrs. Van Johnson, so she continued to be treated with deference in restaurants like Chasen's and the Bistro, but she was no longer invited to the most fashionable parties in Hollywood. "Something was different," Ned said. "Van was gone. Many avenues, both personal and financial, closed and remained that way."

Tracy was then attending Menlo College in northern California, but Ned and Schuyler bonded during the period of readjustment to survive the craziness around them. Evie dyed her hair blond and began wearing orange lipstick, and there seemed to be a steady stream of gay men through the house in Beverly Hills. Ned concluded that his mother must have decided that the best cure for heartbreak was homeopathy: the way to get over abandonment by a gay husband was to play hostess to other gays.

Henry Willson, the agent who had discovered Rock Hudson, "had his stable of tan young men," Ned recalled, "prancing through our house like a tiny herd of carousel ponies." They commiserated with Evie about her errant husband and drank her scotch. "In return for her feeding and watering them," Ned said, "they smiled and told her she was gorgeous, she didn't deserve such treatment, and Van was a prick." They swarmed over Schuyler like aphids, while Eve appeared unaware of their exploitation. "Our house was like a popular nightspot," said Ned. "There were parties all the time. . . . The house was thronged with young boys and their priapic, ramp-sandaled old queens, screeching and twittering in the halls or lolling around the pool."

Whenever he could, Ned fled to his father's house or spent time with friends at the beach. The boy roamed the California coast, bodysurfing and playing volleyball, sometimes sleeping on the sand or in his car. "I still lived inside the emotional skin of a child," Ned said. Eve got her older son a summer apprenticeship at the La Jolla Playhouse, but the boy showed little interest in anything that involved work. "For me," Ned said, "summer stock was another version of camp, a way of getting me out of everyone's hair. It was like a jail sentence." He wanted to stay away from the movie business and the people associated with it and felt more comfortable with songwriters and musicians. "I preferred their avant-garde attitudes, their freer society, their looser women, and their high-class dope," Ned said.

Tracy grew up in the drug generation but hated that whole lifestyle. Succumbing to peer pressure, the younger Wynn boy wore his hair down to his shoulders at one point and smoked pot at parties, but he soon shied away from the drug culture and rejected its propaganda. "Many people my age seem so damned weak," Tracy said later, "and the reason they're weak is that they've been very lazy, very nihilistic, and very indulged."

Van was reluctant to talk about Evie, Schuyler, or his stepsons, and in 1963 he confessed that he did not know where any of them were. "Don't feel sorry for me," Johnson said. "I have many friends and I'm deeply grateful to all of those who came to cheer me." Any spare time

Van had was spent at the movies, his traditional form of escape. "I could see them all day," he said. The middle-aged star now had gray in his hair but appeared to be more at peace with himself than he had been in years. "The process of growing and maturing seems to have taken me a long time," Johnson said. "I don't take myself seriously. I never did." He was still grateful for what MGM had done for him and repeatedly talked about how the studio had turned "a nobody into a somebody." Yet he had no desire to continue living in Los Angeles.

In September 1962 Van's mother died of a heart attack at her home in El Cajon, California. Loretta Neumann was seventy years old at the time. She had suffered a stroke six months earlier and on that occasion was found lying helpless beside an uncradled telephone receiver by a repairman who had been called when someone else on Loretta's party line complained about not having service. Evie maintained that Van's rejection of his wife and daughter stemmed from his intense hatred for his mother. Not only did Van refuse to have anything to do with Loretta himself, he would not let Eve take Schuyler to visit her grandmother.

In October 1962 Van appeared in a new play by Garson Kanin at the Morosco Theater on Broadway. Called *Come on Strong,* the show unfortunately came on weak and closed after a short run. Johnson had accepted the role without reading the final script, enticed in part because Carroll Baker was to be his costar but mainly by the knowledge that Kanin planned to make the comedy into a movie after it closed in New York.

The show opened during a newspaper strike in New York, which proved a mixed blessing since the reviews that appeared were not good. "It is distressing to believe that Garson Kanin could perpetrate *Come On Strong,*" Howard Taubman wrote in the *New York Times.* "It is equally incredible that actors like Carroll Baker and Van Johnson would be accessories to it. . . . If Miss Baker or Mr. Johnson can act, there is nothing in this play or performance to prove it."

Van claimed that he never read "those drama critic creeps," but the newspaper strike meant that *Come on Strong* received little advertising and consequently had few advance ticket sales. Around six o'clock each evening people started lining up for the play, much like they would for a movie, attracted mainly by the stars' names. "Van and I managed to keep it running day by day for five months," Carroll Baker said, but *Come on Strong* proved a disappointment to everyone involved.

The only positive thing to come out of the experience for Van was that producer Hal Wallis saw the show and offered him a role in his upcoming film *Wives and Lovers*. Janet Leigh would again be Johnson's costar, and John Rich, who later did many of the *All in the Family* episodes on television, directed the movie. *Wives and Lovers* would be Van's first motion picture in two years. He was hired at a weekly salary of five thousand dollars, plus expenses, and agreed to appear at Paramount Studios on January 21, 1963, for preproduction services.

Johnson stayed at the Beverly Hills Hotel while he was making *Wives and Lovers*. "Until now, there has been one Jack Lemmon," Wallis said. "Now I think I've got another one in Van. I don't know what happened to him in those years he was away, but he's come back as a superb, suave actor-comedian. That's how I intend to use his talents." In Wallis's film Johnson portrays a harassed young writer whose first novel hurls him into sudden wealth, family strife, and the arms of another woman. The script was charming and funny, and its cast included Shelley Winters, Ray Walston, and Wallis's wife, Martha Hyer. Burt Bacharach was commissioned to write a title song for the picture, and *Wives and Lovers* was viewed from the outset as an important film.

Shelley Winters and John Rich became antagonists during the making of the movie, but Van got along splendidly with everybody. "Van Johnson's smile, his positive attitude, and his upbeat personality endear him to everyone he meets," Martha Hyer said. "He's a big marmalade pussycat—professional, fun, considerate."

In March, while still working on *Wives and Lovers,* Van discovered that a blemish on his inner thigh had begun to spread. The spot was getting rough on the outside, had turned dark brown, and itched. Doctors in-

sisted that the growth must be removed, and while Rich shot around him,
Rosalind Russell accompanied Johnson to Cedars of Lebanon Hospital,
where he tested positive for skin cancer. After minor surgery, Van remained
in the hospital for another week. Russell visited him every day during his
convalesce, but neither Evie nor Schuyler came to see him. As Johnson
left the hospital, he flashed reporters a V-for-victory sign, dressed in a
bright checkered jacket and wearing red socks and black slippers.

He was soon back on the set of *Wives and Lovers*, ready for the final
week of shooting. Van never talked about his surgery to fellow workers,
nor did he complain. He finished the picture in high spirits and left for
San Francisco, where he was to appear in a stage production of *Bye Bye
Birdie*. "I'm convinced his affirmative outlook and cheerful disposition contributed to his recovery," Hyer said.

Wives and Lovers did not live up to its producer's expectations, however, and Van comes across as rather supercilious in his role. In his review,
Bosley Crowther found the picture reminiscent of the sophisticated comedies in the 1930s, when a whole school of Hollywood writers seemed to
emulate Noel Coward. "It's incredible that a screenplay as hackneyed and
witless as this one could get past a first front-office reading in this rigid
day and age," Crowther wrote of the film in the *New York Times*, "and it is
pathetic that it should be directed as woodenly as this one has been by
John Rich."

Van opened a six-week engagement in *Bye Bye Birdie* in early April
at the Sheraton Palace Theater in San Francisco, where he was well received. After the closing performance of the musical in May, Johnson was
rewarded by an outpouring of affection from the audience, and the con-
ductor and the entire cast took curtain calls wearing red socks. "It was so
touching," the show's producer wrote Hedda Hopper, "to see this much
love that it surpassed even the excitement of six sold-out weeks and a
wonderful performance by one of your best examples of what Hollywood
is and what it means to the millions and millions of real people in this
country."

Johnson spent the summer of 1963 appearing in four different musicals—*Birdie, Damn Yankees, The Music Man,* and *Guys and Dolls*—in tents and auditoriums across the country, playing in such cities as Indianapolis and Milwaukee. "I have no home," Van said. "I loathe every hour of these road tours. I'm so sick of hotel rooms. But I'm making money out of it, so why complain?" He did not want to discuss his upcoming divorce but expressed regret that he no longer heard from the two Wynn boys.

In October Johnson returned to nightclub work, opening at the Shoreham Hotel in Washington, D.C. Columnist Dorothy Kilgallen saw his act and declared it "nothing less than a sensational success." Then he went into the Latin Quarter in New York. The pace was grueling, but Van seemed to thrive on the receptions he got. "I've worked hard all my life to get where I am," he said. "I like people. I suppose working, and liking people, will keep anybody fit. The most deathly thing a man can do is to retire."

He was stunned to learn in December that he had to have another operation. This time a lymph node on his left thigh had caused concern. In January 1964 he entered Memorial Hospital in Manhattan for exploratory surgery. "They're slowly chopping me away," Johnson said. But doctors gave him the good news that there was no sign of the cancer that physicians had found ten months earlier. Still, doctors recommended that a lymph gland be removed as preventive treatment against any future recurrence. Van canceled his opening at Harrah's Club in Lake Tahoe and returned to Memorial Hospital in March for the advised surgery. Rosalind Russell sent him a pair of silk pajamas, and Van greeted reporters when the operation was over wearing the pajamas Russell had given him and his perpetual red socks. "When this thing hit me," he said, "when I first got the news in my doctor's office in Beverly Hills, my stomach spun just once, and I remember thinking that the one thing I didn't want was a Hollywood funeral." Johnson explained to the press that he was a fatalist and that after a moment of panic he accepted that the cancer had to be removed and that he must maintain a positive attitude. "They cut me wide open," he said of his second surgery, "and had me on that table for four hours. They went through me with a fine tooth comb, and I'm clean clear through."

When Van left the hospital in Manhattan, he hugged and kissed the nurses who had looked after him, then returned to a midtown hotel where there was no one except staff members to welcome him. Sad and perhaps lonelier than he had ever been in his life, he tried to keep up a courageous front. He thanked God for getting him through the cancer siege. "God has been good to me," he told the press. "It's Christmas every day and I still believe in Santa Claus. I've been very lucky. . . . I've led a charmed life."

The flowers and cards he received during his convalescence helped ease the pain of aloneness, but sustaining a good mental attitude proved to be a struggle. "You get pretty lonesome," Van admitted. "I have faith in God. Norman Vincent Peale helped me. Not many people remember the guy upstairs." He tried to keep in mind how lucky he had been. He had enjoyed the best of old Hollywood and had a good career still in front of him. Rather than focusing on his shortcomings and past mistakes, he reminded himself, he needed to become self-sufficient, believe in himself, and enjoy what lay ahead.

Of marriage Van repeatedly said, "Once was enough." Yet in 1964 he was still wearing his wedding ring. "Why shouldn't I wear it?" he said. "I'm still married to my wife." Yet he refused to talk about Evie and had little or no contact with Schuyler, which left the girl hurt and confused. "I want to thank you for writing the true things in your paper about my father and me," Van's sixteen-year-old daughter wrote to Hedda Hopper in July 1964, after the columnist had defended Eve and Schuyler in print. "I've called him and written him, but I guess he's too busy to answer me." Bruised by remarks that her father had made about her and her mother and fearful of making him angry, the girl felt abandoned. She wanted no more of his angry outbursts. "Why does he do that?" Schuyler wrote in a letter to Hopper. "I love you for standing by Mom and [me] and letting people know the truth about things."

Life was not going well for Evie financially. Ned returned to Beverly

Hills to find a chain on the front door of the house on Foothill Road and a sign tacked up indicating that the property had been condemned to satisfy a federal lien. "They took the Palm Springs house, too," Eve told her son. "They left me a car. That's all. And I'm still liable with Van for a quarter of a million dollars." Ned was shocked to find his mother taking such a defeatist attitude. "For the first time in my life I watched my mother simply shrug and shake her head," he said. "Something was different."

Divorce proceedings would drag on until 1968. Meanwhile, Eve accused her estranged husband of hiding his money in a Swiss bank, and she hired a team of lawyers to delve into the matter. Van remained secretive, even touchy, about his private life, but his bitterness toward Eve became more public and biting. He began referring to his wife as the "dreaded Evie," and she later described him as "selfish, cheap, unfeeling, and meanspirited."

Van decided to make New York his permanent home, and he eventually bought a penthouse overlooking the East River. He hired a hypnotist to help him stop smoking and said that he had learned the importance of living each day to the fullest. "Fortunately, I'm a loner," Van said. "I have my books and I paint and I ride the horses in Central Park." He also walked and went to galleries and museums. "I have to see something beautiful every day," he said, "even if it's just a child looking at a toy in a window." Watching his old movies on television sometimes caused him to laugh and scream. "Let's face it," Johnson said, "I was a male Doris Day."

Van admitted that he was happiest when he was working and looked forward to playing again to live audiences. After his surgery he resumed his nightclub tour, did *A Thousand Clowns* in Skowhegan, Maine, and made some guest appearances on television. A self-professed ham, he seemed eager to entertain crowds of any size. "I made a lot of money," he said, "and being a Yankee, it's all invested. I have my first buck, believe me. Most of it is in real estate."

Evie and Schuyler moved several times, eventually settling into a tract house in Coldwater Canyon, a modest place by Beverly Hills standards. No longer were there servants, except for a maid who came in once or twice a week. Many of Eve's former friends no longer seemed to know her, and some neglected to return her phone calls. The former Hollywood hostess who at one time appeared to hobnob with everyone of importance suddenly found herself ignored by filmland's inner circle.

In November 1964 Charles Johnson, Van's father, died at age eighty-two. Charlie had continued to live quietly in Newport and had been in poor health for some time. When he was hospitalized, Van sent him flowers and called to protest when he found out that his father was not in a private room. Van came from New York to attend his dad's funeral, which was held in St. Mary's Church in Portsmouth, Rhode Island.

Van hid his emotions by keeping busy. In February 1965 he went to Honolulu, later made a trip to Rio de Janeiro, and performed that summer on the borscht circuit, where he scored repeated successes. In the fall he returned to New York to prepare for another Broadway show, *Mating Dance*. The play opened at the O'Neill Theater in November but failed miserably. Van played a publisher in the light comedy, although critics claimed that his performance lacked conviction. "The going is so sleepy in this unfunny comedy that even the stage hands are affected," Howard Taubman reported in the *New York Times*. At the end of the first scene on opening night, leading lady Marian Hailey delivered a curtain line and left the stage, leaving Van standing alone, waiting for the curtain to fall. When it did not, he shrugged his shoulders, indicated that the scene was over, and walked into the wings. "It would have been a fine time for the rest of us to pick up the cue," Taubman said.

In the spring of 1966 Johnson was back in Hollywood to make his first feature film in three years, *Divorce American Style*, written and produced by Norman Lear. Van plays Big Al, a Southern California used-car dealer, and has love scenes with Debbie Reynolds, whom he had known at Metro. Jason Robards and Dick Van Dyke also appear in the comedy. "I loved working with that cast," said Reynolds. "It was a chance to work with Van Johnson, who was a big star when I first went to MGM. . . . Dramatically it was a good film for me." The satire had some truthful comments to make about American marriages and divorce problems, and even though Van handled his humorous supporting role adeptly, the picture did little to revive his movie career in this country, except for occasional parts arranged by old friends.

Johnson found less glamour in the Hollywood of the mid-1960s and soon went to Germany to shoot a television special. In Hamburg he spent an evening at a variety show watching jugglers, trapeze artists, singers, dancers, and magicians. "It was a tonic," Van wrote to Hedda Hopper, "and yet a little sad." He missed the nearly forgotten world of vaudeville and found himself nostalgic for the old days when life everywhere seemed simpler.

He appeared in two episodes of *Batman* on American television and appeared in the telefilm *The Doomsday Flight,* aired in 1967 on NBC. He did two pilots for series that did not sell and continued to make guest appearances on weekly shows. But the stage had become the venue Van liked best. "Funny thing," he said, "but I have a great loyal following among those gals who were bobby-soxers. They bring their own teenagers around to the stage door to say hello or to get an autograph. That's very gratifying."

Lucille Ball and Desi Arnaz hired Van in 1967 for a supporting role in their movie *Yours, Mine and Ours,* a story they had bought several years before from *Life* magazine. The couple originally had planned to star together in the film, but by the time the picture was made, they had divorced, and Henry Fonda plays opposite Ball in the comedy. Based on a real family, *Yours, Mine and Ours* deals with an ex-navy man with ten children who marries a widowed woman with eight children of her own. Director Mel Shavelson wrote the final screenplay with Mort Lachman, but during the shooting of the production Shavelson had trouble with Ball, who had grown used to running her own shows during her successful television career. "I wouldn't stand for it," the director said, "so there was a constant battle. Lucy even wanted to tell me where to put the camera."

When *Yours, Mine and Ours* proved a huge box-office success, all was forgiven, and Shavelson and Ball remained friends. Critics were less enthusiastic about the film than were general audiences, but even Renata Adler, noted for her tough reviews, admitted in the *New York Times* that Ball had funny moments in the picture and that Fonda contributed a calm presence to what otherwise seemed to be a protracted television sitcom. "Van Johnson also does his best," said Adler. "But nothing can keep this old-fashioned comedy all right."

In late 1967 Van's devoted friend Rosalind Russell recommended him for *Where Angels Go, Trouble Follows,* a sequel to the actress's highly successful *The Trouble with Angels* (1966), in which Russell played a mother superior. Van was cast in the follow-up as a priest in charge of a boys' school, but *Cue* magazine remarked that he persisted in looking at Russell in her nun's habit "with the same expression he used talking to June Allyson" back in his heyday. Like Lucille Ball, Rosalind Russell had become a keen film technician as well as a fine performer, and she knew about lighting and camera placement, although she rarely interfered the way Ball did. Russell was also a great baseball fan and spent most of her time between takes on *Where Angels Go* in her dressing room watching games on television. Unfortunately, the film did not meet its predecessor's standards.

Van went to London in early 1968 to tape a television special and enjoyed a short vacation in Lisbon before returning to the summer theater circuit in the United States. He performed in *Bells Are Ringing* with Patti Karr in Dallas and repeated the musical with Sheila MacRae elsewhere. "I'm hoofing it all the time," he said. "I just grab the money and run." When fans reminded Johnson of the many war movies he had made at Metro, he smiled and assured them that those days were over. "I believe like that song," Van said, "what the world needs is love. There's already too much war in the world for me."

Van and Eve's divorce became final in 1968, and the property settlement their lawyers worked out stipulated that she was to receive 15 percent of Van's gross income and that real estate owned by the couple was to be divided equally. He often referred to the split as the "ugliest divorce in Hollywood history" and claimed that Evie wiped him out financially. "I make out checks every week to the Dragon Lady," Johnson said, "and carry them through the snow at 4 A.M. if necessary to get them in the mail on time." But Eve claimed that Van lied about his finances and that she got practically nothing in the divorce. "He conned the judge and everyone involved," Evie wrote in 1999. "He's a fine actor off screen, in the courtroom!"

Van claimed that it had become necessary for him to live in the east because his ex-wife had instituted such financially complicated divorce proceedings in California that he could not linger in the state without facing a prolonged court battle. "I'll never get married again," he said, "and if I do, throw something at me." In the fall of 1968 the Internal Revenue Service was hounding him for back income taxes, this time for fifty-seven thousand dollars.

Johnson understood the drug culture and social unrest of the 1960s no better than Evie did. He realized that the Hollywood he knew was no more. Van disliked most current movies and missed the wholesome family pictures that he and June Allyson and Esther Williams had made at Metro. "I'll be glad when the pendulum swings back," he said. Like many of his generation, he was tired of beatnik actors and appalled at the way people dressed and behaved in public. He did not go to the theater much in New York because getting into the crowded theater district was such a hassle. When he was not performing, his life became increasingly reclusive. "In the next world," Johnson said, "I want to be a writer."

In December 1968 Van finished location work in Denver on *Company of Killers,* a CBS television feature that eventually had spasmodic bookings on double bills in theaters when the story was judged too brutal for network airing. During the making of the film Johnson had been hospitalized for ten days with influenza and a mild case of pneumonia, but he returned to the set shortly after Thanksgiving. Ray Milland, John Saxon, and Diana Lynn were also featured in the movie, in which Van played a tough cop. His role was secondary, but he handled the assignment with his customary skill and looked convincing coping with hoodlums. Van considered made-for-television movies unglamorous work and turned out too quickly for inspired results, but he remained the consummate professional. "It's a whole new business," Johnson said of the current entertainment industry. "You can do anything you want now," referring to the plethora of sex and violence that had become the norm in filmmaking.

Van much preferred the stage and the social outlets that stage work provided. He delighted in winking at "his girls," the matronly former bobbysoxers who still adored him and came to his performances in droves, and he frequently joked about his expanding weight and famous freckles in curtain speeches. "I get a dollar a freckle," Van said of his nightly fee. In public he appeared jovial, less beguilingly innocent and more openly campy and gay among fellow workers. Yet there were indications of emotional suffering and a touch of the stoic in his presence.

Ned Wynn ran into Van once when Schuyler had gone into the hospital and her father came to visit. It would be one of Johnson's last contacts with his daughter. Ned had been part of the hippie counterculture for about a year by then, and Van greeted him with, "Look at the beatnik." The three of them giggled nervously as they talked in Schuyler's hospital room. Although Sky was flustered, it was apparent that the girl was excited to see her father again. "I realized then that she worshipped him," Ned said. "He was the whole universe to her, and he had simply, drastically, removed himself from her without an explanation." Van had made no permanent arrangement for his daughter to spend time with him; he simply called her whenever the inclination hit him, which was seldom. "Schuyler might wait for a year or more before he called or wrote," Ned said. "Her own calls and letters to him went unanswered. Her perplexity and confusion [were] painful to see. My father had taken over in part, acting as the dad as best he could." But Schuyler needed the love and support of her own father.

Evie claimed that her parental family paid for Schuyler's college education and that Van was "less than friendly" whenever his daughter sought him out. The Wynn boys made little effort to continue contact with their stepfather, nor he with them. Ned produced rock-and-roll records with Doris Day's son, Terry Melcher, before becoming a screenwriter, and Tracy attended the UCLA Film School, became the first college graduate in his family (although he found academics a waste of time), and went on to win two Emmy awards for scripts he wrote. "I never really cared about acting," said Tracy, "but I've always enjoyed talking with actors, not stars." Tracy would later settle in Colorado.

During 1969 and 1970 Van went to Italy and made three films whose titles translate as *Battle Squadron, The Price of Power,* and *The Eye of the Spider.* Italian actor Giuliano Gemma had been a Van Johnson fan before they made *The Price of Power* together and found working with the American star pleasant and exciting. The production crew spent two months in Spain and Italy filming the Western, shooting exteriors in the south of Spain and interiors in Rome. Van lived alone while he was in Europe and spoke no Italian, but he conducted himself like a dedicated professional. Since *The Price of Power* depicted a presidential assassination in frontier Dallas, the story too closely paralleled the killing of John F. Kennedy for Van's comfort. He worried that the picture might cause grief for the Kennedy family, many of whom had become his friends. Gemma pointed out to Johnson that the family would probably never see the movie, since it was not likely to play in American theaters. The Italian actor had assumed that Johnson was rich, but Van said that he was not and that he needed to keep working.

On other occasions, however, the divorced star maintained that he was "too old and too rich" to concern himself with fighting for choice parts in Hollywood. Van claimed that he liked playing heavies and supporting parts since they were often more intriguing and challenging than leading roles. He said that he loved living in New York, read five to seven books a week when not working, arose early in the morning but took naps in the afternoon, and had become a gourmet chef, with a particular appetite for Mexican dishes. He worked out regularly in a gym not far from his penthouse on Manhattan's East Side and continued to write notes to friends who were ill and to spouses of recently deceased acquaintances.

In public Johnson seemed to be comfortable with himself, although he remained too fearful of damaging his image to come out of the closet fully where his sexual preferences were concerned. He admitted that he was spoiled and blamed Metro-Goldwyn-Mayer. "They carried me around on a velvet pillow," Van told a colleague after a dinner playhouse rehearsal. "And I still expect that when I play a theater engagement. You'll have to forgive me."

He kept busy, primarily in regional theater, and had the capacity to draw sizable audiences and enchant them with his genial performances. By the early 1970s Van accepted that his career would wax hot and cold from that point on. "You can't let it get you down," he said. He gave no thought to moving into directing, as many of his contemporaries had, and offered as explanation, "I want somebody to tell me what to do."

Van seemed little concerned about his advancing age or bulging waistline and often acknowledged his passion for desserts with a pat on the stomach and an impish grin. In his middle fifties Van seemed secure in his talent, was master of his craft, and seldom fluffed a line or a cue. But the fun-loving side of his personality was more than ever a mask. Free of his wife and family, Van played the imperishable star yet remained a prisoner of his celebrated image. Any guilt or self-hatred he felt was kept under wraps. Always a great mimic, he began to mimic himself, sometimes even talking about himself in the third person. He liked to think of himself as unchanged. "I'm still the same schnook I was when I left Rhode Island," he frequently said. But by the 1970s the posture of Van Johnson, former movie star, the abiding sweetheart of aging dowagers, had become the spine that held him erect. "I knew them all," producer A. C. Lyles said, "Cagney, Bogart, Hope, Crosby. And of all the celebrities I knew, no one enjoyed being a movie star more than Van Johnson." That was the role Van played best, the only identity with which he felt completely comfortable.

CHAPTER 9

Later Years

In the 1970s Van Johnson became the self-proclaimed king of the dinner-theater circuit. He was ideal for such bookings, since he was familiar to middle-aged audiences and came across as warm and nonthreatening to average people who wanted to enjoy an evening out. Most of the plays in which he performed were comedies. "I'm not interested in doing anything that has to get across some kind of message," Van said. After the show he took pleasure in meeting the fans who had watched his movies in their youth. Many of his admirers brought along their children and grandchildren, and Van would hold court backstage and greet everyone in an affable manner. "I feel like I know each and every one of you," he said in frequent curtain speeches. "After all, we grew up together."

The pay was good for appearances in dinner theaters, and Van found sporadic travel a welcome relief from the solitary life he led in New York. Having learned that approachability was the key to return engagements, he seemed to enjoy signing autographs, which he did with a red marker, and projected the demeanor of a contented, "together" person delighted to be with old friends. "Be happy inside," Van said in interviews. "It shows." He had the freedom to work when he wanted and to travel to faraway places between commitments. "I'm a terrible gypsy," he said. "Thank God, the jobs are still available. I love to work—in anything—stage, screen, television, or industrials. But if I want to go off to Europe to loaf or paint, I can do that, too."

Johnson was featured on the straw-hat circuit in such lighthearted diversions as *There's a Girl in My Soup, Help Stamp Out Marriage,* and *Forty Carats,* which consistently drew capacity crowds. A critic once complained that Johnson evidenced only two emotions on stage, "worried and happy," but the public adored Van, which is what counted to theater managers. "He's fifty-five going on twelve now," a reviewer for the *Chicago Tribune* wrote in 1971, "but he's lost none of his buoyant charm."

Although Van exuded affection from the stage, a colleague said that Johnson was petrified in his early live engagements that someone would ask him about his divorce or mention rumors of his homosexuality. On his initial outings he spent a great deal of time secluded in his dressing room. "He didn't want to be anywhere near the public," said Richard Lederer, who acted with Johnson in *There's a Girl in My Soup* at a dinner theater in New Jersey. "He had a limousine that picked him up after the show to take him into Manhattan," Lederer said. "He didn't want to answer any questions." But Van gradually learned to relax and came to understand that his public wanted to believe he was still the boy next door who had simply gotten older as they had.

At his penthouse in New York, Johnson painted, read, cooked, and did needlepoint between out-of-town engagements and travel. All of the pillows on the sofa in Van's living room were his creations. Actress Hermione Gingold was one of his neighbors, and he occasionally had lunch or went shopping with Greta Garbo. "She leaves me messages on our special tree in the park," Van said. "The messages usually say something like, 'V meet G for lunch.' It's lovely." More frequently, he and Garbo ran into one another on the street, since both enjoyed taking long walks.

Van occasionally had a one-man show of his paintings, but he claimed that he was too lazy to be a truly fine artist. He jokingly referred to himself as the "Grandma Moses of Nantucket" when he arrived on the resort island, off the coast of Massachusetts, loaded down with paintings for a showing of his work in July 1970. The paintings sold well, even though Van claimed they were junk. "I'm sorry I ever agreed to put on a show," he said. "I'll never do that again." He eventually grew less critical of his work.

Johnson and Keenan Wynn remained friends, although they lived on different coasts. Keenan was still into motorcycling, an interest he shared with such friends as Lee Marvin, Marlon Brando, and Steve McQueen. Wynn had disregarded ear protection through the years, with the result that excessive noise left him with a severe hearing loss in his final years. By the early 1970s Keenan and his wife, Sharley, had scaled down their life-style, and the couple ultimately settled into a modest house in Brentwood.

Eve and Van remained in a constant financial battle, which involved periodic court dates. Evie and Schuyler were reduced to sharing an apart-ment in Beverly Hills, and Johnson's ex-wife was later forced to declare bankruptcy. "Van has been less than honest and very nasty," Eve wrote in 1999 from Palm Beach Gardens, Florida, where she was then living. "I've been reduced to near poverty. [He is] complex—as well as devious, with-out a conscience, and egomaniacal."

During one of the last times Ned Wynn saw his stepfather, Van seemed "powered up, rouged, florid, and soft. The old combination of good looks, size, and presence, was now an overstatement," Ned wrote in his book, "a gauche and stagy misrepresentation of the man I had always known. His attitude was stiff, almost silly." Van no longer seemed to know what to say to his daughter on their infrequent meetings, and he conse-quently ceased to have any contact at all with Schuyler. The girl hid her pain with food, anger, and finally indifference. Ned admitted that he under-stood Van's position. "I had the same kind of fear and terror of emotional attachment," Wynn said, "of giving love, and worse, of receiving it, that Van had. I would have run, too."

Johnson claimed that he no longer found joy in making movies. "It is hurry up and wait," he explained, a process that quickly became a bore for most performers. Van laughed about his recent experiences while filming pictures in Europe. "No one spoke English very well," he said, "and everything there is mañana." He much preferred to make guest appearances on Doris Day's or Dean Martin's television shows but said that he had no interest in doing a weekly series of his own. He appeared on *McMillan and Wife* with Rock Hudson in 1974 and played a politician on the television hit *Rich Man, Poor Man* in 1976.

Yet Van devoted himself primarily to regional theater and was booked solid season after season. He costarred with Linda Lavin in *On a Clear Day You Can See Forever* in 1973 and did a production of *The Prisoner of Second Avenue* in San Diego that same year. In 1974 he appeared in *6 Rms Riv Vu* in Chicago and Tampa and *Boeing Boeing* on the dinner playhouse circuit, where "Standing Room Only" signs were posted outside most perform-ances. The following year he had success with *Send Me No Flowers* in dinner theaters, alternating the comedy with other family shows that he had al-ready performed. Most of the facilities in which he played were small, with audiences seated at tables around the playing area. "The people are so close to you," Van said, "and you can really feel the audience contact."

Johnson was earning about $250,000 a year, but he said in 1976 that he would like to slow down for a while and just relax. "I thought the other day," he said, "that if I ever plan to see the world, I'd better hurry up and get moving." He looked back on his heartthrob years with mixed emotions. "I wouldn't want to live through that again," Van told reporters. "I'm happier now. But I must say that MGM was fair to me." He hated watching his old movies on television, he said, because "they remind me of how young I used to look."

Johnson saw few current films, since he deplored four-letter words on the screen and said that he had no interest in seeing cars smashed or someone getting stabbed to death. "Whatever happened to sweet, roman-tic films?" Van asked. "I wouldn't do anything myself I couldn't take the family to see. I've never even seen a stag movie." He professed that he was into positive thinking and credited comedienne Phyllis Diller with teaching him the importance of always focusing on "a perfect picture."

Soothing platitudes, however, could not erase Van's imperfect being or the struggle that existed within him. At a press luncheon the actor attended in 1976, an observer noted that Johnson, aged sixty, punctuated every point he made by patting the leg of the male reporter seated on his right. Van had grown more openly gay in his mannerisms through the years, particularly within the confines of a working environment, and an actor hired to read lines with him in the 1980s remembered how Johnson often laced his dialogue in run-throughs with ad-libbed sexual innuendoes. In public Van usually maintained a squeaky-clean image, although a Neiman-Marcus salesman in Dallas told his wife that Johnson had propositioned him in the store.

In 1978 Van played host on a cruise up the Mississippi on the *Delta Queen,* departing from New Orleans, and made television guest appearances on *Quincy* and *The Love Boat.* Dieting had become a constant part of his life, although it was a losing battle since he very much enjoyed eating. Otherwise, Van took care of himself, got plenty of rest, and despite his heavy performing schedule in theaters, he contended that he was not a night person.

With Ronald Reagan's election to the presidency, reporters frequently asked Van to comment on the former movie star's political career. "Listen, when someone asks me about politics I say I voted for Dennis Morgan," Johnson said. "I don't think actors should ever tell who they voted for. I think they can have so much sway they shouldn't try to influence people in those matters." Van's political beliefs were never strongly defined, although he reputedly voted for Adlai Stevenson in the 1952 presidential election.

In 1980 Johnson returned to Los Angeles to make *The Kidnapping of the President,* a movie that dealt with Third World terrorism. Van plays the U.S. vice president and the husband of Ava Gardner, a friend from Metro days. Johnson and Gardner had their first rehearsal in David Selznick's old office in Culver City. The chandelier in the once posh office was hanging out of the ceiling, plaster was cracking on the walls, and there was no carpet on the floor. Van asked his costar, "What do you do now when you have to pass MGM?" Gardner replied, "I just turn my head the other way." Johnson nodded his understanding. "I hate to drive by there because it's all been flattened out," he said. Much of MGM had already been turned over to real estate developers.

The Kidnapping of the President also featured Hal Holbrook as the nation's president and William Shatner as the Secret Service chief. Because of political uprisings around the world at the time and the danger of reality imitating events depicted on the screen, *The Kidnapping of the President* was rushed into the theaters and quickly forgotten, although it is not a bad action film.

In September 1980 Van launched a six-month national tour in Bernard Slade's play *Tribute*, which had starred Jack Lemmon on Broadway. The company opened at the Hanna Theater in Cleveland, played five weeks at the Blackstone in Chicago, then went on to St. Louis, Pittsburgh, Washington, D.C., and several Florida cities. Gloria DeHaven, another of Johnson's pals from Metro, was his costar. Van earned $7,500 a week during the tour and insisted on wearing red socks in the show, even though he played a leukemia victim. "Here's a comedy of hope," he said, "and I want people who see it to realize that cancer is something that one can get through. I want people to look at me, Van Johnson, the aging movie star, . . . and know I got through it."

He admitted that every time he walked on stage in *Tribute*, he thought of his own cancer bout. "Sometimes I just have to be alone after the performance," he said. In St. Louis with the show, Van stepped off a curb and broke his foot. He continued his performances in a wheelchair. "I'm still here," Johnson said. "I've been in and out of hospitals all my life." The actor had a complete physical checkup every six months and seemed in robust health, despite his expanding paunch. "Van is the survivingest damned survivor of us all," Lucille Ball remarked.

Johnson acknowledged that he was a workaholic. "I work fifty-five weeks a year," he said, "and I'm not complaining. When I drop dead, it'll be on an airplane—on the way to my next job." In a campy moment Van said that he felt like the "Last of the Red Hot Mamas." He had been in show business for nearly fifty years and was grateful that people still wanted to see him perform. "It's been good to me," he said of his career. "I have no beefs, no complaints. I have to say that all my dreams came true."

In 1981 Evie sued Van for seventy-five thousand dollars in back payments. She wanted five thousand dollars a month in alimony, and her demands meant another trip to the Los Angeles Superior Court for him. Ned remembered seeing his stepfather in the crowded hallway outside the courtroom. "The clutches of people, mostly Latino and black, don't recognize the stout, florid-faced man who puffs along in his black suit and hamburg toward the courtroom," Wynn wrote of the occasion. "Twenty-five years earlier they would have besieged him for autographs; now he evokes only the most cursory of glances."

Van seemed old, almost sexless, to Ned that day. Evie remarked that her former husband looked like a rabbi. After being closeted with his attorney, Eve, and her attorney for half an hour, Van came out of the courtroom. He ran into Ned, whom Van did not recognize at first. "It's me, Ned," his stepson said. Van eyed Wynn with almost complete indifference. "Gawd, you look old," Johnson said, then turned and walked away.

Van declined a 1982 offer to tour in *The Best Little Whorehouse in Texas* because he objected to saying four-letter words on stage. He said that his fans might disapprove and that he would be uncomfortable using bad language. He participated in "Night of the 100 Stars" at Radio City Music Hall that year and later appeared as Captain Andy in several productions of *Show Boat* around the country. Van and Ethel Merman played former lovers on another episode of *The Love Boat,* he guest starred as Shelley Fabares's father on *One Day at a Time,* and he teamed with June Allyson on a *Murder, She Wrote* sequence in 1984, during the series' first month on the air. "My friends sit around their swimming pools in California waiting for the phone to ring," Van said. "I stay alive in television movies, an occasional *Love Boat*, and the miracle of dinner theaters. I never thought I would last this long."

He welcomed the love he received from live audiences. Unable to sustain intimate relationships with individuals, male or female, in his private life, he let his aging fans satisfy his craving for affection. They gave him approval without demanding much more from him than a smile and possibly an autograph. His female admirers particularly supplied him with an ardor that not only made his lonely life tolerable but validated his existence. Dinner-theater audiences were friendly and accommodating. "They've had food and wine," Van said, "and they're so excited waiting for you to come out that by the time you make your entrance, they're already applauding." He needed their reassurance, enjoyed the attention he got from the media and local actors, and delighted in the royal treatment and perks he received from regional management.

Having basked in adulation and backstage commotion for an extended period on the road, Van was ready for the seclusion and comfort of his Manhattan penthouse, with its wraparound terrace and view of the East River. There he lived with three cats—Fred, Kitty, and Bo—surrounded by his needlepoint and walls filled with gold-framed photographs of stars he had known and worked with through the years. In a bookcase were the red leather–bound scripts of the movies he had made. He spent a great deal of time in New York cooking, did his own marketing, usually walked in the afternoons from four o'clock until six, then took a hot bath and settled down for an evening by himself. Johnson's friend Sylvia Syms once said, "Van never goes out after dark unless heavily veiled." He enjoyed his home and passed the time working crossword puzzles, looking over his collection of cookbooks, and reading. He usually drank a glass of wine before going to bed and retired early.

"I'm a Virgo," Van said, "and a Swede. I go it alone. . . . I'm content at home these days with my memories." By the 1980s he did not like to be photographed, rarely visited Broadway haunts like Sardi's, where he might be recognized, and said that he had no intention of ever writing his memoirs. "I don't want to hurt anybody, and I don't need the money," he said. "I don't want to go over the marriage and the ex-wife and all that. It's very traumatic to go over your life."

Van claimed that his cardinal rule was to never look back. "I'm not nostalgic about the old days," he said. Hollywood was no longer any fun for him; it had become a rat race. "There's a whole new breed out there," Johnson said. "I'm not condemning it, but I don't understand it, and I don't like the products they are turning out." In interviews he stressed how much he cherished his freedom, how lucky he had been, and how unflappable he had become. "The idea is to just get out of the damned spotlight while you can still be remembered for your earlier glories," he said, "not as some old relic."

In 1985 Van took over the role of Georges in the musical version of *La Cage aux Folles* at the Palace Theater on Broadway, following Gene Barry and Keith Michell in the role. He signed for a year's run in the show and maintained that appearing at the Palace was the realization of a lifelong dream. Johnson said, "I stand on that stage and think of the stars who've stood there before me—Sarah Bernhardt, Judy Garland, Sophie Tucker, Josephine Baker. . . . It's magic time." The Palace engagement would be the highlight of his later career and bring him more national attention than he had had in years.

Johnson's part in *La Cage aux Folles* was the more masculine of the show's two homosexual lovers. Agreeing to play the role was a bold step for Van and seemed to free him from some of his earlier repressions. But aside from the fact that its central characters are lovers of the same gender, *La Cage aux Folles* is an old-fashioned musical comedy, full of heart, with dazzling costumes and lovely, singable melodies.

The show's producers had sent Johnson tickets to see the production, trying to entice him to consider the assignment, and Van went to a matinee performance with his manager. "I thought it was beautifully done,"

Johnson said, "and I wanted to be part of that troupe. When I walked home, back to the East Side, I couldn't get that music of Jerry Herman's out of my mind." The producers asked him to audition for the musical, which he did three times before getting the part. Then he went to Venice to learn the script and Herman's songs, taking with him the original cast recording. "I had to get out of New York," Van said, "away from the phones."

During the rehearsal period in Manhattan he walked home from the theater reading the script aloud. "People would say, 'Look at that fat old man talking to himself,'" Van joked. He took lessons to improve his singing and got his dancing up to speed. "Gene Kelly I'm not," he said, "but I can still move these buns."

He found the preparation exhilarating. "It has been my dream to be a Broadway leading man," Van said, "someone all the nice ladies would come to see." He fell in love with the show and felt comfortable in the part. "It's a wonderful love story," he said. "It's really like a big, old-fashioned MGM musical. It picks you up, lets you down. . . . It makes you cry, makes you laugh . . . and it has no four-letter words." He also found *La Cage aux Folles* liberating. Playing a gay man night after night before a cheering audience did much to bring the sixty-eight-year-old star to accept publicly his homosexual tendencies. Times had changed, and most Americans were more accepting of alternative sexual preferences than they once had been.

George Hearn, who won a Tony for his performance, played Albin, the flighty, flamboyant homosexual in the musical, and Van had nothing but praise for his costar's professionalism. "George is a very dear man, underrated, understated," said Johnson. "He holds the cast together." Yet Van was a strong box-office attraction for out-of-town patrons, and his critical notices were good. "He is not so commanding as Barry or as moving as Michell, and he cannot act as well as either," Clive Barnes wrote in the *New York Post*. "But he remains a real personality, and a charming one at that."

Van later claimed that it took him six months to hit his stride and find his pace and tempo in the show. "I'm nervous every night," he said, "but opening night I was scared to death." The producers slipped him into the production three days ahead of his scheduled opening, which gave him an opportunity to settle into the part before reviews were written. "No one knew I was on Broadway," Van said. Gene Barry told him, "Don't forget, Van, when you come through that curtain, you set the pace for the whole show." Johnson rose to the occasion.

He arrived at the Palace Theater two and a half hours before curtain time to vocalize, look over the script, and limber up as best he could. "Then it takes half an hour to fill in the cracks when I put on my makeup," Van said. Giving eight performances a week took discipline, but he liked having a structure to his life. "I've never felt as happy, as uplifted as in this show," Johnson said. "It's like Disneyland." The company of La Cage became Van's family. "I haven't had one since I was divorced," he said, and he interacted cordially with other actors and seemed cheerier than ever.

On matinee days he stayed in the theater between shows. Gallagher's sent over potato skins and a salad for him to eat. "Energy is what it's all about," Van said of his rigorous routine. "When people are paying $47.50 for a ticket, it's your responsibility to give them the best you've got." He exercised regularly, took all manner of vitamins, and got plenty of sleep. "I take better care of myself now," he said. "This may prolong my life." Each time the curtain came down, Van retired to his dressing room with applause ringing in his ears, content that he had given a satisfying performance. "I have everything to be happy about," he said. "I've paid my dues, and can enjoy myself now."

Yet the pace of appearing in a big Broadway musical was grueling. By May, after five months in La Cage, Van needed a vacation. "I still have my Christmas tree up with the red lights," he said. "I'm too tired to take it down." After a short break, Johnson returned to the show and performed until mid-November, when he abruptly left the cast two weeks before his contract expired. An ear infection affected his equilibrium and made him apprehensive about continuing in such a demanding role. He was exhausted and needed prolonged rest.

Not only had Van given eight performances a week for nearly a year in *La Cage aux Folles,* he also managed during that period to appear in Woody Allen's film *The Purple Rose of Cairo.* Johnson found making the movie a joy. "It was like the old days," he said, "no one raised his voice. It was great fun." Allen maintained that he was not looking for big names when he cast the picture but was simply trying to find appropriate people to play the key roles. Someone had suggested Van, pointing out that Johnson was in New York and currently visible. "He hadn't acted in films for some time," Allen said, but "he seemed just fine." The movie was an artistic success.

After a busy 1985 Van was happy to concentrate more on painting. He had a one-man show in 1987 in Dallas, where sixty-three of his works were exhibited. Prices ranged from $1,200 to $10,000, while subjects included his pet cats, brightly colored flowers, urban scenes, sun-drenched villages, and landscapes, all in what Johnson called his "Van Go" style. "I paint to express my own inner happiness," he said. "Painting makes me feel young and close to the creative source. I have learned much about myself through canvas and brush. No deep hidden meanings, but a celebration of my love affair with life."

Van usually completed a painting in one day, starting work around nine in the morning and finishing the picture by bedtime. "I get nervous at the start of each new canvas," he said. Painting heightened his senses and, according to Van, gave him the power to stop time. "In painting," he said, "each stroke is new, unconditioned and very exciting." Flowers were a favorite motif. "I've been to so many Hollywood funerals," Van said. "I want to see the flowers now, when I'm alive."

Death seemed to become a more immediate consideration for him. Keenan Wynn died of cancer in October 1986 at seventy years of age. For months Keenan sat in the small cottage in Brentwood he and Sharley rented, seeing very few people. "There was no pain," Ned Wynn said of his father, "just fear and worry." Toward the end, after being sober for seven years, Keenan realized that his drinking had caused most of his problems. "Keenan was a wonderful guy," said Van, "we were still friends to the end. He always left me notes, saying, 'Thanks a lot, Van—for taking Eve off my hands.'"

Long before Evie had moved to Florida, she stopped giving parties, although she still liked to be included on Hollywood guest lists. Cesar Romero, a favorite Hollywood escort, served as her frequent date on social outings, although Eve claimed that many hostesses made a point of not inviting widows and divorcées to their parties. "They're all so afraid you're going to steal someone's husband," she said. "Having been on both sides of that game, it's something I could never, ever do." Rocky Cooper, Gary Cooper's widow, remained Eve's close friend, as did actor Jim Backus and his wife. Of the many others who had once been frequent guests in her home, Evie said, "When I run into them now about the best I get is a vague invitation to lunch. Lunch! I gave black tie dinners, dinner dances, and big parties. It's a 'What have you done for me lately?' town, believe me."

Whenever reporters asked Van about Schuyler, he generally replied, "We don't go into that. Just say she's thirty-two. Come to think of it, I've been saying she's thirty-two for a long time now. Maybe she's older." In September 1998 Johnson's daughter had a complete hysterectomy as a result of cancer, but Van neglected to contact her.

Modern life seemed more and more to bewilder the veteran actor. He went out less in New York, except to go to church. "I thank God for every day," he said. "Every time I pass St. Patrick's I tip my hat and thank God. . . . I've had so many chances." In 1988 he said that he had been celibate for ten years but was not lonely. "I'm an aging star in menopause," said Van.

He and June Allyson occasionally gave talks on cruise ships together, and Johnson continued to make infrequent television appearances. He ended 1987 by performing in a musical, *The Twelve Dreams of Christmas,* in Richmond, Virginia. Despite his reclusive nature, Van always gave his all on stage. "Once that curtain goes up," he said, "I belt." In the summer of 1988, he played Father Moon in a production of *Anything Goes* at Casa Mañana in Fort Worth, Texas, with the role built up for him. On the closing night of the engagement, a cake was brought on stage during curtain calls to celebrate the star's seventy-second birthday. "I hope to live to be seventy-three," he said. "You know, folks, a lot of you thought I was older, didn't you?"

By 1989 Johnson's hair had turned white, and for a time he wore a beard. His jowls had grown thicker, and he claimed that he had not had cosmetic surgery on his face except what was necessary after his 1943 automobile accident. In November 1989 he went to Rome to make a movie, *Killer Crocodile,* directed by Fabrizio De Angelis. On the Italian set Van proved gracious to fellow actors, who were eager to listen to how he used to kiss Elizabeth Taylor one day and swim with Esther Williams the next.

Northwood Institute presented Johnson with a Lifetime Achievement in the Arts award in 1990 at the Players Club in New York. Van appeared that summer in *No, No, Nanette* with Marge Champion and Carol Lawrence at the St. Louis Muny Opera, and when he returned home, he told reporters, "I was not Nanette." He made two inexpensive films in Europe that year, *Escape from Paradise* and *Delta Force: Commando 2,* looking puffy and paunchy in both. In the latter, made in Italy, he plays the villain, and the scars from his automobile accident are quite apparent.

In 1991 Van again played Captain Andy in a production of *Show Boat* in Pasadena, performed at a salute to Cole Porter at the Palladium in June, and made a movie, *Three Days to a Kill.* He also put together a one-man show, *The Best of Times: A Musical Odyssey,* which re-created highlights of his career. One of his most pleasurable engagements that year was a reunion with Janet Leigh for a performance of *Love Letters* in Beverly Hills. "I loved doing that and loved Van in the role," Leigh said. "He was so funny." The actors' dressing rooms were downstairs in the theater, and

Leigh recalled that the stairs were dark when she and Van came up after the intermission. Neither of them could see, and Johnson had forgotten his glasses and talked loudly since he wore a hearing aid in one ear. "Where the fuck is the flashlight?" Van bellowed as they made their way up the steps. When the two came on stage, the audience was hysterical, having heard Van's expletive on the stairs.

By then Johnson seemed to need the support of his friends in professional situations. Elliott Reid, who had known Van for years, worked with him at a theater in Florida in the 1990s. "I've got to have you there," Johnson told Reid, and he even supplemented his friend's salary out of his own pocket to make the job more attractive. "Van was delightful," the actor said, "a truly sweet guy." Others found the star easy to work with, a master at stage technique, able to ad-lib his way out of any gaffes that might occur during performances.

Van seemed to enjoy laughing about his age and said he could read lips even if he could no longer hear. He claimed that the only part of him that still worked was his memory. "I'll stop performing only when they run me over with a bulldozer," he told the press. "Thank God for the little old gray-haired ladies." He joked that his own hair was blonder than Catherine Deneuve's and that his eyes required more makeup than hers. "Darling, old Vanny's lashes disappear without mascara," he told a reporter in his increasingly campy way in 1992. "I'm a genuine antique."

Mary Sharmat and Frank Vohs acted with Van in *Lend Me a Tenor* at the Hampton Playhouse in New Hampshire during June 1992 and had occasion to observe the star's love for his fans. Van would talk to audiences for about forty-five minutes after each show and was honest about his age and deafness. "I can't hear a thing," he said in his curtain speech. One evening in Hampton a busload of women arrived for the play, and Van went outside and greeted them in his robe and red socks. He got aboard the bus and walked down the aisle, individually welcoming each one of "his girls."

Lend Me a Tenor is a complicated show with many entrances and exits. At the playhouse where Van acted in New Hampshire the crew put strips of different colored paper under the door to signal for him which member of the cast was about to enter, since there had been little time for rehearsal. Supporting players had to touch Johnson on the shoulder to give him cues when he was not in a position to read their lips. Yet Sharmat and Vohs agreed that Van was a magnetic personality on stage. He seemed comfortable with himself, not neurotic, yet very much a loner.

In 1993 Johnson had a reasonably large part in an Australian movie, *Clowning Around,* in which he plays a circus owner doubling as the ringmaster. He also joined Kathryn Grayson in Australia during the early 1990s for a song-and-dance revue called *Red Socks and Roses,* which highlighted their two careers. "I love my work," said Van, who often referred to himself as an "old gypsy." He and Grayson were the celebrity guests aboard the *Delta Queen* on the Mississippi River in 1997, and during the trip Johnson frequently turned up in the public areas of the steamer, greeted passengers with affection, and signed autographs. There was a West Coast exhibition of his paintings in 1997, and two years later Van appeared at Carnegie Hall for a tribute to musical movies and their stars, hosted by Michael Feinstein and June Allyson. Johnson had recently undergone hip surgery and walked with a noticeable limp, but he was otherwise in fine form, winning over the audience with improvisations and double takes as clips from his films were shown.

Retirement remained a dirty word to Johnson, even though on a trip to Los Angeles in 1996 he greeted film authority Robert Osborne with, "Mygawd, Osborne! I'm eighty, can you believe it?" Van had become very conscious of age, even though he retained a boyish quality that enchanted fans. He could be relied on to muster a gregarious personality and a ready wit in public, although friends were frequently stunned to find him looking so red faced and fat.

Johnson had always been a private person, but his hearing problem caused him to avoid socializing in crowds. Talking to him on the telephone became nearly impossible. Johnson told Eddie Bracken that his deafness was causing him to lose friends, and by 1996 it was a surprise to see Van at parties or dinners. "I have to be alone," he said. "It's the only way I can recharge my batteries." He seldom answered letters and invited few people to his apartment.

Now an octogenarian, Johnson still awakens automatically at five A.M. and says that he often dreams of his leading ladies and costars back on the MGM lot. He continues to walk a great deal and never takes a cab if he can help it. In his opinion, he is still a conventional New Englander, and intimate friends say that Van sometimes kids himself that he was never homosexual. Sexuality does not fit in the movie in his mind, and like the films from Hollywood's golden era, Van would rather ignore an aspect of his life that might cause controversy or damage his image.

Johnson has spent decades going out among his fans, meeting them with smiles, and cultivating a loyal following. After dinner-theater performances he has frequently heard daughters of former bobby-soxers ask, "Is this the man you get the scrapbooks out to see on a rainy day, Mommy?" The answer is usually yes. Yet Van has probably lingered too long in the public eye to become the icon that Rudolph Valentino, James Dean, and Marilyn Monroe have, and he is not reflective enough of cultural values to be the folk hero that John Wayne is. Johnson's appeal is far more frozen in time.

Van's charisma on screen is undeniable, even if he seems too cute for some. Yet aside from a handful of solid performances, Johnson's impact on screen history has been slight, and, despite his onetime popularity, he failed to make the American Film Institute's list of all-time great movie stars. Personally, Johnson remains an enigma. Basically a timid soul, he has spent a lifetime hiding his loneliness and sexual ambivalence behind a mask of superficial charm. Van Johnson endures in films of the 1940s and 1950s as Mr. Nice Guy. For many of his contemporaries he is a symbol of eternal youth, but for most members of younger generations he is a pleasant face on classic movie channels. Yet somehow the personality does not ring true.

BIBLIOGRAPHICAL ESSAY

Van Johnson's film and stage career is far easier to track than is his private life. Whatever personal papers exist have not found their way into public repositories. Of necessity a biographer must therefore rely on clipping files, interviews with friends and colleagues, and published memoirs of Johnson's friends, associates, and the one family member who has written a book. Occasional mentions of the actor are found in such collections as the George Cukor and Hal B. Wallis papers at the Margaret Herrick Library of the Academy of Motion Picture Arts and Sciences in Los Angeles, the Henry Hathaway collection at the Mayer Library of the American Film Institute in Los Angeles, and the Greer Garson collection at the Hamon Arts Library at Southern Methodist University in Dallas. The Hedda Hopper papers held by the Margaret Herrick Library are illuminating in key moments of the star's life.

The Herrick Library has extensive clipping files on Johnson's life and films. The theater arts section of the New York Public Library has files covering these areas as well as his later stage work. Regional material is on file in the fine arts division of the Dallas Public Library. Not to be overlooked is the Constance McCormick Collection, a series of scrapbooks containing a wealth of clippings on luminaries of Hollywood's golden age, housed in the Doheny Library at the University of Southern California in Los Angeles. Also valuable are the Doheny Library's Warner Bros. and Twentieth Century–Fox production files, which include data on the films Johnson made for those studios.

Johnson's associates were not as readily available to be interviewed for this book as I would have liked, but I gleaned a great deal from the people to whom I talked. Some would discuss only their professional relationships with the actor; others were willing to divulge what private insights they could. Among those most helpful in writing this book were Eddie Bracken (New York, 1999), Mildred (Toddy) Burns (by telephone from Stroudsburg, Pa., 1999), Rosemary Clooney (Los Angeles, 1999), Sandy Descher (Los Angeles, 1999), Anne Dimery (Newport, R.I., 1999), Giuliano Gemma (by telephone from Rome, Italy, 1999), Eve Wynn Johnson (multiple telephone conversations from Palm Beach Gardens, Fla., 1999), Martin and Erin-Jo Jurow (Dallas, 1999), Richard Lederer (New York, 1999), Janet Leigh (Los Angeles, 1999), Leonard Panaggio (Newport,

R.I., 1999), Elliott Reid (Los Angeles, 1999), Mary Sharmat (New York, 1999), Barbara (Mrs. Marshall) Thompson (by telephone from Danville, Calif., 1999), Frank Vohs (New York, 1999), and Jane Wyman (by telephone from Rancho Mirage, Calif., 1999). Eve Johnson's candid note to me of August 30, 1999, proved of vital importance.

Interviews containing information and background data on Johnson's life and career taped for the Southern Methodist University Oral History Collection on the Performing Arts include those with George Abbott (Miami, Fla., 1979), Leon Ames (Corona Del Mar, Calif., 1983), Lucille Ball (Los Angeles, 1980), Pandro S. Berman (Los Angeles, 1978), Ralph Blane (Broken Arrow, Okla., 1979), Frederick Brisson (Los Angeles, 1981 and 1982), Robert Buckner (San Miguel de Allende, Mexico, 1988), Lillian Burns (Los Angeles, 1986), Edward Buzzell (Los Angeles, 1982), Joseph J. Cohn (Los Angeles, 1991), Donald Curtis (Dallas, 1988), Arlene Dahl (Dallas, 1975), Dan Dailey (Dallas, 1974), Rosemary DeCamp (Los Angeles, 1982), Don DeFore (Los Angeles, 1986), Armand Deutsch (Los Angeles, 1982), Edward Dmytryk (Austin, Tex., 1979), Stanley Donen (Los Angeles, 1983), Joanne Dru (Los Angeles, 1991), Irene Dunne (Los Angeles, 1982), Julius J. Epstein (Los Angeles, 1986), Mike Frankovich (Los Angeles, 1985), John Green (Los Angeles, 1975), Henry Hathaway (Los Angeles, 1983), June Havoc (Stamford, Conn., 1990), Marsha Hunt (Los Angeles, 1983), Martha Hyer (Los Angeles, 1982), Gene Kelly (Dallas, 1974), Ruth Kobart (Dallas, 1982), Stanley Kramer (Los Angeles, 1988), Fernando Lamas (Los Angeles, 1981), Piper Laurie (Los Angeles, 1989), Mervyn LeRoy (Los Angeles, 1977), Norman Lloyd (Los Angeles, 1979), Mary Anita Loos (Los Angeles, 1990), John Lund (Los Angeles, 1988), Betty Lynn (Los Angeles, 1984), Mary Martin (Dallas and San Miguel de Allende, Mexico, 1984 and 1988), Dorothy McGuire (Los Angeles, 1986), Vincente Minnelli (Los Angeles, 1980), Tharon Musser (New York, 1986), Robert Nathan (Los Angeles, 1981), Barry Nelson (Dallas, 1985), Richard Ney (Los Angeles, 1983), Robert Pirosh (Los Angeles, 1986), Jean Porter (Dallas and Austin, Tex., 1980 and 1981), Ella Raines (Los Angeles, 1983), Joseph Ruttenberg (Los Angeles, 1978), Lizabeth Scott (Los Angeles, 1984 and 1985), Vivienne Segal (Los Angeles, 1981), Melville Shavelson (Los Angeles, 1991), George Sidney (Los Angeles, 1980), Leonard Sillman (New York, 1979), Robert Stack (Los Angeles, 1975), Ann Straus (Los Angeles, 1985), Marshall Thompson (Los Angeles, 1980), Emily Torchia (Los Angeles, 1984), Al Trescony (Los Angeles, 1986), Nancy Walker (Los Angeles, 1978), Hal B. Wallis (Los Angeles, 1982), Charles Walters (Los Angeles, 1980), Marie Windsor (Los Angeles, 1983), and Keenan Wynn (Los Angeles, 1984).

Interviews in the Columbia University Oral History Collection with material on Johnson include those with Henry Hathaway (1971), Joseph Pasternak (1971), Mary Rodgers (1982), and Carey Wilson (1959). Screen biographer Robert Nott forwarded to me insights from his sessions with A. C. Lyles and Don Weis. Rudy Behlmer interviewed assistant director Rideway Callow (1976), who had pertinent observations to make about the filming of *Plymouth Adventure*, and that interview is in the American Film Institute's Mayer Library in Los Angeles.

For more exact citations, see the following.

Introduction
The roller coaster incident comes from the author's oral history with actor Marshall Thompson. Johnson's despondency in Geneva is reconstructed primarily from a May 1962 interview the star granted to gossip columnist Hedda Hopper.

Chapter 1: Newport
My background reading on Newport, R.I., included C. P. B. Jefferys, *Newport: A Short History* (Newport, R.I.: Newport Historical Society, 1992); Leonard J. Panaggio, *Portrait of Newport II* (Newport, R.I.: Bank of Newport, 1994); and Richard H. Rudolph, "Eighteenth Century Newport and Its Merchants," *Newport History* 51, pt. 2 (spring 1978). City directories in the Newport Historical Society also were helpful.

Valuable in understanding Johnson's Swedish heritage were Jonas Frykman and Orvar Lofgren, *Culture Builders: A Historical Anthropology* (New Brunswick, N.J.: Rutgers University Press, 1987); and Richard F. Tomasson, *Sweden: Prototype of Modern Society* (New York: Random House, 1970).

The Binnacle, the Rogers High School yearbook, conveys much about Johnson's teenage school activities in Newport. "On Travelling," by Van Johnson, appeared in the May 17, 1934, edition of *The Red and Black*, a Rogers High School publication, and an interview with Van's father was published in *The Red and Black* in 1946. Pat Tierney Schlicher, a Newport resident, sent me her recollections of young Van and his father.

Johnson's own observations about his boyhood were gleaned mainly from articles based on interviews given to writers for fan magazines and national periodicals. I have tried to use these sources cautiously, taking into account the tendency of stars and studio publicists to exaggerate and sanitize such writings before publication. Those articles shedding most light on the actor's years in Newport include Roger Butterfield, "Van Johnson," *Life* 19 (November 5, 1945): 114–25; Van Johnson as told to Ruth Waterbury, "My Life," *Photoplay* 26 (February 1945): 32–34, 111–112 and (March 1945): 46–47, 66–69; Pete Martin, "Bobby-Sox Blitzer," *Saturday Evening Post* 217 (June 30, 1945): 16–17, 54–57; and Alice L. Tildesley, "The New Van Johnson," *Movieland* 2 (August 1944): 34–35, 67–68. I also found useful many magazine clippings in the scrapbooks assembled by Constance McCormick.

Chapter 2: New York
Information on Johnson's participation in *New Faces of 1936* was largely derived from my interviews with Leonard Sillman, Ralph Blane, and particularly Mildred Burns, al-

though Sillman's book, *Here Lies Leonard Sillman . . . Straightened Out at Last* (New York: Citadel, 1959), supplies details on the production.

The author's long interviews with Eddie Bracken and Martin Jurow yielded intimate details about Johnson's life during the preparation and run of *Too Many Girls*, whereas general information on the production is drawn from my oral history with George Abbott. In her interview for SMU, Lucille Ball talks about the making of the RKO film based on the show, but she says little about Van Johnson. Desi Arnaz comments more on the young performer's work in *Too Many Girls* in his autobiography, *A Book* (New York: Warner, 1976).

Gene Kelly and June Havoc discuss *Pal Joey* at length in the oral histories I taped with them, and Stanley Donen added his recollections in my interview with him. The homosexual lifestyle favored by Lorenz Hart and others involved with the Rodgers and Hart shows is described in Frederick Nolan, *Lorenz Hart: A Poet on Broadway* (New York: Oxford, 1994).

Dan Dailey's oral history in the SMU collection delineates the work of choristers in the stage shows presented at the Roxy Theater in New York, and the interview I conducted with Mary Martin provides data on her act in the Rainbow Room, although she does not mention Van Johnson.

Keenan Wynn discusses his friendship with Johnson in *Ed Wynn's Son* (Garden City, N.Y.: Doubleday, 1959), and June Allyson wrote about her relationship with the young performer in *June Allyson* (New York: Putnam's, 1982) but gave more details about her friendship with Van for an article published in the *Hollywood Reporter* and reproduced in Tichi Wilkerson and Marcia Borie, *The Hollywood Reporter: The Golden Years* (New York: Coward-McCann, 1984).

Useful articles in fan magazines and national periodicals on Johnson's early life in New York include those listed for chapter 1 as well as Alyce Canfield, "Every Mother's Son," *Liberty* 22 (October 13, 1945): 38–39, 83–86; and "Van Johnson: He's Riding High," *Look* 9 (November 13, 1945): 34–40.

Chapter 3: Early Hollywood

The Warner Bros. production file for *Murder in the Big House* provides a wealth of material on Van Johnson's first starring role in Hollywood, and the second volume of June Havoc's memoir, *More Havoc* (New York: Harper and Row, 1980), gives vivid insight into Van's private life during his initial months in Hollywood. Billy Grady's autobiography, *The Irish Peacock: The Confessions of a Legendary Talent Agent* (New Rochelle, N.Y.: Arlington House, 1972), details Johnson's introduction to Metro-Goldwyn-Mayer and the grooming process the actor received at the studio. Martin Jurow, talent scout Al Trescony, and drama coach Lillian Burns Sidney also supplied useful information on Johnson's early period under contract to MGM in the oral histories I conducted with them. The interview with Carey Wilson in the oral history collection at Columbia University contains a thorough narrative of how Johnson was selected for the part of Dr. Red Adams in the later *Dr. Gillespie* series.

Excellent background data on the big studio system may be found in Gary Carey, *All the Stars in Heaven: Louis B. Mayer's M-G-M* (New York: Dutton, 1981); Bosley Crowther, *The Lion's Share* (New York: Dutton, 1957); Bosley Crowther, *Hollywood Rajah: The Life and Times of Louis B. Mayer* (New York: Holt, Rinehart, and Winston, 1960); Ronald L. Davis, *The Glamour Factory: Inside Hollywood's Big Studio System* (Dallas: Southern Methodist University Press, 1993); James Robert Parish and Ronald L. Bowers, *The MGM Stock Company: The Golden Era* (New Rochelle, N.Y.: Arlington House, 1973); and Thomas Schatz, *The Genius of the System* (New York: Pantheon, 1988).

Johnson's relationship with Keenan and Evie Wynn is discussed in Keenan Wynn's autobiography, *Ed Wynn's Son* (Garden City, N.Y.: Doubleday, 1959), and in Ned Wynn's discerning book, *We Will Always Live in Beverly Hills: Growing Up Crazy in Hollywood* (New York: Morrow, 1990). My oral history with Keenan Wynn includes cogent biographical statements but little discussion of Van Johnson. Eddie Bracken's interview for this book disclosed more about Keenan and Van's relationship, and telephone conversations with Eve Wynn Johnson were essential in gaining her point of view. Slim Keith's book with Annette Tapert, *Slim: Memoirs of a Rich and Imperfect Life* (New York: Simon and Schuster, 1990), describes the Sunday-morning motorcycle rides of Slim's then husband, Howard Hawks, who was part of the Hollywood biker crowd in the 1940s. Biographer Todd McCarthy also gives an account of these Sunday gatherings in *Howard Hawks* (New York: Grove Press, 1997), and Robert Stack mentions them in the oral history he and I taped.

Another side of Johnson's early social life in Hollywood is suggested in Joan and Jack Benny, *Sunday Nights at Seven* (New York: Warner, 1990).

Barry Nelson talks about the making of *The Human Comedy* in the interview he granted to Southern Methodist University, and George Sidney assesses *Pilot No. 5* in his oral history. Irene Dunne and Don DeFore discuss working on *A Guy Named Joe* in theirs. Esther Williams writes of her meeting with Van on the set of *A Guy Named Joe* in her book with Digby Diehl, *The Million Dollar Mermaid* (New York: Simon and Schuster, 1999).

Johnson's automobile accident during the filming of *A Guy Named Joe* is widely covered in the clipping files at the Margaret Herrick Library, and Johnson himself describes the car wreck in an excerpt in Doug McClelland, *Forties Film Talk: Oral Histories of Hollywood* (Jefferson, N.C.: McFarland, 1992).

Pertinent secondary works for this chapter include Michael Troyan, *A Rose for Mrs. Miniver: The Life of Greer Garson* (Lexington: University of Kentucky Press, 1999) for the making of *Madame Curie;* and Bill Davidson, *Spencer Tracy, Tragic Idol* (New York: Dutton, 1987) for the filming of *A Guy Named Joe.*

The *Life, Movieland, Photoplay,* and *Saturday Evening Post* articles cited for chapter 1 also rendered information for this chapter, as did the *Liberty* article cited for chapter 2.

Dora Albert, "Death Was So Close," *Movieland* 11 (February 1953): 42–45, 76–77, was also useful.

Chapter 4: Heartthrob

The description of adolescent fans' reactions to Van Johnson during the early 1940s is based largely on fan-magazine articles and clippings in the Herrick Library and the theater arts section of the New York Public Library, and the December 21, 1944, *New York World-Telegram* quotes several young women who considered the redheaded movie star their ideal man. Dana Welborne Pickett described for me her memories of her childhood idol, and June Allyson recalls how she and Van were mobbed by fans in her autobiography, referred to in the notes for chapter 2.

Constance McCormick's scrapbooks contain information on Johnson's social life during the heyday of his career, and Martin and Erin-Jo Jurow gave me personal recollections of the Hollywood social scene of which Van Johnson became part. The actor's continuing relationship with Keenan and Eve Wynn is depicted at length in contemporary fan magazines and newspaper clippings, but the friendship is probably most reliably reported in Keenan Wynn's autobiography and Ned Wynn's memoir, cited earlier.

The shift in Johnson's attitude toward the roles MGM assigned him is described in Billy Grady's book, mentioned in the notes for chapter 3.

Ava Gardner discusses working with Van Johnson in *Three Men in White* in *Ava: My Story* (New York: Bantam, 1990). Joe Pasternak, who produced *Two Girls and a Sailor, Thrill of a Romance*, and other Johnson movies, briefly mentions the star in his memoir, *Easy the Hard Way* (London: Allen, 1956), and Mervyn LeRoy goes into detail on the filming of *Thirty Seconds over Tokyo* in his autobiography, *Mervyn LeRoy: Take One* (New York: Hawthorn, 1974), written with Dick Kleiner. Former actor Donald Curtis related anecdotes about working on *Thirty Seconds over Tokyo* in the oral history I conducted with him, and Bruce Cook analyzes the script of that wartime classic in his biography of the screenwriter, *Dalton Trumbo* (New York: Scribner's, 1977).

Esther Williams remembers making *Thrill of a Romance* and *Easy to Wed* in her autobiography, cited in the notes for chapter 3, and Jean Porter and Edward Buzzell related incidents that occurred during the production of *Easy to Wed* in the author's oral histories with them.

Memos from the Office of War Information concerning *Two Girls and a Sailor* and *Thrill of a Romance* may be found in the manuscript holdings on film in the Doheny Library at the University of Southern California.

Relevant fan-magazine articles for this chapter include Alyce Canfield, "Are You the Girl for Van?" *Movieland* 4 (September 1946): 28–29, 65–66; Van Johnson, "I Was Just Thinking...," *Photoplay* 24 (June 1944): 44–45, 110–11; Mme. Margaret Mamlok, "Van—Hands Down," *Photoplay* 29 (September 1946): 44–45, 105–8; Louella O. Parsons, "Untold Story," *Photoplay* 30 (December 1946): 38–39, 111–12; Florence Pritchett, "Van

Gets Clubby," *Silver Screen* 15 (August 1945): 22–23, 64–67; Adela Rogers St. Johns, "Heart of a Yankee," *Photoplay* 28 (February 1946): 30, 119–22, (March 1946): 34–35, 129–31, and (April 1946): 42–43, 111–15; and Adela Rogers St. Johns, "The Truth about Van Johnson's Health," *Photoplay* 27 (July 1945): 28–29, 89–90. Helpful, too, was "New Matinee Idol," *Life* 17 (November 13, 1944): 47–50.

Excellent background material for this period is supplied by Clayton R. Koppes and Gregory D. Black in *Hollywood Goes to War* (New York: Free Press, 1987); and John Morton Blum, *V Was for Victory* (New York: Harcourt Brace Jovanovich, 1976).

Chapter 5: Trouble in Paradise

Johnson's relationship with Sonja Henie is covered in multiple clippings in the Herrick Library and the theater arts section of the New York Public Library as well as such magazine articles as Sheilah Graham, "People Will Say They're in Love," *Photoplay* 29 (June 1946): 32–33, 78–79. Raymond Strait and Leif Henie also discuss the friendship in their biography of the skater, *Queen of Ice, Queen of Shadows* (New York: Stein and Day, 1985).

Johnson's wedding is reported in numerous newspaper articles in the various clipping files, and the consequent commotion is evidenced in endless fan-magazine articles, among them Sheilah Graham, "The Verdict on Van," *Photoplay* 32 (February 1948): 48–49, 84; Sally Jefferson and Florence Pritchett, "The Van Johnson–Evie Wynn–Keenan Wynn Triangle," *Photoplay* 30 (March 1947): 34–35, 113–14; Kenyon Lee, "Is Van Johnson Dead at the Boxoffice?" *Screen Guide* (February 1948): 25–27, 82–84; "Mrs. Van Johnson Takes Her Life in Her Hands," *Movieland* 6 (February 1948): 25, 86; and Louella O. Parsons, "They've Had to Take It," *Photoplay* 34 (March 1949): 46–47, 104–5. Johnson supposedly replied to his followers' concerns about his marriage in Kate Holliday, "Van Johnson Talks to His Fans," *Movieland* 5 (June 1947): 36–37, 96–97; and Van Johnson, "My New Life," *Photoplay* 30 (September 1948): 38–39.

Eve Wynn Johnson explained the reasons for her sudden marriage to Van to writer David Heymann, quoted in Heymann's *Liz: An Intimate Biography of Elizabeth Taylor* (New York: Birch Lane, 1995) and in her August 30, 1999, note to me. Playwright Arthur Laurents gave his version in his autobiography, *Original Story By: A Memoir of Broadway and Hollywood* (New York: Knopf, 2000).

Insight into gay Hollywood may be gained from David Ehrenstein, *Open Secret: Gay Hollywood, 1928–1998* (New York: Morrow, 1998); and Willima J. Mann, *Wisecracker: The Life and Times of William Haines, Hollywood's First Openly Gay Star* (New York: Viking, 1998). Also worth consulting on this subject are Tom Clark with Dick Kleiner, *Rock Hudson, Friend of Mine* (New York: Pharos, 1989); and Phyllis Gates and Bob Thomas, *My Husband, Rock Hudson* (Garden City, N.Y.: Doubleday, 1987), although Hudson came onto the Hollywood scene several years later than Van. Martin and Erin-Jo Jurow and Barbara Thompson gave me their observations about Hollywood's public attitude toward homosexuality in my interviews with them.

Billy Haines's contention about an actor with the same initials as one of the celebrations at the end of World War II appears in an interview with Haines published in Boze Hadleigh, *Hollywood Gays* (New York: Barricade, 1996). The reaction of Peter Lawford's mother to the Van Johnson–Keenan Wynn–Evie Wynn triangle is recorded in Lady Lawford and Buddy Galon's book, *"Bitch!": The Autobiography of Lady Lawford* (Brookline Village, Mass.: Branden, 1986). For Lucille Ball's response to Johnson's decision to marry Evie Wynn, see Jim Brochu, *Lucy in the Afternoon* (New York: Morrow, 1990); and Lucille Ball with Betty Hannah Hoffman, *Love, Lucy* (New York: Putnam's, 1996).

By far the most complete account of life in the Johnson and Wynn households after Van married Eve appears in Ned Wynn's remarkable book, *We Will Always Live in Beverly Hills: Growing Up Crazy in Hollywood,* supplemented by Keenan Wynn's autobiography, *Ed Wynn's Son,* and a discerning interview with Johnson's younger stepson, Tracy Keenan Wynn, published in Raymond Strait, *Hollywood's Children* (New York: St. Martin's, 1982).

Information on Keenan Wynn's later marriages is contained in the various clipping files mentioned earlier.

Janet Leigh recalled making *The Romance of Rosy Ridge* in her oral history for Southern Methodist University and went into more detail on the subject in the 1999 interview I did with her. Leigh also discusses the picture in her first book, *There Really Was a Hollywood* (Garden City, N.Y.: Doubleday, 1984), and describes her affection for Johnson in Doug McClelland's *Forties Film Talk,* cited previously. Screenwriter Lester Cole recalls writing and preparing *The Romance of Rosy Ridge* for production in his autobiography, *Hollywood Red* (Palo Alto, Calif.: Ramparts Press, 1981); and Marshall Thompson discusses location work on the film, along with his observations of making *Command Decision,* in his Southern Methodist University oral history.

Director Frank Capra makes interesting comments about filming *State of the Union* in his book, *The Name above the Title: An Autobiography* (New York: Macmillan, 1971). Mary Anita Loos and Betty Lynn discuss *Mother Was a Freshman* in their interviews for Southern Methodist University; and Arlene Dahl and Norman Lloyd do the same for *Scene of the Crime* in the oral histories I taped with them. The quote from Johnson about working with Judy Garland comes from Doug McClelland's *Forties Film Talk.*

The 1949 reunion photograph of the 1934 graduating class exists in the Rogers High School archives in Newport.

Chapter 6: Resilient MGM Star

The most insightful source on Van Johnson's family life during the last half dozen years he was under contract to MGM is again Ned Wynn's *We Will Always Live in Beverly Hills,* although Tracy Keenan Wynn's interview in Raymond Strait's *Hollywood's Children* remains an important complement. Clipping files in the Herrick Library and the theater arts section of the New York Public Library also proved invaluable in writing about this period of Johnson's life.

In her autobiography, *"Bitch,"* written with Buddy Galon, Lady Lawford states that her son, Peter, was sometimes thought to be homosexual because of his friendship with Van Johnson; and Phyllis Gates discusses agent Henry Willson's circle of homosexuals in *My Husband, Rock Hudson,* written with Bob Thomas.

Johnson talks about his interest in painting in "Reel Life Legend Van Johnson Frames a New Career," *People Weekly* 29 (January 11, 1988): 109–12.

Dore Schary reflects on his years as head of production at Metro-Goldwyn-Mayer and the making of *Battleground* in *Heyday* (Boston: Little, Brown, 1979). Most of the material on *Battleground* in this chapter comes from the excellent oral history I conducted with Robert Pirosh, although the interviews I taped with Marshall Thompson and Leon Ames were helpful as well. So were George Murphy's *"Say . . . Didn't You Used to Be George Murphy?"* (n.p.: Bartholomew House, 1970), written with Victor Lasky, and Frank T. Thompson's *William A. Wellman* (Metuchen, N.J.: Scarecrow, 1983).

Rosemary DeCamp provided anecdotes on the filming of *The Big Hangover* in her oral history for Southern Methodist University; and in their interviews, Armand Deutsch and Charles Walters discussed the making of *Three Guys Named Mike.* Jane Wyman recalled making *Three Guys* as well as her respect for Johnson as a performer in our 1999 telephone conversation. Esther Williams recalls production details on *Duchess of Idaho* and *Easy to Love* in her book, *The Million Dollar Mermaid.* Charles Walters gives his evaluation of *Easy to Love* in the oral history I taped with him.

Robert Pirosh discusses his work on *Go for Broke* and *Washington Story* in his oral history for Southern Methodist University; and Patricia Neal remembers the latter in *As I Am: An Autobiography* (New York: Simon and Schuster, 1988), written with Richard DeNeut. Mervyn LeRoy states his reaction to the script of *Plymouth Adventure* in his book, *Take One,* and assistant director Rideway Callow includes his observations about making the film in his interview with Rudy Behlmer in the Mayer Library at the American Film Institute. Janet Leigh talks about *Confidentially Connie* both in her autobiography and in the interviews she granted me. Angela Lansbury's assessment of *Remains to Be Seen* comes from Rob Edelman and Audrey E. Kupferberg, *Angela Lansbury: A Life on Stage and Screen* (New York: Birch Lane, 1996).

Extensive production files exist on *The Siege at Red River* in the film holdings of the Doheny Library at the University of Southern California.

In my 1999 interview with her, Sandy Descher recounted seeing Clark Gable saluting the Thalberg Building before leaving MGM.

Fan-magazine articles consulted for this chapter include Fredda Dudley Balling, "The Sky's the Limit," *Movieland* 9 (September 1951): 26–27, 69; "How the Van Johnson Rumors Start," *Movieland* 11 (May 1953): 40–45, 64; Jane Kessner, "'Mr. Congressman' at Home," *Movieland* 10 (April 1952): 62–65, 75; and Joseph Henry Steele, "Rhode Island Redhead," *Photoplay* 40 (October 1951): 50–51, 70–71, 73.

Lana Turner recalls her final months at Metro in *Lana: The Lady, the Legend, the Truth* (New York: Dutton, 1982).

Chapter 7: Freelance Actor

The production information on *The Caine Mutiny* was drawn principally from Edward Dmytryk, *It's a Hell of a Life but Not a Bad Living* (New York: Times Books, 1978); the oral history I taped with Dmytryk; and Stanley Kramer's autobiography, *A Mad, Mad, Mad, Mad World: A Life in Hollywood* (New York: Harcourt Brace, 1997), written with Thomas M. Coffey. The discussion of the problems while preparing to film *Brigadoon* came mainly from my oral history sessions with Gene Kelly and cinematographer Joseph Ruttenberg, augmented by Vincente Minnelli's book, *I Remember It Well* (Garden City, N.Y.: Doubleday, 1974), written with Hector Arce. Sandy Descher gave me touching anecdotes about the making of *The Last Time I Saw Paris* in our interview, and Billy Grady recounts Metro's problems with Van Johnson at the beginning of the film in his memoirs, *The Irish Peacock,* cited earlier.

Dmytryk also talks about *The End of the Affair* in his autobiography; and Eric Braum included a great deal of information on the making of the movie in *Deborah Kerr* (New York: St. Martin's, 1977). Extensive production files exist on *Miracle in the Rain, The Bottom of the Bottle,* and *23 Paces to Baker Street* in the film archives at the University of Southern California. Jane Wyman provided me with additional information on *Miracle in the Rain* in our telephone interview, and Lenore Coffee makes some cogent remarks about the script of *The End of the Affair* in Pat McGilligan, *Backstory: Interviews with Screenwriters of Hollywood's Golden Age* (Berkeley: University of California Press, 1986).

Robert Stack mentions replacing Van Johnson in *The Untouchables* on television in his memoir, *Straight Shooting* (New York: Macmillan, 1980), written with Mark Evans, as well as in the oral history he did for Southern Methodist University.

Ned Wynn's book and Tracy Keenan Wynn's interview in Raymond Strait's *Hollywood's Children* remain the major sources on life and family problems in the Johnson home, although Rosemary Clooney shared with me her observations of Van and Eve's marriage in the interview I conducted with her in 1999.

The newspaper article, dated June 20, 1955, claiming that the vice squad was watching Johnson's activities is among the clippings on file in the theater section of the New York Public Library.

Biographical and production files at the Margaret Herrick Library proved essential to this chapter, as did the Constance McCormick collection at the University of Southern California.

Fan-magazine articles for this period of Johnson's life include Margaret Gardner, "New Deal for Van," *Movieland* 12 (December 1954): 16–17; Evie Johnson, "Portrait of the Man I Love," *Photoplay* 49 (June 1956): 52, 109–12; Dee Phillips, "Van Johnson Learned No Man Walks Alone," *Photoplay* 47 (March 1955): 46–47, 94–98; and Ruth Rowland, "Van, the Man," *Movieland* 14 (August 1956): 44, 74, 81.

Chapter 8: Holding Together

Information, including reviews, about Van Johnson's London appearances in *The Music Man*, his real estate problems there, and his accident on stage were drawn from the *Daily Herald, Daily Mail, Guardian, London Daily Mirror, London Daily Telegraph, London Sunday Telegraph, London Times, Queen,* and *The Tatler.* The actor's performances in the show at the Cocoanut Grove in Los Angeles were extensively covered by the local press, and most of those articles are on file in the Herrick Library.

The Johnsons' final separation, Van's relationship with the boy dancer in *The Music Man,* and subsequent family complications are discussed in detail in Ned Wynn's *We Will Always Live in Beverly Hills.* The interview with Tracy Keenan Wynn in Raymond Strait's *Hollywood's Children* adds to an understanding of the family situation after Van and Eve parted, although his tone is gentler than his brother's. Eve's August 30, 1999, note to me reflects her continued bitterness toward her second husband, whereas Van's later attitude toward his former wife was recounted in interviews I conducted with his friends and colleagues, who prefer to remain nameless on this point. Insights into Evie's later life are broached in Richard Lamparski, *Whatever Became of . . . ?* (New York: Crown, 1985).

Johnson's many appearances in regional theaters during the 1960s are covered sporadically in the clipping files in the Herrick Library and the theater arts section of the New York Public Library, and Van's final performance in *Bye Bye Birdie* in San Francisco is detailed in a telegram from theater manager Iggie Wolfington to Hedda Hopper, May 13, 1963, in the Hopper papers at the Herrick Library.

Carroll Baker recalls working with Johnson in *Come on Strong* on Broadway in *Baby Doll: An Autobiography* (New York: Arbor House, 1983). Janet Leigh talked about making *Wives and Lovers* with Van in my 1999 interview with her; and the film is discussed by Martha Hyer Wallis in *Finding My Way* (New York: Harper Collins, 1990) and by Shelley Winters in *Shelley II: The Middle of My Century* (New York: Simon and Schuster, 1989).

Debbie Reynolds mentions working with Johnson on *Divorce American Style* in her book, *Debbie: My Life* (New York: Morrow, 1988), written with David Patrick Columbia. Rosalind Russell recalls the lack of success of *Where Angels Go, Trouble Follows* in her autobiography, *Life Is a Banquet* (New York: Random House, 1977), written with Chris Chase; and Binnie Barnes talked about making the movie in the oral history I conducted with her for Southern Methodist University. Melville Shavelson related the problems he had with Lucille Ball during the making of *Yours, Mine and Ours* in the oral history we taped, and Giuliano Gemma discussed working with Johnson in our 1999 telephone conversation.

Magazine articles on the actor's life and career during the 1960s are headed by Chrys Haranis, "Thoughts on an Old Wedding Ring," *Photoplay* 65 (June 1964): 72–74. "Reel Life Legend Van Johnson Frames a New Career," *People Weekly* 29 (January 11, 1988): 109–12, also contains pertinent data on this period of the star's life. Johnson's bout with skin cancer was reported at length in the national press, and a plethora of articles on his hospital stays are preserved in the various clipping files.

A. C. Lyles's remark about Van's capacity to enjoy his stardom came from writer Robert Nott's interview with the ubiquitous Hollywood producer.

Chapter 9: Later Years

Van Johnson's more recent activities are best covered in the clipping files in the theater arts section of the New York Public Library, although the Herrick Library has some material and the Dallas Public Library's holdings includes articles based on interviews with the actor during his engagements in nearby Fort Worth. Johnson's demonstration of affection for his fans in Hampton, N.H., was recalled by his colleagues Mary Sharmat and Frank Vohs in an interview with me, and Janet Leigh talked about working with Van in *Love Letters* on the stage in Los Angeles during our 1999 conversation.

Johnson's performances in *La Cage aux Folles* were thoroughly reported in the New York press at the time, as were his attitude toward the show and details of his work routine. The quote from Van expressing his enthusiasm for a chance to play the Palace Theater on Broadway is taken from Harry Haun's article in the March 1985 *Playbill*.

On the making of *The Purple Rose of Cairo*, see Woody Allen, *Woody Allen on Woody Allen* (London: Faber and Faber, 1994); and Mia Farrow, *What Falls Away* (New York: Doubleday, 1997).

Johnson's later life and particularly his career as a painter are discussed in the January 11, 1988, article in *People Weekly* cited previously.

Ned Wynn's book includes poignant glimpses of the star during his declining years, and Johnson's friends Richard Lederer, Eddie Bracken, Elliott Reid, and Erin-Jo Jurow and his business manager, Alan Foshko, talked about the older Van in their conversations with me.

The observation that Johnson punctuated every point he made by patting the leg of the male reporter seated next to him at a press luncheon in 1976 comes from an article, authored by Steve Warren, in the clipping files at the New York Public Library.

Eve Wynn Johnson's later life is outlined in the 1985 edition of Richard Lamparski's *Whatever Became of . . . ?*, referred to previously. Eve's claim that she was forced to declare bankruptcy and the contention that Van ignored his daughter during her 1998 hysterectomy are stated in Eve Johnson's August 1999 note to me.

Quotes throughout the text from reviews of Van Johnson's appearances in films and Broadway shows came from the *Beverly Hills Daily News Life, Christian Science Monitor, Cue, Film Daily, Hollywood Reporter, Los Angeles Daily News, Los Angeles Examiner, Los Angeles*

Times, Mirror-News, Motion Picture Herald, New York Herald Tribune, New York Post, New York Times, New Yorker, Showman's Trade Review, Time, and *Variety.*

At the height of the actor's popularity, *Van Johnson: The Luckiest Guy in the World* (Racine, Wis.: Whitman, 1947), a supposed biography by Elizabeth Beecher, appeared, but the book is highly fabricated and of little use to a serious researcher.

Additional background material on Johnson's time in Hollywood may be gleaned from Rudy Behlmer, ed., *Memo from Darryl F. Zanuck* (New York: Grove, 1993); George P. Erengis, "MGM's Backlot," *Films in Review* 14 (January 1963): 23–37; Christopher Finch and Linda Rosenkrantz, *Gone Hollywood* (Garden City, N.Y.: Doubleday, 1979); James Harvey, *Romantic Comedy* (New York: Knopf, 1987); Jack McElroy, "Breakfast in Hollywood," *Photoplay* 36 (June 1949): 54–55; Richard Schickel, *The Stars* (New York: Bonanza, 1962); and the made-for-television documentary *MGM: When the Lion Roars,* in which Johnson appears.

Additional biographies and autobiographies that provided fragments of information about Johnson's life and career or added to the context of the star's Hollywood career include Donald Dewey, *James Stewart: A Biography* (Atlanta: Turner, 1996); Gerold Frank, *Judy* (New York: Harper and Row, 1975); Jay Fultz, *In Search of Donna Reed* (Iowa City: University of Iowa Press, 1998); Fred Lawrence Guiles, *Tyrone Power, the Last Idol* (Garden City, N.Y.: Doubleday, 1979); Kitty Kelley, *Elizabeth Taylor, the Last Star* (New York: Simon and Schuster, 1981); Patricia Seaton Lawford with Ted Schwarz, *The Peter Lawford Story* (New York: Carroll and Graf, 1988); Jeffrey Meyers, *Bogart: A Life in Hollywood* (Boston: Houghton Mifflin, 1997); Ann Miller with Norma Lee Browning, *Miller's High Life* (Garden City, N.Y.: Doubleday, 1972); Joe Morella and Edward Z. Epstein, *Jane Wyman: A Biography* (New York: Delacorte, 1985); Barry Parks, *Garbo: A Biography* (New York: Knopf, 1995); Jane Russell, *My Path and My Detours* (New York: Franklin Watts, 1985); Stephen M. Silverman, *Dancing on the Ceiling: Stanley Donen and His Movies* (New York: Knopf, 1996); and Bob Thomas, *King Cohn: The Life and Times of Harry Cohn* (New York: Putnam, 1967).

FILMOGRAPHY

1940
Too Many Girls (RKO)

1942
Murder in the Big House (Warner Bros.)
Somewhere I'll Find You (MGM)
The War Against Mrs. Hadley (MGM)
Dr. Gillespie's New Assistant (MGM)

1943
The Human Comedy (MGM)
Pilot No. 5 (MGM)
Dr. Gillespie's Criminal Case (MGM)
Madame Curie (MGM)
A Guy Named Joe (MGM)

1944
White Cliffs of Dover (MGM)
Three Men in White (MGM)
Two Girls and a Sailor (MGM)
Thirty Seconds Over Tokyo (MGM)

1945
Between Two Women (MGM)
Thrill of a Romance (MGM)
Weekend at the Waldorf (MGM)

1946
Easy to Wed (MGM)
No Leave, No Love (MGM)
Till the Clouds Roll By (MGM)

1947
High Barbaree (MGM)
The Romance of Rosy Ridge (MGM)

1948
State of the Union (MGM)
The Bride Goes Wild (MGM)

1949
Command Decision (MGM)
Mother Is a Freshman (Twentieth Century-Fox)
Scene of the Crime (MGM)
In the Good Old Summertime (MGM)
Battleground (MGM)

1950
The Big Hangover (MGM)
Duchess of Idaho (MGM)

1951
Grounds for Marriage (MGM)
Three Guys Named Mike (MGM)
Go for Broke (MGM)
Too Young to Kiss (MGM)

1952
It's a Big Country (MGM)
Invitation (MGM)
When in Rome (MGM)
Washington Story (MGM)
Plymouth Adventure (MGM)

1953
Confidentially Connie (MGM)
Remains to Be Seen (MGM)
Easy to Love (MGM)

241

1954

The Siege at Red River (Twentieth Century-Fox)
Men of the Fighting Lady (MGM)
The Caine Mutiny (Columbia)
Brigadoon (MGM)
The Last Time I Saw Paris (MGM)

1955

The End of the Affair (Columbia)

1956

Miracle in the Rain (Warner Bros.)
The Bottom of the Bottle (Twentieth Century-Fox)
23 Paces to Baker Street (Twentieth Century-Fox)

1957

Slander (MGM)
Kelly and Me (Universal)
The Pied Piper of Hamelin (originally shown on television)
Action of the Tiger (MGM)

1958

The Last Blitzkrieg (Columbia)

1959

Subway in the Sky (United Artists)
Web of Evidence (Allied Artists)

1960

The Enemy General (Columbia)

1963

Wives and Lovers (Paramount)

1967

Divorce American Style (Columbia)

1968

Yours, Mine and Ours (United Artists)

Where Angels Go, Trouble Follows (Columbia)

1969

La Battaglia d'Inghilerra (Italian, Spanish, French)
El Largo Dia Del (Spanish-French)

1970

Il Prezzo del Potere (Italian)
Company of Killers (Universal)

1971

L'Occhio del Ragno (Italian)

1976

Rich Man, Poor Man (made for television)

1980

The Kidnapping of the President

1981

Absurd!

1985

The Purple Rose of Cairo

1987

Down There in the Jungle

1988

Taxi Killer

1989

Killer Crocodile

1990

Escape from Paradise
Delta Force: Commando 2

1991

Three Days to a Kill

1993

Clowning Around

INDEX